JUVENILE VIOLENCE IN A WINNER–LOSER CULTURE

D0596290

JUVENILE VIOLENCE IN A WINNER–LOSER CULTURE

SOCIO-ECONOMIC AND FAMILIAL ORIGINS OF THE RISE IN VIOLENCE AGAINST THE PERSON

OLIVER JAMES

Free Association Books / London / New York

Published in 1995 by
Free Association Books Ltd
Omnibus Business Centre
39–41 North Road
London N7 9DP
and 70 Washington Square
New York, NY10012-1091, USA

ISBN 1 85343 309 8 hbk

A CIP catalogue record for this book is available from the
British Library.

Designed and produced for Free Association Books Ltd by
Chase Production Services, Chipping Norton, OX7 5QR
Printed in the EC by TJ Press, Padstow, England.

*To My Mother Lydia – at seventy-eight years old,
still the most intellectually stimulating person I know.*

CONTENTS

ACKNOWLEDGEMENTS

I have Jane Hewland (ex London Weekend Television) to thank for my first interest in this subject. Anne Barrowclough was the original impetus for a book and I am grateful for her work with me in the early stages. David Farrington was exceptionally encouraging and helpful in orientating my earliest researches.

Marvin Wolfgang, Gerry Patterson and Peter Townsend were all kind enough to read the first draft and stimulated further research. David Downes's detailed critique was highly influential in focusing the thesis and he freely and frequently gave of his time in further discussing it. Likewise, thanks to Simon Field for putting up with my periodic phone calls.

Alex Stitt bravely took the book on for publication originally and when this did not work out he continued to act supportively. Sara Menguc, my literary agent, has stuck with it through thick and thin, with minimal reward. I am extremely grateful to Gill Davies at Free Association Books for feeling there was the germ of something publishable in the end.

I am indebted to Jemima Biddulph, Lucy Gibbons, Sarah Pope, Natasha Galloway and Alex Hope for their various secretarial and other help in preparation of the manuscript. Thanks also to the staff of The Print Gallery in Pembridge Road, London, for all their photocopying work.

ACKNOWLEDGEMENTS

INTRODUCTION

This book has two aims. The first is to provide a comprehensive explanation of the causes of male violence against the person, complete with reviews of relevant scientific literatures. The phenomenon seems to attract books purporting to explain it but this one has some distinctive features. At the broadest level, violence is strongly associated with being male, young and from a low income family. The review of the literatures presented herein reveals that the great majority of the variance between violent and non-violent males from low income families is explained by the presence of parental abuse, disharmony and irritability. Studies of biological or other differences suggest that they account for little of the variance. Violence-inducing parenting is shown to be far more common in families with low incomes. It follows that the more boys there are being raised in low income homes in a society, the larger the number of violent men there will be a few years later. However, this lagged theory of violence has a limited capacity to explain varying prevalences in violence between nations and across history. There is substantial evidence that the greater the degree of inequality in a society, the more violent it is. Thus, in the explanation presented in this book, inequality is held to be a direct, immediate cause of violent behaviour in young men of low income as well as affecting them indirectly through the parenting they receive.

The second aim of the book is to test this thesis in explaining the unprecedented increase since 1987 in the raw numbers and rates per 100,000 of notifiable offences of male violence against the person that has occurred in England and Wales (henceforth denoted as Britain for reasons of economy; figures for Scotland are excluded because of differences in the legal systems and for Northern Ireland, because of the distorting effect of 'the Troubles' there since 1969). 'Violence against the person' is the formal term used to summarize some three-quarters of all violent crimes recorded in the annual government publication *Criminal Statistics*. While it encompasses a great variety of offences from homicide to domestic assaults, it mostly entails young men from poor backgrounds punching, kicking and stabbing each other. I have focused on violence against the person because, compared with other forms of violence, it is the most likely to come to the attention of the police and, where it occurs out of doors, it is a highly visible offence – 75 per cent were cleared up in 1992 (compared with 22 per cent of robberies and 24 per cent of thefts/the handling of stolen goods). Reporting of the domestic variety of violence against the person, such as child abuse and wife beating, is much more erratic because it usually happens behind closed doors. Likewise sexual violence often occurs in domestic settings and victims are understandably reluctant to report events like rape, whatever their location. In addition, this book does not explain civil violence, like inner city riots, or industrial conflicts such as miners' strikes. Nor does it consider state-sanctioned military acts, like those in Ulster, the Falkland Islands or the Gulf.

Employing the rise in violence against the person as the index, Britain has become thirty times more violent since 1950. Something similar has happened throughout most of the developed world, although personal violence was actually falling for the 160 years prior to 1950. Intriguing though this fall and the international increase since 1950 may be, I have chosen as my main subject the unprecedented increase in England and Wales since 1987 – a threefold rise in the rate of increase.

The explanation is two pronged. On the one hand, the proportion of boys being raised in a low-income family rose from 19 per cent to 30 per cent between 1979 and 1981, and it has stayed at this higher rate ever since. My analysis of the criminal statistics for juvenile male violence against the person reveals that they rose substantially (by 40 per cent) after 1987, having remained static from 1980 to 1986. The increase in the number of violent juvenile males after 1987 – swelling the overall statistics for violence against the person – is attributed to the increase in the number of low-income families at the start of the decade. On the other hand, after 1979 Britain became more unequal than at any time since the Second World War. Unemployment and low pay increased and the quality of available employment for the lowest social classes fell. Among the lowest paid, state benefits and housing provision decreased as a consequence of a deliberate government policy to reduce welfare dependency. The physical health of the lowest paid underwent a measurable deterioration. Alongside these material changes there emerged a 'winner–loser' culture which took hold in the mid- to late 1980s. Where previously people of low income were regarded with respect and no blame attached to their low status, the new culture judged them inadequate morally, intellectually and emotionally. The word 'loser' replaced words like 'disadvantaged' as a common way of denoting them. The winner–loser culture may have caused a change in the way males in the poorest sections of British society interpreted the new inequalitites: when feeling frustrated and angry, it may have made them more likely to respond with physical violence.

Since the second aim of this book is to explain the rise in violence against the person since 1987, it is important at the outset to establish what this rise consisted of. As we shall see, there is also some debate as to whether the statistical increase truly reflected a change in behaviour in the real world.

THE UNPRECEDENTED RISE IN VIOLENCE AGAINST THE PERSON SINCE 1987

Looked at only in percentage terms, the figures for increases in violence against the person are less remarkable than they would be if considered in raw terms. The 10 per cent annual rise throughout the 1950s took the raw incidence of crimes of violence against the person from 6000 crimes a year in 1950 to 12,000 in 1959 (*Criminal Statistics*, 1970); for the incidence to rise by 1 per cent in 1950 needed only sixty crimes more. In 1993, 2050 were needed – over thirty times as many. A 1 per cent rise in 1993 would have represented 3 per cent more crimes in 1950.

Between 1979 and 1993, 95,000 crimes became 205,000, with the majority increase occurring in the second half of the decade. In 1986 there were 125,000 crimes. In 1993, 80,000 more crimes were committed – an increase not much smaller than the total of crimes committed in 1979. This rate of increase is way beyond anything seen before. Its significance is clearest when presented in terms of the annual rise in thousands of crimes of violence against the person recorded by the police (rounded up to the nearest thousand):

Years	Rise between year
1950–55	+200 (average rise per year)
1955–60	+1000 (average rise per year)
1961–65	+2000 (average rise per year)
1965–69	+1000 (average rise per year)
1970–79	+6000 (average rise per year)
1980	+3000
1981	+3000
1982	+8000
1983	+3000
1984	+3000
1985	+7000
1986	+4000
1987	+16,000
1988	+17,000
1989	+19,000
1990	+9000
1991	+6000
1992	+11,000
1993	+3000
1994	+14,000

The average rise between 1950 and 1986 was 3000 crimes per year. It was 5000 per year between 1970 and 1986 and 4000 per year between 1980 and

1986. The average rise between 1987 and 1993 was 12,000 per year – over twice as many as 1970–86 and three times the 1980–86 average. These differences cannot be explained by increases in the total population, which rose by 15 per cent between 1950 and 1989 (from forty-four million to fifty million, [OPCS, 1993]). Thus the rate of increase in the upward trend of recorded violence against the person since 1950 has accelerated unprecedentedly since 1987.

Of course, this does not prove that there has been an increase in the number of such crimes in the real world. It is possible that these statistics do not reflect actual changes in the number of people who have been committing acts of violence but that they reflect the way these statistics are defined, reported and gathered. Since the object of this book is to explain why a real rise in violence has occurred – rather than an artefact of statistics – it is important to establish that the increase is, indeed, real. Appendix 1 is devoted to this issue and those interested in the detailed argument need to read it. Here I shall restrict myself to conclusions.

Home Office researchers have claimed that the official statistics greatly exaggerate the extent of violence against the person and that the recorded increase since 1987 largely reflects a greater preparedness on the part of women to report incidents of domestic violence. In Appendix 1 I offer substantial reasons for rejecting this view. Indeed, if anything the evidence suggests that there has been an even more substantial increase in the violence of young men than the statistics indicate. 1987 was the year in which recorded violence against the person began its unprecedented rise; it was also the year when the numbers of young men at large in England and Wales – the people most often committing these crimes – began to decrease sharply. Fewer young men should have meant less violence against the person.

Ten to twenty-year-olds accounted for 38 per cent of males cautioned or convicted for indictable offences of violence against person in England and Wales in 1993. Between 1987 and 1993 the total number of fourteen- to twenty-year-olds fell by over one million, or 20.8 per cent. While we would not expect the equation to fit exactly because crime has risen steadily since 1950, if no other factors intervened and pure logic applied there should have been 20.8 per cent of 38 per cent (7.9 per cent) fewer crimes of violence against the person in 1993 than in 1987. Nothing of the sort happened and there were few signs in the violence against the person statistics that there were 20.8 per cent fewer in the single most criminogenic age group (the peak age for the offence of violence against the person is eighteen).

Most significantly for my thesis, explained in detail in Appendix 2, there was a remarkable increase in the amount of juvenile (ten- to sixteen-year-old) violent offending after 1987 running flatly against the overall trend for juvenile crime: the number of juveniles cautioned or found guilty at a court of any crime – not just violence – decreased by thirty-one per cent between 1987 and 1993 and the rate of offending per 100,000 juveniles (usually regarded as the best index of crime) fell by twenty-six per cent from 1987 to 1993. The figures for juvenile violence against the person are in the opposite direction; substantially so. The analysis in Appendix 2 of the criminal statistics for juvenile violence against the person reveals the following:

1 Between 1987 and 1993 the rate per 100,000 of recorded juvenile violence against the person increased by 40.5 per cent – despite the 26 per cent decrease for all juvenile offenses. The number of recorded violent juveniles increased by 34 per cent.– despite the 31 per cent decrease for all offenses.

2 Between 1980 and 1987 the rate of juvenile violent offending rose by only 2 per cent and the number of offenders fell by 15.5 per cent: juveniles have been significantly more violent since 1987 compared with the period from 1980 to 1987.

3 Comparison of the figures for juvenile violence with those for theft and handling stolen goods highlights the extent of the increase in violence: between 1987 and 1993 theft/handling of stolen goods decreased by over 40 per cent – about as much as the increase in violence.

4 The proportion of juvenile crime that is violent has increased significantly since 1987, suggesting that they have become more violent as a group. Violence made up 4 per cent of all crimes committed by ten- to thirteen-year-olds in 1987, whereas it made up 9 per cent of all crimes in this age group in 1993; the increase among fourteen- to sixteen-year-olds was from 8 per cent to 13 per cent. By contrast, the proportion of crime that was violent in older age groups (seventeen to twenty, and twenty-one and over) did not change significantly between 1987 and 1993. Nor did the proportion of juvenile crime that was violent change significantly between 1980 and 1987, again strongly suggesting that the post-1987 cohort of juveniles was more violent.

This analysis is powerful evidence of the extent to which boys who reached age ten in 1987 – sometimes referred to as 'Thatcher's children' – were more violent than those whose tenth birthday was in 1980.

THE EXPLANATION FOR THE RISE IN JUVENILE AND ADULT VIOLENCE

THE ARGUMENT IN MORE DETAIL: THE INDIRECT EFFECT OF THE NEW INEQUALITY

A review of the scientific literature (presented in chapters 1 and 2) suggests that three characteristics distinguish the families of the boys from low-income homes who become violent from those who do not: severe, frequent and erratic punishment (mostly physical; bordering on the abusive), disharmonious parental relationships (often involving physical assaults in sight of the son) and high parental irritability (often caused by depression, especially in mothers). Boys from homes where parenting is of this kind are significantly more likely to be aggressive. While not all boys who are aggressive become violent men, very few violent men were non-aggressive boys. Childhood aggression is one of the strongest predictors of adult violence. It is not sufficiently appreciated just how extensive and soundly based this scientific literature is, and chapters 1 and 2 are intended as a comprehensive review. There is also a tendency to overlook the fact that studies of biological factors, whether genetic, neuroanatomical or physiological, strongly suggest that they play little or no part in explaining the differing degrees of violence between men (made clear in chapter 6), although they may explain a significant part of the variance between genders (see chapter 5). Boys may be born more aggressive and prone to violence than girls, but the difference in the degrees of violence between two boys is largely, or wholly, not genetically inherited.

The most detailed and revealing studies of what happens in the families of violent boys have been conducted by Patterson (chapter 1). All families have what he calls 'coercive processes' (Patterson, 1982) – methods for getting your way like whining, teasing, disapproval, yelling, humiliation, negative commands, non-compliance and hitting. We all do these things but they happen significantly more often in families with aggressive boys. In such families there is a stream of parental 'nattering': continual threats and scolding of the child at the smallest sign of trouble, but the threats are not carried out or are done so inconsistently. The punishments don't work because what was punished yesterday is rewarded today and the parents are inept at providing good models of behaviour. The parents' aggression is irritable rather than educational; punishments express anger rather than being instruments for altering the child's behaviour. Gradually, the amount of aggressive behaviour escalates until the family seems to be permanently on a war footing.

The constant anger and negativity amplifies otherwise harmless acts into the cause of major rows. Words cease working and to make a point the parent is forced to become physical. The levels of violence inflate as the disciplinary currency becomes devalued.

Both parents, but especially the mother, report feeling down – depressed and irritable. Until now, parental depression, especially that of mothers, has been accorded a minimal role in the familial causes of violence. Chapter 2 brings together for the first time the disparate evidence which suggests that it is a key variable, demonstrating surprising similarities between the psychology of depressed mothers when dealing with their children and the attitude of violent men to their victims. Depressed parents find themselves attributing malevolent intentions to the child with no real basis for doing so. Two-thirds of attacks in such families are unprovoked – as are so many of the boys' attacks when they, in turn, become violent men. Having been brought up in a chaotic world where they may be assaulted at any moment without warning, violent criminals have been demonstrated to be far more paranoid than non-violent ones in experiments conducted in prisons. Like their parents, they have come to attribute malign intentions where none exist. That may help to explain the most common comment preceding a city-centre violent incident: 'What are you looking at?' More often than not, the innocent bystander to whom this was addressed intended no insult or other communication at all by 'looking'.

Statistically, 'out of control' families are far more common when parents are living with the stress of a low income (the subject of chapter 3). Not many public-school-educated boys were routinely beaten up throughout their childhood. Parents on low incomes are far more likely to erratically brutalize their sons in the pattern described by Patterson than parents on high incomes.

The logic of this model would suggest that the more low-income families there are in a society, the more aggressive boys there are, and, a few years later, the more violent men there will be. The proportion of British children living in a family with a low income (defined as less than 140 per cent of supplementary benefit) rose from one fifth (19 per cent) in 1979 to nearly one-third (30 per cent) in 1981, and it has stayed thereabouts ever since. The vastly increased number of boys raised in low-income families (the kind most likely to have the patterns of coercive processes that create violent men) have begun to swell the statistics for violence against the person. The increase in the proportion of boys being raised in families that are violence-inducing has caused an increase in the amount of violence recorded several years later.

DIRECT EFFECTS OF THE NEW INEQUALITY

Not all the average of 12,000 more crimes of violence against the person per year since 1987 can be attributed to juveniles (the subject of Appendix 2: 'How much of the increase in violence against the person since 1987 is explained by juveniles?'). Increased inequality does not only affect the violence statistics indirectly through parents, it has a direct effect as well (discussed in chapter 4). The generalization holds that the more unequal a nation and the poorer the social class or family within the class, the more violent it is. Historically, as nations become more prosperous they become less violent. Today's wealthy nations are on the whole less violent than poor ones – a fifty-nation comparison shows a simple correlation between decline in homicide rates and growth of Gross National Product per capita. While this is true of the overall picture, it is often pointed out that all the developed nations (with the exceptions of Japan and Switzerland) have become substantially more violent since 1950, despite three- to fourfold increases in wealth. The explanation lies in the form that modern socio-economic inequality has taken. Advanced industrialization is liable to cause the breakdown of traditional social networks and of neighbourhood identity and loyalty. Violent subcultures thrive in these conditions. However, the extent to which these factors occur varies consid-erably between technologically-developed nations according to the extent and form of their inequality. Large cross-national surveys reviewed in chapter 4 show that there is a straightforward correlation between high homicide rates and large gaps between rich and poor and disparities in income between workers in different sectors of industry. Likewise, homicide rates are lower in countries with employment and training policies that keep unemployment low. The higher the proportion of Gross National Product that is devoted to social service programmes ensuring the well-being of the work force, the less violent the society. This even applies within nations. In comparisons of different States within America, levels of State aid to families with children vary considerably; the higher the levels of benefit, the lower the levels of violence in the State.

In Britain since 1979 there have been profound changes in all these respects. The gap between rich and poor has increased enormously, as has the proportion of people on low incomes (however defined); in both respects Britain has returned to the position found prior to the Second World War. Twenty-five per cent of Britons were living with an income of less than half the average in 1991–92, compared with 9 per cent in 1979. The real income of the poorest 10 per cent of Britons fell by 17 per cent during this period compared with a 62 per cent rise in real income for the wealthiest 10 per cent. State benefits have been reduced and, as the British Medical Journal (1994) has chronicled, the health of the poor has worsened dramatically. That young British men would become more violent is exactly what the studies of the inequality–violence correlation would have predicted.

ALTERNATIVE EXPLANATIONS

Many factors other than inequality could account for the rise in violence since 1987 and these are addressed as they arise within this book. While there is no doubting the evidence that abusive, disharmonious and irritable parenting are strongly associated with low income, this is not necessarily a causal relationship. Other factors which also co-vary with low income could be the cause of the parenting. Three that have been given considerable prominence in recent years are: the rise in single-parent families; the thesis that inherited low intelligence accounts for the greater violence of low-income men; and the alleged development of an underclass. These are addressed in detail in chapters 3 and 7 and are shown to be unlikely to explain even a small proportion of the rise in violence.

In the case of single-parent families, while there has been a significant increase in this family form during the 1980s, the main proponents of this view are shown to have confounded the effects of fatherlessness with the effects of low income and divorce. Single parenting is shown to have had a potential effect on the violence statistics only insofar as it is mostly a consequence of divorce (which increases aggressiveness in boys) and causes low income.

The low-intelligence thesis does not take sufficient account of detailed studies which demonstrate that it is the pattern of coercive child-rearing which correlates with aggression in boys and subsequent violence in men. While low IQ scores do undoubtedly correlate with delinquency in boys and men, these are shown principally to be an effect rather than a cause of delinquency. Boys whose delinquency has been caused by the patterns of the coercive process described by Patterson are difficult to train by parents and teachers; as a result they underachieve academically and in the verbal sections of IQ tests.

Finally, the thesis that an underclass culture in a special portion of the poorer sections of society has developed which causes men to reject job opportunities and to become addicted to state benefits is shown to have no empirical basis. There is no scientific evidence that such a group actually exists at all or that the people living in the lowest social class are any more coercive in their patterns of child rearing, more averse to steady employment or more violent than their predecessors. Far too much weight has been placed on such 'moral' factors in recent years; driven more, perhaps, by biased newspaper articles, written for the most part by authors of politically motivated and scientifically questionable books, than by any newly-published scientific evidence.

The fourth factor which could account for the rise in violence since 1979 is short-term shifts in the business cycle. In the final chapter I suggest that this may indeed be the case to a small degree but, even after this is taken into account, a large proportion of the increase still remains unexplained. The direct and indirect effects of the new inequality emerge as the most likely candidates.

The reader will appreciate, then, that there are several building blocks to the argument. Chapter 1 reviews the evidence that parental abuse, disharmony and irritability explain a large proportion of the variance between violent and non-violent men. Chapter 2 presents a new view of the importance of parental depression in causing violence-inducing childcare. Chapter 3 demonstrates that low income – not single parenting, low intelligence or an underclass culture – is the main cause of the abuse, disharmony and irritability which causes individual differences in male violence. Chapter 4 shows that inequality is the single best predictor of the prevalence of violence in a given society and points to the large increase in inequality in Britain during the 1980s as a direct cause of increased adult as well as juvenile violence. Chapters 5 and 6 are slight but necessary detours from the main argument, explaining the roles of gender and biology respectively in causing violence. Finally, chapter 7 presents the full argument: that the rise in violence since 1987 was principally caused by the direct and indirect effects of the large increase in inequality in Britain since 1979.

1 PARENTAL CAUSES OF INDIVIDUAL DIFFERENCES IN VIOLENCE: ABUSE, DISHARMONY AND IRRITABILITY

Every murder committed not directly in self defence but on innocuous surrogate objects is the expression of an inner compulsion, a compulsion to avenge the gross abuse, neglect, and confusion suffered during childhood and to leave the accompanying feelings in a state of repression . . . It is absolutely unthinkable that a human being who, from the start, is given love, tenderness, closeness, orientation, respect, honesty, and protection by adults should later become a murderer.

Banished Knowledge
Alice Miller

The aggressive boy is father to the violent man. Whatever explains the difference between aggressive and unaggressive boys largely accounts for why men are violent as well. The nearest thing to a racing certainty in this field of research is that aggressive men were aggressive boys (Olweus, 1979). Boys who are aggressive at home are more likely to be so at school and at play with other children than unaggressive schoolchildren (Manning *et al.*, 1985; Manning and Herman, 1981), and this remains true down the years (Patterson *et al.*, 1990). When they are followed into adulthood, as several large representative samples have been, the aggressive eight- to ten-year-olds almost invariably become the violent eighteen-, twenty- and thirty-year-olds. Likewise, unaggressive eight-year-olds rarely become violent adults (Farrington *et al.*, 1988).

This chapter reviews the empirical evidence that childhood aggression is caused by parental (the word 'parents' will be used henceforth as synonymous with the more general term 'primary caregivers') behaviour and goes on to review further evidence that violent men are more likely than non-violent men to have been subjected to this behaviour. This latter evidence divides into retrospective and prospective studies.

THE CAUSES OF CHILDHOOD AGGRESSION

BOYS FROM CONFLICT-RIDDEN COUPLES ARE MORE AGGRESSIVE

If children look up to their parents and what they see is mostly bickering and anger, they might be influenced to behave in this way in their own relationships. Nine studies suggest that this is so.[1] Cummings et al. (1985), for example, orchestrated angry verbal exchanges between unfamiliar adults in front of two-year-old children. Afterwards the toddlers were more aggressive in their play with peers than toddlers who had witnessed friendly exchanges. When the same procedure was repeated a month later these differences were even more marked. It was concluded that the children were imitating the adults' behaviour. The naturally occurring version of this artificial experiment is to see whether children of disharmonious couples are more aggressive than those of the harmonious. In a sample of sixty-four troubled families, Porter and O'Leary (1980) found that the greater the degree of marital discord, the greater the likelihood that five- to ten-year-old boys were liable to suffer from conduct disorders. Likewise, in thirty-one families containing boys with conduct disorders, Johnson and Lobitz (1974) found a strong correlation between the extent of marital dissatisfaction and the amount of aggressiveness, destructiveness and temper tantrums when directly observing the children at play. Oltmans et al. (1977) repeated this finding but with the additional rigour of a comparison group of harmonious families: the boys from discordant homes were significantly more conduct-disordered. Dodge's study of 309 children took this a step further by tracing a chain from marital violence to abuse of children to aggressive outcome in the child (Dodge et al., 1990).

Another group of studies looked at the behaviour of boys before, during and after marital separation. Separating couples are usually discordant, and eight studies suggested separation increases aggressiveness in sons.[2] Block et al. (1986) assessed at intervals 110 families with children from age three to fourteen of which forty-one families were broken by the end. Boys whose parents parted were found to have significantly more, 'undercontrol of impulse, aggression and excessive energy' than those where the parents had stayed together. Hetherington's (1979) studies of separating couples concluded similarly that, 'a conflict-ridden intact family is more deleterious to family members than is a stable home in which parents are divorced'. More recent work (Wallerstein et al., 1988; Cockett and Tripp, 1994) questions whether actual separation of parents is not at least as distressing for children in its own right as living with an unhappy but intact couple, in the long term. Clearly, neither promote emotional security in children.

If witnessing parental discord encourages aggression in boys we might expect that witnessing actual violence between parents would do so even more. Seven studies suggest it does.[3] Wolfe et al. (1985) compared the behaviour of 102 children in shelters for battered women who had not been abused with that of children from non-battering families. The boys whose mothers had been battered had significantly more behaviour problems. Jaffee *et al.* (1986) took this a stage further, comparing thirty-two children in shelters who had not been abused but had witnessed violence, with eighteen abused children and a control group who had experienced neither. Both abused and witness-to-battery groups were significantly more aggressive than the controls, displaying more cruelty, fighting and destructiveness of objects like toys. Of the two, the abused were more aggressive than the witnesses. Another study, by Rosenbaum and O'Leary (1981), found similar differences between control and witness groups but not statistically significant ones, possibly because of small samples. The conclusion was that, 'while marital discord and violence may contribute to the behaviour problems of children, other factors are also involved'.

It seems clear that being in the company of warring parents – whether they actually hit each other or not – plays a significant role in making boys aggressive. However, common sense suggests that the effect of being the direct victim of maltreatment would be greater than that of witnessing it.

MALTREATED BOYS ARE MORE AGGRESSIVE THAN NON-MALTREATED BOYS

Aggressive boys almost invariably turn out to have had different care to unaggressive ones. When parents and teachers are asked to rate the aggressiveness of their charges and when independent observers rate the behaviour of the same children at play, all three sources agree. Statistically the aggressive boys are significantly more likely to have been maltreated by parents compared with unaggressive boys in almost every study making this kind of comparison, of which there are at least twenty-six.[4] Maltreatment is defined very broadly in these studies, incorporating physical or sexual abuse as well as emotional neglect or deprivation, but it seems beyond doubt that boys who are aggressive have been subjected to a different quality of care than the unaggressive. For example, Herrenkohl and Herrenkohl (1981) twice observed the play of seventy-two maltreated children comparing it with 174 non-maltreated ones. The maltreated were significantly more likely to be . aggressive when interrupted by peers or when frustrated by a difficult task. However, there are numerous studies which show that this tends to be true of delinquent children as a group (for example, Loeber and Stouthamer-Loeber [1987] list eleven). The 'antisocial tendency' – a generalized propensity towards criminality, including stealing, poor discipline at school and hostility to all authority, as well as aggressiveness – is much more likely if a child has been maltreated (Patterson *et al.*, 1990). The crucial question from our point of view is what, if anything, is specifically different about the aggressive's maltreatment, as opposed to that of the more globally antisocial child? One possibility is abuse as opposed to neglect.

ABUSE VERSUS NEGLECT AS CAUSES OF CHILDHOOD AGGRESSION

Many of the studies listed above lumped abuse and neglect victims together and simply compared them en masse with non-maltreated children. More specific attempts have been made to see if there are differences in aggressiveness between children who have only been abused as opposed to solely neglected in early life. In later life, it has been suggested, the neglected tend to turn into antisocial stealers more than the abused, who are thought to become violent (Bowlby, 1944; Patterson, 1982). Since the abused are often neglected also, this distinction has been criticized as too crude and poorly defined (Cicchetti and Rizley, 1981). None the less, there have been at least twelve attempts to select separate samples of non-abused but neglected, and abused but not neglected, children and make comparisons of their aggressiveness. In four of them[5] no significant differences were found. However, three of these had very small samples of twelve or less children in each subgroup and relied not on direct observation of the children's behaviour to evaluate their aggressiveness, but on parents' second-hand reports. The eight where differences were recorded[6] suffered less from these methodological shortcomings. In two pioneering studies, Jenkins (1966, 1968) looked at the case records of 800 and 1500 children referred for psychiatric assessment at the ages of eight to eleven. He identified clusters of symptoms in the children and showed that their parents differed in specific ways, two being especially pertinent. The 'socialized delinquents' were aggressive, extrovert, stole, ran away from home a lot, truanted from school and tended to have three or more siblings. Their mothers were neglectful, cold, distant and tended to delegate responsibility as much as possible. The mothers were likely to be delinquent themselves, promiscuous and not married to the child's father, who was himself liable to be rigid, punitive, neglectful and overtly rejecting. Jenkins's other relevant category, the 'unsocialized aggressives', were markedly more hostile and provocative to the investigator. They were more defiant of authority; vengeful, malicious, sullen and prone to temper tantrums. They were more likely to be only-children. The aggressives' parents were much more likely to use extensive physical punishment than the delinquents' and to employ physical or emotional isolation as methods of control. The mothers rather than the fathers tended to be more punitive, in contrast to the paternal punitiveness of the delinquents' families. The mothers were highly critical, conspicuously inconsistent and more often diagnosed as suffering from mental illness. Thus, childhood stealing was associated with parental neglect, and childhood malignancy and hostility with physical punishment, cruel deprivations of love and forced isolation by parents.

Not all the other studies which found the abused to be more aggressive than the neglected confirmed Jenkins's detail. In Crittenden's study (1982) the neglected children were 'passive' where Jenkins's had been extrovert and in Burgess and Conger's study (1978) it was the mothers of the neglected – not the abused – who were more 'negative'. All the children in these samples were selected by welfare professionals through clinical judgements about the kinds of maltreatment. It is highly likely that big differences in applying criteria existed and that the various labels used do not mean the same things. Above all, there is little guarantee that the abused children were not, in fact, also neglected, and vice versa.

A more recent attempt to address the question which was specifically designed to avoid methodological shortcomings was Widom's (1989a) examination of the criminal outcomes of 809 abused and neglected children. All cases of recorded abuse or neglect processed between 1967 and 1971 in a town in the Midwest of the USA were subsequently checked for criminal records. The proportions with different kinds of childhood maltreatment who were subsequently convicted of a violent crime were as follows:

Physical abuse	15.8%
Neglect	12.5%
Physical and neglect	7.1%
Sexual and other abuse	7.1%
Sexual only	5.6%
Controls (no maltreatment)	7.9%

This suggests that neglect and physical abuse alone are independently implicated in violence (but also that, perhaps curiously, together they are less likely to cause it). Because the sex, age and race of the offender all independently determined criminal outcomes, Widom conducted a further analysis: after allowing for these, statistically both neglect and abuse were still significantly related to a violent outcome.

That abuse causes childhood aggression more than neglect is not certain on the evidence of these studies alone, although six suggest that it does, and it is certainly highly significant that none of the ten suggested that neglect was more likely to. In Widom's study overall, 19.4 per cent of the neglected and abused males were convicted of violent crimes (statistically significantly different from the 13.4 per cent of non-abused, non-neglected controls). Of course, many violent men are never convicted of the crime so it is almost certain that a far higher percentage would have been violent. Likewise, the control group were selected purely on the grounds that as children they were not in court as victims of neglect or abuse – many of them may have been maltreated; particularly the 13.5 per cent who were subsequently convicted of violent crimes. None the less, it shows that while neglect and abuse increase the likelihood of a violent criminal conviction, it does not have this outcome in four-fifths of cases. As Widom pointed out (1989, p. 164): 'the intergenerational transmission of violence is not inevitable'. Neither abuse nor neglect in themselves necessarily cause violence and it is only when we look at the dynamic processes in families that we begin to see what makes the difference between a violent and a non-violent outcome.

WHEN IS A PUNISHMENT AN ABUSE?

Child physical abuse is usually justified by the aggressor as a necessary disciplinary measure provoked by the child's naughtiness. Most of the blows struck against a child are done ostensibly because the child 'deserved' it. The line between abuse and punishment can be thin.

Most children are physically chastised at some point, with as many as 18 per cent suffering a 'severe violent act' (11 per cent in the previous year) according to one national sample in the USA (Straus and Gelles, 1988). Normal four- to six-year-olds do something their parents regard as deviant or naughty on average once every three minutes (Johnson *et al.*, 1973) and they comply with 60–80 per cent of parental commands (Johnson *et al.*, 1973; Forehand *et al.*, 1975). Aggressive children are significantly less compliant with parental commands than these normal children. Problem children responded to only 42 per cent of parents' commands compared with 62 per cent for non-problem children in one study (Forehand *et al.*, 1975) and this finding has been repeated (Patterson *et al.*, 1990). If their children are less compliant, it is also true that the mothers of those diagnosed as having conduct problems do react differently. Observed during free play sessions they issue more direct commands and make more criticisms than mothers of unaggressive children (Forehand *et al.*, 1975). Haverson and Waldrop (1970) compared the behaviour of mothers when with their aggressive offspring to their behaviour with children who were not their progeny. They displayed significantly more aggression towards their own children. Overall, families with problem children offer more negative and less positive responses when the child acts in a socially acceptable fashion ('prosocially') and offer more encouragement and less criticism if the child acts deviantly, compared to families without problem children (Snyder, 1977).

On the one hand, these studies suggest that aggressive children are more provocative than normal ones; on the other, that their parents are more critical and negative, and do not encourage them in the right ways at the right times. A cycle of child aggression–inadequate response–child aggression arises, escalating to the point where an abusive level of violence by the adult seems to them the only way of breaking it. A punishment becomes an abuse.

WHICH COMES FIRST: THE CHILD'S AGGRESSIVENESS OR THE PARENTS' NEGATIVITY?

It is easy to believe that there exists the child born with an impulsive, bloody-minded intolerance of frustration or an innate aggressiveness; one who rapidly drives his parents to extremes of anger and despair. It is equally imaginable that some parents create this state in the child by not meeting his needs, or by abuse. The two are not mutually exclusive; is it not always 'a bit of both'? It is perfectly possible that in most cases it is not. In theory it is possible, for instance, that the vast majority of aggressive children genetically inherit higher levels of certain hormones than the unaggressive and, therefore, that the method used to punish them makes only a negligible difference to how they behave. Or it could be that parental responses are critical and inheritance is largely irrelevant – an equable temperament is made monstrous where it would otherwise, in a different family, have turned out fine; or the opposite – where initially irascible babies are made equable by families that are facilitating.

Bernal *et al*. (1974) found the aggressiveness of a sample of non-compliant and disruptive boys to be greater at home with their mothers than at school. Something about home was different. Kuczynski *et al*. (1987) found marked differences in the styles of negotiation used by thirty-seven children aged two to three to get their way when with their depressed mothers, compared with that of thirty-two non-depressed mothers and their toddlers. Mothers who used reasoning, suggestion and polite commands (for example: 'Could you please put it there?') had children who bargained and offered alternative, compromise solutions when disputing a parental injunction, whereas those children whose mothers employed direct methods, such as physical interventions with no accompanying explanation (for example, pulling a hand away) or incontestable commands ('Put it there!', for instance) tended to use direct defiance such as overt refusals to comply, and angry, defiant, negative affects often amounting to temper tantrums. Kuczynski (*et al*. 1987, p. 805) concluded that his findings were 'consistent with the hypothesis that childrens' interactive strategies may derive from parental models'.

A longitudinal study by Dodge *et al*. (1990) of 309 four-year-old children (almost equally divided between boys and girls) bears out Kuczynski's view. Subjects were video-recorded at home and parent and child were interviewed. Six months later, the children were assessed by teacher ratings, peer nominations and direct observation. Early abuse significantly predicted later observed aggression towards peers and teacher and peer ratings of high aggressiveness. None of five child biological variables (maternal health problems in pregnancy or at birth; children's health problems; maternal recall of a child's fussiness, unadaptability and resistance to control during the first year) predicted abuse of a child.

This is also consistent with the evidence suggesting that a child's pattern of attachment is determined by his mother's (or other carer's) relationship to him (Ainsworth *et al*., 1978), the evidence that positive (so-called 'prosocial') behaviour by children reflects their parents' behaviour (Radke-Yarrow *et al*., 1983; Rheingold and Emery, 1986) and that which shows that a child's degree of impulsivity depends on the family environment (Olweus *et al*., 1986). There is a strong probability that if you exchanged at birth 100 boys from families with hostile, depressed parents with 100 from unaggressive, non-depressed families, regardless of early temperament the boys in the depressed families would become more aggressive. In short, childhood aggressiveness is mainly caused by differences in family relationships; not in genes (see chapter 6). Insofar as 'impulsivity' is ever inborn, the key determinant of whether it is manifested at all in later life is the responses of those who care for the child.

The most robust advocacy for this view comes from Patterson who concludes: 'If our society has antisocial children it is the fault of the adults . . . most "difficult" children do not become antisocial . . . mothers of social aggressors are unskilled, irritable and mildly depressed people . . . while some children may, by temperament, be more difficult to control than others, in any given setting it is the adult who is the major determinant of how much aggression will occur' (Patterson, 1982, pp. 269–71).

PATTERSON'S 'COERCIVE FAMILY PROCESSES'

Patterson conducted microanalyses of what members of families with aggressive boys actually do compared with families having unaggressive ones. Working clinically with hundreds of such families Patterson observed them at home and in laboratory settings and provides one of the few systematic bodies of evidence examining how the behaviour in families of normal children, 'stealers' and 'social aggressors' differ.

All families have what Patterson calls 'coercive processes', the most frequent behavioural manifestations of which are whining, teasing, disapproval, yelling, humiliation, negative commands, non-compliance and hitting: 'Taken individually, most of these aversive events are trivial, a psychological mote . . . Rather than cataclysmic episodes, flood tides of rage or crumbling defensive structures, coercive family processes change with glacial slowness, a process that is composed of events that are inherently banal' (Patterson, 1982). In studying the development of these familial glaciers longitudinally, Patterson has established that coercive behaviours are significantly more common in families with aggressive boys. In such families 'the punishments don't work' and the parents are 'inept' at providing good models for behaviour. The parents display irritable aggression, using punishment more to express anger than as an instrument for altering the child's behaviour. Gradually the amount of aggressive behaviour escalates until the family seems to be permanently on a war footing. Both parents, but especially the mother, report feeling down, depressed and irritable. They find themselves attributing malevolent intentions to the child with no real basis for doing so. Two-thirds of attacks in such families are unprovoked – as, indeed, will so many of the boys' attacks be when they turn into violent men. They take place against a background of what Patterson calls parental 'nattering': continual threats and scolding of the child at the smallest sign of trouble, yet the parents do not carry out the threat and are highly inconsistent. The constant anger and negativity amplifies otherwise harmless acts into the cause of major rows. Threats and other non-physical methods cease working and to make a point the parent is forced to go to the extremities of physical coercion to get their way. The levels of physical violence inflate as the currency of parental coercion becomes devalued. Boys from such families are described as suffering from arrested social development, with the relatively uncontrolled social behaviour of a three- to four-year old found in ten-to eleven-year-olds.

DIFFERENCES BETWEEN 'STEALERS' AND 'SOCIAL AGGRESSORS'

Early claims regarding the differences in family experience of different kinds of antisocial boys have often been based on shaky scientific foundations (Bowlby, 1944). Most of the subsequent major studies of delinquents were not designed in such a way that they could distinguish that which causes stealing from that which causes violence. Of the hundreds of boys Patterson treated clinically and studied, about one-quarter were purely given to stealing, another quarter were solely aggressors and the remaining half sometimes did both (Patterson *et al.*, 1990). Both stealers and aggressors shared some characteristics in common compared with normal children: non-compliance; a tendency to maximize short-term gains; a lack of responsiveness to social 'carrots' (rewards) or 'sticks' (punishments); poor attention, and arrested social development.

Statistically, however, there were significant differences between the stealers and aggressors in several important respects. Stealers had parents who were more distant and cold; much less involved in the child. They misclassified dishonest behaviour, often failing to grasp that their child had actually engaged in stealing and consequently not punishing it. Their ideas about ownership of property and what constituted stealing were poorly defined and amoral. When they did recognize that a violation had occurred they 'nattered' rather than imposed an adequate punishment. By contrast, parents of aggressors were intensely 'enmeshed' with their children, continuously punishing them and highly irritable. Their fathers were significantly more likely to physically attack the child, imposing highly inflexible yet inconsistent systems of rules. If stealers' parents' rules were vague and morally weak, aggressors' fathers were the opposite, pathologically so, but it was the aggressors' mothers who made the biggest difference. They were exceptionally irritable and scolding, threatening at the slightest provocation yet, when the child was aggressive, failing to confront him and to enforce clear guidelines of acceptable conduct. The behaviour of the mothers was found to be the key difference between the two groups (accounting for over 40 per cent of the variance). There is a strong case for supposing that the mothers irritability may be due to depression. In the next chapter, I develop the theory that maternal depression may be a major cause of childhood aggression and adult violence.

This account broadly supports the findings of Jenkins (1966; 1968 described above) based on case records of delinquents. Patterson was able to go into considerably greater detail than any previous researchers, and it repays closer inspection.

AGGRESSORS' AGGRESSION IS ENCOURAGED MORE

On the one hand, aggressive boys, when exhibiting aggressive behaviour, have not been adequately punished , in order to discourage it; on the other, they have actually been encouraged to display it. Patterson showed there are big differences between the amount of positive support attendant on an aggressive act in an aggressor's and a normal home.

By the age of six, nearly all children have learnt to employ coercive behaviour to get their way and that different acts work better on different family members. Whining, non-compliance and yelling, for example, are used more by the average child to coerce his mother than teasing, humiliation and negative commands – which they use on siblings. The victim's reaction is a major determinant of how often particular acts are employed. If the child learns that he can always get his way by yelling then the mother is actually encouraging him to yell every time he wants something. Patterson found that coercive acts by child aggressors were significantly more likely to receive a positive response such as giving in to a demand. Indeed, when the aggressors coerced other children, especially ones from another family, they were much more likely to be actually applauded by their parents for displaying manliness. A clearer mandate to fight other children could not be imagined.

However, this encouragement was not as significant in causing aggression as the methods used to punish it.

FAILURE TO PUNISH AGGRESSION

The aggressive child is twice as likely as the normal child to continue with coercive behaviour after a punishment. Patterson (1982) suggests there are two possible explanations for this difference: 'antisocial behaviour occurs because the parents can't (or won't) confront the child in a consistent manner when he is deviant', or: 'antisocial children are [born] less responsive to punishment'. His conclusion is that even if a child is born less responsive, 'inept parenting will be the key variable and the problem child's hypo-responsiveness can be altered by improvements in the parents' child management skills'. This view is based on microanalyses of the numbers of different types of behaviours employed by parents when punishing their children.

At its simplest, punishment is doing something unpleasant to someone and only stopping when a desired response is exhibited. 'Most parental punishment consists of threats to punish, scolding and so on. To be effective these threats must occasionally be paired with back up punishment' (Patterson, 1982). Threats that are not backed so are 'nattering', which merely serves to increase the amount of behaviour that needs punishing because it devalues the punitive currency.

By contrast, the words of skilled parents have force since the child knows that failure to comply will lead to a worse punishment. Their approach is more sophisticated in dealing with trouble. Either they ignore the child's coercive behaviour altogether, thereby avoiding the pitfall of making him into an effective attention-seeker, or they confront and prevent the behaviour. By contrast: 'When parents tried to punish the coercive behaviour of problem children the immediate effect was to make things worse' (Patterson, 1982). This was because the punishment tended to be an expression of the considerable irritability of the parents rather than a step on a reliable gradient of displeasure designed to train the child to behave acceptably. Parents of aggressors 'nattered' more, were less likely to confront coercion, imposed more punishments and finished up using physical beating more often. That one-third of the antisocial boys were classified as having been physically abused is a measure of the extent of the inflation; warnings were not sufficient. For these parents a physical assault gave satisfying expression to their irritability, took little time and effort and gained a brief respite. To enforce the alternatives, such as a deprivation of privileges or enforced 'time out', required them to forego their own pleasures and lacked the short-term pay off of releasing pent-up anger. The concept of training the child by repeating a longer-term punishment was alien. If sent to his room, the child would only misbehave as soon as he came down, so what was the point? The basic principle of rewarding correct responses and punishing incorrect ones was not being applied. The adult's mood at the time determined their response to coercion. Instead of attaching a clearly expressed rule to a punishment and applying it consistently, these parents used punitive behaviour as a vehicle for anger and irritability.

In support of this analysis Patterson was able to point out that families which were offered training in basic precepts of family management soon changed the behaviour of their boys for the better. He found that 'to change the problem child requires that one change the parents' (Patterson, 1982). Four principles of management determined differences in how coercive a child was: the clarity and content of the house rules; their monitoring; the consistency and timing of their application, and the styles of problem solving, negotiation and crisis management employed. When trained to employ these principles, the parents soon changed the boys' behaviour in ten different studies (reported in Patterson, 1994, pp. 38-45).

THE INFLATION OF COERCION IN AGGRESSORS' HOMES

In experiments with animals, aversive, negative stimuli are highly effective in producing desired responses and discouraging others. Positive reinforcement is nowhere near as successful in inhibiting the undesirable, although it works in accentuating the positive once it has been established. The stick works better than the carrot; a rat will do what you want quicker if you punish it for wrong acts rather than reward it for exhibiting the desired ones. But, as noted above, punishment of undesired behaviour only succeeds if you keep it going until the desired result has occurred. If you pull out before then it only serves to encourage the wrong behaviour by giving the wrong signal. The mother who scolds the child for not clearing up but stops doing so when the child protests and instead offers soothing balm may have achieved the short-term goal of stopping the whining but has failed to get the clearing up done. In the process the child has had a lesson in the effectiveness of whining. Parents of aggressors use a greater frequency of aversive stimuli and punish their boys far more, yet they are ignored twice as often because they also back down and mistime their coercive interventions much more. The result is out-of-control boys in out-of-control families, and escalating violence.

The rate at which animals learn when being negatively reinforced depends on the intensity of the punishment. Electric shocks of low intensity get results slower than higher amplitude ones. In the out-of-control family, higher and higher wattages of punishment are required as the parents' punitive equipment becomes less and less effective and more and more short-term in its goals. Trunk loads of punitive currency become necessary to buy even a modicum of purchase. Furthermore, it takes increasingly less on the boy's part to provoke an increasingly extreme punishment, as mere verbal threats become redundant and the parent feels obliged to move straight to the ultimate deterrent of physical coercion: 'Where escalation is an accepted means for problem solving then physical violence is a predictable by-product' (Olweus et al., 1986). In the normal family, if a parent spanks a child he submits, but if the parent of a socially aggressive child tries to spank: 'he or she is met with anything but submission. The child may respond in a synchronous fashion by hitting back. The reaction may be a temper tantrum, loud yelling, or whatever, but it is very probable that the child will respond in some high-amplitude coercive fashion.'

Nor is the difference between aggressors' families and normal ones purely a matter of degree of intensity of punishment. Quantity, as in the length of the chains of violence, plays a crucial role as well.

LONGER CHAINS OF VIOLENCE IN THE HOMES OF AGGRESSORS

'Socially aggressive children live in aggressive families. Members of these families are disposed to react irritably with each other. They are more likely to persist in their irritable reactions regardless of how the other person reacted . . . the mothers', and to a lesser extent the fathers' disposition to continue their irritable reactions account for the largest portion of the variance in the performance of the child's behaviour' (Patterson, 1982). So once a row has broken out in an aggressor's home it lasts longer as well as being bloodier.

Patterson completes this picture when he looks at the way aggressors' attempts to be positive are responded to.

POSITIVE, 'PROSOCIAL' BEHAVIOUR BY AGGRESSORS RECEIVES LESS ENCOURAGEMENT

When couples are solving problems together, one of the best indices of the likely outcome is the way emotion is handled. If there is a shift from positive or neutral effects to negative ones then the problem is much less likely to be solved. The irritability of the parents of aggressors means that they are worse at finding happy solutions. They are more likely to regard their child as 'bad' before anything has happened and this inevitably means the aggressor gets less positive encouragement when problems are encountered. Being deemed a 'good' child for successful collaboration also happens less. This is exacerbated by the way parents of problem children tend to define what is good and bad. Highly restricted definitions are used so that there is simply less behaviour that such children can do which might give the parent cause to let the child know they are pleased by him. Whereas a normal child need do little to receive parental support and enthusiasm, the aggressor must perform like the paragon that he is already conspicuously far from being, in order to attract praise. Not surprisingly, the incidence of positive, prosocial communications by the parents of aggressors is significantly less.

SUMMARY

The evidence reviewed thus far indicates that childhood aggression, as opposed to antisocial behaviour in general, is caused primarily by patterns of family coercion (rather than, for example, by variations in DNA or RNA). The key factors can be summarized under three headings:

1 *Extensive use of physical punishment* to the point of abuse, made necessary by 'nattering', failure to employ more skilful methods, encouragement of aggressive behaviour and insufficient encouragement of prosocial behaviour.
2 *Disharmony between parents*, especially when it gives rise to physical fighting between them.
3 *Irritability in both parents*, but especially mothers. In Patterson's studies their irritability is significantly greater compared with partners or mothers of stealers and normal boys (see chapter 2 for further consideration of this factor).

There are a number of unresolved questions in this scientific literature, such as the precise role of emotional neglect versus deprivation, and the extent to which merely witnessing violence promotes it. It is not wholly clear if there are reliable differences in the family experience of boys that are solely aggressive, boys who steal, boys who do both and those who do neither. Abuse does not in itself lead to a violent outcome in more than half of cases; the coercive family processes described by Patterson may be crucial in distinguishing violent from non-violent outcomes of abuse. One thing seems beyond reasonable doubt: most childhood aggression is caused primarily by the way parents relate to their children.

FROM CHILDHOOD AGGRESSIVENESS TO ADULT VIOLENCE

We began this chapter with the established fact that aggressive boys continue to be so (Olweus, 1979) and that it is a rarity for an unaggressive boy to become a violent man (Farrington et al., 1988). It followed that the causes of childhood aggression and those of adult violence may be one and the same. What is the evidence for this proposition?

A paper by Curtis in 1963, entitled 'Violence breeds violence – perhaps?', was one of the first to set out the hypothesis in formal terms. Since then there has arisen a substantial, methodologically two-tiered, edifice built largely of sound scientific materials which supports it.

One tier consists of asking adolescents and men who are already violent about their experiences as children (retrospective); the other is to regularly sample the behaviour of selected boys from a young age until they grow into more or less violent adults (prospective). Both supply abundant evidence of differences in childhood treatment, but the prospective method is the more reliable since it avoids the distortions inevitably arising where the only evidence is the man's memory (although there are studies showing that memory is often reliable [Yarrow et al., 1970]) or the ambiguity and incompleteness of official records. The prospective method could provide definitive proof of such things as whether five-year-old boys that were hit a lot or whose parents were irritable are more likely, ten years later, to be violent, violent thieves, exclusively felonious, or sometimes none of these. Regrettably, no prospective studies have yet been constructed that are capable of answering such specific questions and it is the retrospective method which has provided the strongest evidence.

RETROSPECTIVE EVIDENCE

Eight studies have found significant differences in the recollections of violent delinquents as against non-violent ones concerning their childhoods.[7] Comparison of violent and non-violent delinquents is more important than comparison with non-delinquents because it has been well established that, whether violent or not, delinquents tend to have had different parenting from normal children (Loeber and Stouthamer-Loeber, 1987; Robins et al., 1975;

Glueck and Glueck, 1950; Wolfgang *et al.*, 1982). The question is, do *violent* delinquents differ?

All eight studies examined the case records of, or administered questionnaires to, large samples of delinquents to see if there were differences in the amount of childhood abuse and neglect between the violent and non-violent. When added together, a total of 8887 delinquents were examined and in all of them, the more abused the child, the greater his likelihood of being violent or aggressive. The most telling was that by Geller and Ford-Somma (1984) who administered detailed questionnaires to 224 incarcerated juveniles concerning their past family lives. To check that the responses were broadly honest, they interviewed twenty-two of the boys personally and also cross-checked the responses with welfare records so that, for example, if a boy claimed to have been physically abused and hospitalized as a result, it could be verified. The findings were unequivocal: 'There was a close relationship between the violence offenders experienced in their homes and violent delinquency; the more offenders were abused the more violent crimes they committed' (Geller and Ford-Somma, 1984). Taken as a whole this body of evidence potently supports Patterson's and Jenkin's formulations concerning the differences between stealers and aggressors, reliably demonstrating that relentless physical punishment subsequently results in violent, as opposed to other, misdemeanours in adolescence. Furthermore, it supports the hypothesis that violent adolescents are likely to have been aggressive boys. We know that abused boys are more likely to be aggressive so it is reasonable to infer that since they were abused, these violent adolescents were aggressive as boys.

There is one tangential study (Gutierres and Reich, 1981), of 774 delinquents which conflicts with these results. Although the aim of the study was to investigate the differences in background of 'runaways' (children who leave their homes, truant and so forth), along the way they found that aggressiveness in the children did not correlate with the amount of abuse they had endured; if anything, the abused children were actually less likely to engage in violent crime than the non-abused. However, when set alongside the sheer weight of numbers found in the studies mentioned above and the fact that they were designed specifically to test this theory rather than to look at runaways, it must be improbable that the Gutierres finding is generalizable.

A second set of retrospective data ignores delinquency and simply compares violent with non-violent adolescents or men. Again the method is to ask two samples about their past lives and to see if there are differences in the kind of care received. Monane *et al.* (1984) compared 166 abused and non-abused adolescents and children and found a significant relationship between abuse and aggressiveness. Comparing aggressive and unaggressive adolescents or men, four studies showed the aggressive to be more likely to have been harshly punished or abused.[8] Most strikingly, Widom (1989a) found that 809 children who had been abused as children were more likely to become violent offenders in adulthood than controls; the younger the abuse, the greater the likelihood. Widom's study is the strongest support yet that 'violence breeds violence'.

A third set of retrospective data are nineteen studies of the backgrounds of murderers, some including comparison groups.[9] They, too, support the general notion that childhood violence breeds violence: murderers are more likely than non-violent criminals to have been abused or to have suffered other maltreatment as children.

A final group of retrospective studies addresses the more detailed question of whether specific kinds of abuse, such as child physical abuse or witnessing parents fighting, increase the likelihood of repetition of that particular type of violence. While they leave little doubt that they do, it is by no means invariably so. Men do not always repeat precisely what was done to them. Whether being abused as a child leads to child abusing, for example, seems to depend on a great many factors. One (Kaufman and Zigler, 1987) of several reviews (Spinetta and Rigler, 1972; Friedrich and Wheeler, 1982) of the literature on this subject estimated that only 30 per cent of the physically abused become child abusers. This is a far higher proportion than the non-abused but raises questions: 'The rate of abuse among individuals with a history of [being] abuse[ed] is approximately six times higher than the base rate for abuse in the general population . . . being maltreated as a child puts one at risk for becoming abusive but the path between these two points is far from direct or inevitable' (Kaufman and Zigler, 1987). Six studies bear out this conclusion particularly forcefully.[10] The conclusions regarding the witnessing of wife-beating are similar. Although Stark and Flitcroft's (1985) review of this literature casts doubt on the relationship, there are several convincing studies (Straus, 1983; Straus and Gelles, 1988) which strongly suggest that those whose parents fought are more likely to do so themselves with lovers in later life. Kalmuss (1984), for example, showed that wife beaters who had only witnessed it as children were more likely to follow suit in later life than men who had actually been directly abused themselves. Being hit yourself was less likely to result in you hitting lovers than seeing your parents hit was. While this remains a controversial finding, since other studies suggest that abuse is the key variable (Kratcoski, 1985), the tendency for witnesses to become perpetrators is supported. Whilst the exact proportion of specific abuses that are likely to be repeated is a matter for future research, the existing retrospective studies strongly support the violence-breeds-violence thesis.

PROSPECTIVE STUDIES

Whereas retrospective studies start with a violent man or adolescent and work backwards, the prospective approach starts with the boy before he has got into trouble. Numerous large samples have been followed from childhood into adulthood in order to see if the ones who turned out delinquent (or 'antisocial' or 'conduct disordered') had different early care and familial characteristics, and manifested their deviance in consistent ways from before they started to break the law (Farrington, 1987; Loeber and Stouthamer-Loeber, 1987; Robins *et al.*, 1975; Glueck and Glueck, 1950; Wolfgang *et al.*, 1982). Predictors have been developed in the hope of picking out the boys most likely to become delinquent years before they actually do so (Farrington, 1987). In several of them, a tiny proportion of boys (5–7 per cent) account for as much as half of all crime. Many predictors of delinquency have been identified but, unfortunately, most of these studies are of little help in discriminating between the violent and the non-violent delinquent or man because they were not designed to do so. There has been a tendency in this literature to argue that because, in a very general sense, boys who commit property crimes also tend to be violent as compared with non-delinquents, and because both tend to come from the same sort of background, there are probably no significant differences between them; that violence is just one manifestation of an all-encompassing 'antisocial tendency'. Being sociological in nature, the studies were not designed to tease out the subtle differences in the behaviour of families that produce the violent rather than the property criminal. None began observing the behaviour of families before the child was aged five, all but one beginning at age eight, presumably because it was believed that preschool experiences were not important determinants of later behaviour, a view with which few would now concur.

There are five prospective studies that observed boys and their parents in some detail from a young age, and were designed, at least in part, to examine the factors which could affect violence/non-violence as an adult outcome.

McCord (1979)

Between 1939 and 1945, 201 American boys aged five to thirteen from poor homes were visited twice monthly by trained observers in their schools, at home and at play. Ten years later the criminal records of the boys were checked, and in 1975 – now in middle age – those who were still alive were re-traced and interviewed (98 per cent were identified) and their criminal records were examined again. By the average age of forty, fifty-three of the men had been convicted of serious property crimes, thirty-four of crimes against the person, and fifteen of both. When the familial experiences of the men were examined, it was found that 'the boys who lacked maternal affection, who lacked supervision, whose mothers lacked self-confidence and whose fathers were deviant were more often subsequently convicted of property crimes' (McCord, 1979). The boys who became violent criminals also lacked supervision and had mothers lacking self-confidence, but in addition they had been exposed to parental disharmony and to aggression (harsh discipline and physical punishment). This is all that McCord's report tells us about the difference between these two types because there is no other breakdown of the delinquents into violent and non-violent in the presentation of results.

Eron (Lefkowitz et al., 1977)

In 1960, all 870 of the third-grade (average age eight) children in a New York semi-rural school were asked to rate each other's aggressiveness and 80 per cent of their parents were interviewed. The children were extensively reassessed at ages nineteen and thirty, when their spouses were also asked to judge their aggressiveness. The results supplied a definitive demonstration that aggressive boys become violent adults but they revealed less about the causes of aggression. At age eight, there was a powerful correlation between how severely parents had punished the child and how aggressive peers rated them. However, by age nineteen parental punitiveness was less predictive than the extent of identification of the child with the parents (Lefkowitz *et al.*, 1977). Children who had displayed their parents' sense of right and wrong at age eight (in that they were prepared to confess to wrongdoing and displayed guilt) were significantly less likely to be violent at age nineteen. Those who were lowest in identification with mother at age eight were the most violent later on. None the less, severity of punishment at age eight was correlated with nineteen-year-old aggressiveness and, of particular interest in terms of the abuse-breeds-abuse hypothesis, it also correlated with the severity of punishment they employed in disciplining their own children.

Whereas McCord had studied the boys with spectacular thoroughness (twice monthly for five years) but not looked at the crucial parenting variables that might have caused violence, Eron's study lacked this element of repeated first-hand observation; its reliance on peer assessment and parental interviews means it is weak on the question of what really was different in the childhood families of the subsequently violent and non-violent.

Magnusson (Magnusson et al., 1983)

412 Swedish children were assessed for aggressiveness at ages ten and thirteen by teachers and followed up at ages eighteen to twenty-six. The finding that aggressive youths become violent adults was again confirmed but little of importance investigated regarding the causes of aggression. The most significant finding was that boys who went on to commit crimes against the person in later life were more aggressive at ages ten to thirteen than those who committed only property crime. This adds to the body of evidence that the two groups of criminal should not be assumed to be essentially the same people.

Newson and Newson (1989)

700 children in Nottingham were followed from birth to age nineteen. Physical punishment by parents at ages seven and eleven predicted later convictions. Forty per cent of offenders had been smacked or beaten at age eleven compared with 11 per cent of non-offenders.

Farrington (1975)

All 411 boys from one year in six London primary schools were interviewed every two to three years from ages eight to twenty-one and followed up at regular intervals until the age of thirty-two. As with all the other studies, aggression at a young age was significantly correlated with subsequent aggression. By the age of twenty-one, twenty-seven of the boys had been convicted of seriously violent crimes, and these were compared with the ninety-six convicted of non-violent crimes, who were more aggressive than non-delinquents but less so than those convicted of violent crimes. The only childhood factors which significantly distinguished the two groups was the harshness and coldness of the parents' attitude and the severity of their methods of punishment. The violent criminals were almost three times more likely to have been heavily subjected to these at age eight compared to the non-violent delinquents. In general, by the end of the study when the boys were thirty-two, these factors, along with parental disharmony and poor supervision, were predictive of subsequent aggressiveness. However, in concluding the study Farrington did not feel that violent men stood out from the delinquent crowd: 'aggression and violence are elements of a more general antisocial tendency . . . the predictors of aggression and violence are similar to the predictors of antisocial and criminal behaviour in general' (Farrington, 1989a. Patterson *et al.*, 1992, came to a similar conclusion). While there is no question that antisocial men also tend to be aggressive, it remains very possible that a prospective study of a large sample of boys which observed them intensively from birth (rather than aged eight) would reveal significant differences between the family experiences of the solely violent, the violent felon and the felon.

Indeed, despite Farrington's conclusion, and despite their focus on delinquency in general, these prospective studies do reveal some significant differences already between the delinquent and the violent delinquent: severity of punishment comes through in three of those discussed here and such factors as parental disharmony and lack of supervision are also significant in some.

CONCLUSION: FROM CHILDHOOD AGGRESSIVENESS TO ADULT VIOLENCE

Violent men were aggressive boys. The reason boys become aggressive is the way their parents relate to them and to each other. Their irritability, disharmony and abusiveness are markedly greater. They explain the difference between aggressive and unaggressive boys. By no means all boys who were abused become violent adults. The crucial difference may be found in the patterns of coercive process described by Patterson. It seems likely that where abuse is part of a consistent, structured regime it is much less likely to have a violent outcome.

There can be little doubt that, whether delinquent or not, violent adults had different boyhood care from non-violent ones. In particular, both the retrospective and prospective studies reveal that they were punished more severely and were more likely to have been abused. There is also evidence that their parents were more disharmonious and irritable.

WIDER IMPLICATIONS

In chapter 3 I shall present persuasive evidence that parental irritability, abuse and disharmony are more common in families with low incomes. It follows that the more families there are on low incomes, the more parents there will be displaying these characteristics to their sons. The more of such families, the higher the proportion of aggressive boys and the greater the number of violent adolescents and adults several years later.

2   IRRITABILITY IN DEPRESSED MOTHERS: A HIDDEN CAUSE OF VIOLENCE?

And she was doing everything at 'ome, vacc'ing, washing and ironing, out of routine. Right? And she were taking pills like they were going out of fashion – sleeping pills – and she was becoming nothing more than a zombie.

A murderer describing his mother.

Q: Was she quite cheerful?
A: Ach, she was always, the world on her shoulders at that time. She really did have.
Q: Do you think she was quite depressed really?
A: Aye. Terrible mixed up, struggled to live.
Q: She had two children die and her husband dead. Were you close to her?
A: No.
Q: Did she used to cuddle and kiss you?
A: No.
Q: Can you remember any time in your childhood when you had a happy occasion with your mother, a day out together or something like that, a holiday . . .
A: No.

An habitually-violent Glaswegian.

The title of this chapter may cause some readers to emit a despairing sigh: 'It's always the woman's fault, that's right, blame it on that most defenceless of the sex, the depressed mother.' On the contrary, my objective here and in chapter 5 is to chart and explain the flow of aggression and depression in families, up and down the generations, across the genders and between the classes. If depression in mothers is a major cause of aggression in their sons it is only because mothers become the 'storm centres' (Patterson, 1982) for the torrid emotions stirred up in families in difficulties. Murder of children is the only violent offence that women are more likely to commit than men (*Criminal Statistics* 1993). Abuse in the earliest years is more likely to be by the mother than the father (Geller and Ford-Somma, 1984). We have also seen that irritability in mothers is the single most significant factor distinguishing aggressors from stealers in Patterson's studies, more so than paternal irritability. The most common reason why these mothers hit their children and are so irritable is depression.

CHILDCARE IS DEPRESSING AT THE BEST OF TIMES

Patterson maintains that childcare is inherently depressing work, inverting the word euphoric to call it dysphoric:

> At least a dozen longitudinal studies have shown that the first year or two after birth is associated with maternal depression. Under the best of conditions (i.e. normal mothers, intact families) raising a normal infant is highly stressful. This seems to be a well kept secret . . . because most adults are unwilling to face the fact that family life is characterized by a high density of daily aversive events. A normal mother will experience a trivial aversive event about once every three minutes; the rates are even higher for younger children or mothers with large families. The daily round of aversive events . . . lead twice as many wives as husbands to report being depressed. (Patterson et al., 1990).

There are more than passing connections between the black feelings of depressed mothers and the destructive behaviour of their sons.

Patterson has looked closely at the relationship between maternal irritability, childhood aggression and maternal depression. First of all, the irritability clearly causes aggression in the boys: 'The mother's disposition to continue in her irritable reactions, regardless of the child's reaction, was significantly greater for the antisocial samples than for the normal sample . . . mother-continuance accounted for a major portion of the variance in the child's [aggression] score' (Patterson, 1982). The father's behaviour did not account for that of the child to the same degree. Patterson explains why: 'Rather than train the child she scolds. Rather than confront the child . . . she natters and threatens' (Patterson, 1982). On the one hand, the irritable mother is too permissive and self-preoccupied to confront the child, and on the other, she explodes vesuvially from time to time with a violent aggression that teaches the child no useful lesson. Whatever causes the irritability is the single biggest cause of the child's aggression: 'Irritability reflects internal processes [in the mother] . . . she feels angry about her family and the uncontrollable situation in which she finds herself. Constant conflict plus the lean schedules for positive reinforcement provided for mothers in the families place them at grave risk for depression . . . the ratio of positive to aversive events is very low' (Patterson, 1982). The relentless flow of negativity creates irritability and hostile attitudes to other family members, which in turn means she gets less positive reactions back. The outcome is depression: low self esteem, hopelessness and helplessness.

It may seem an odd idea, but, psychologically speaking, depressed women have a great deal in common with violent men. They share a tendency to attribute malign intentions to acts of others that normal people would have thought benign, and they are conspicuously hostile and avoidant in their personal relationships. These similarities are not coincidental and their implication is that maternal depression plays a hitherto underestimated role in the genesis of violence.

The Attribution of Malevolence by Violent Men

The fundamental process behind all violence involves two mental operations. Step one is the attribution of malign intentions to another with the assumption that that person is to blame for an unpleasant experience. Step two: this provokes frustration and anger. The actual attack comes next. It follows that men prone to imagining malevolence where none exists (paranoia) are more likely to get involved in violence and, indeed, it is the case that such paranoia is commonplace in violent men.

Paranoid ideas amongst aggressive males start in childhood. Dodge (1980) videotaped and compared ninety aggressive boys competing to solve a puzzle with a control group of unaggressive boys. The trick that he played was to interrupt them all when some way into the task and to subject them to one of three possible influences: in the first interruption the boys were unequivocally given to understand that another boy was ruining all their good work on the puzzle; the second was ambiguous, so that the boy might imagine something hostile or supportive was going on, depending on how he chose to intepret it; in the third there was an unambiguously benign intervention. This machiavellian scheme revealed no differences in the ways the aggressive and unaggressive boys reacted when the intervention was unambiguous, whether benign or hostile. But in the ambiguous condition there was a significant difference: the aggressive boys divined a hostile intent and became aggressive, whereas the unaggressive attributed benign intentions and were friendly. To check that the boys' aggression was triggered by their assumption that the intent behind the ambiguous intervention was hostile, Dodge rigged up a further experiment. He asked two similar groups to tell him how they felt a child would react in various hypothetical settings in which they were first the accidental, then the deliberate, victim of another child's actions. Sure enough, the aggressive boys were statistically more likely to attribute malign intentions in the accidental settings, to say they would mistrust its perpetrator as a result and that they would respond to the accident with aggression.

Given the size of the samples used and the care employed in their conduct, Dodge's experiments provide substantial evidence that aggressive boys are more prone to attribute malign intentions and that this attribution is instrumental in making them aggressive. Patterson suggests why: 'Most socially aggressive boys live with parents who initiate negative interactions with them at over twice the rate of well-socialized boys; these boys' siblings initiate

negative interchanges at over three times the rate of well-socialized boys . . .
the paranoia of the aggressive boy may not be paranoia at all but an accurate
representation of his experience' (Patterson, 1982). In short, aggressive boys
need not 'adjust their set' if they espy malignancy in their home, for the odds
are that that is precisely what is going on. Small wonder that when they venture
forth into the world beyond they are liable to suffer delusions of being 'got
at'; and that they grow into the youth who asks completely innocent strangers
'What are you looking at?', immediately before pre-empting anticipated attacks
or indignities with a fist or knife (as Poyner (1980) reported in one study of
street violence).

Direct evidence of the paranoia of violent men – as opposed to boys – is
plentiful in clinical literature (Gallwey, 1985; Glaser, 1983; Storr, 1968), but
it has been demonstrated experimentally as well. Some of Dodge's paranoid
boys become the psychopathic, mentally ill adults studied by Blackburn and
Lee-Evans (1985) in controlled conditions in two secure prisons. They compared two samples of twenty-eight psychopaths' and non-psychopaths' reactions to hypothetical situations. They were asked how they would react to
various stimuli ranging from the mildly annoying to the highly threatening.
The psychopaths were significantly more likely to say they would respond
with aggression and to perceive malevolence behind the stimulus. In a further
study of 282 patients, Blackburn (1986) compared the reactions of two
different kinds of psychopath and found that all were prone to hostility or
rejection of others and easily aroused to anger. While they were divided
between a withdrawn, over-controlled and especially paranoid group, as
opposed to a friendly, sociable under-controlled one, Blackburn concluded
that: 'Psychopaths as a group more readily interpret provocation or threats
from others as unwarranted attacks' (Blackburn, 1986). These tendencies may
be particularly pronounced in psychopaths, but they are also the norm
amongst most violent men. Patterson again summarizes the position (Patterson, 1982): ' . . . the violent person is more likely to attribute a malevolent
intent to the behaviour of the other person . . . an otherwise simple argument
becomes a potential battleground. These people *all believe they were provoked*' (Patterson, 1982 [Patterson's emphasis]). Having attributed hostility
and malevolence to their victims, violent men feel angered and under threat,
so they go on the attack. For those waiting to learn what all this has to do with
depression, Patterson goes on to explain something else about 'these people':
'It is the person with the low self-esteem who is most likely to be caught up
in the anger/negative attribution cycle.' Enter the depressed woman.

THE ATTRIBUTION OF MALEVOLENCE BY DEPRESSED WOMEN

In studying the families of aggressive boys, Patterson noticed that physically
abusive parents were significantly more likely than normal ones to feel their
children were getting at them: 'The observers often saw the parents hit [their

children]. The parents also seemed to attribute malevolent intentions to the child' (Patterson, 1982). This could be because aggressive boys merit such attributions more; that they are actually more malevolent. However, six studies suggest this tendency – at least in women – is caused by depression.[1] Samples of depressed mothers and their children were observed and compared with normal couples; in all of them, the mothers attributed such things as 'maladjustment' to the child more if they were depressed, regardless of how badly the child actually behaved as measured by the independent observers. It was the level of depression of the mothers and not the difficulty of their offspring which predicted whether they would attribute badness to them (we are assuming here that a mother who makes such attributions is experiencing the child as malevolent). Given how negative that depressed people feel, this is not surprising. It suggests that six further studies,[2] which found a general correlation between maternal depression and negativity towards offspring, but which did not address the question of the child's contribution to this correlation, should be interpreted as further evidence for the view that it is their depression that makes the mothers more likely to attribute malevolence to their children. This may help us to distinguish the chicken of childhood aggressiveness from the egg of maternal negativity. Wahler described the behaviour of three mothers of aggressive children, whom he studied in depth, as follows: 'all three mothers appeared to be chronically depressed and angry . . . [they] seemed disinterested and detached . . . when provoked into extended confrontations [by their offspring] we were struck by the combative, almost sibling like quality of their responses, 'name calling' (e.g. 'you jerk!') or other derogatory language or even taunts (e.g.'you just try it!')' (Wahler and Dumas, 1986).

Of course, it could be that these women had been made depressed by the insufferable behaviour of their children rather than that they were its cause. There are several studies that suggest the possibility that, at least in some cases, babies born 'difficult' could create depression in mothers. Field et al. (1988) showed that when a non-depressed experimenter interacted with depressed mothers' infants their behaviour became less positive and expressive than when interacting with infants of non-depressed mothers.

Cutrona and Troutman (1986) reported that maternal depression was more likely to persist if three-month-old infants were difficult to soothe and cried excessively. Whiffen and Gotlib (1989) found that two-month-old infants of depressed mothers were more tense and less content. However, in each case it is possible that the mother's depression could have caused the infant to be difficult rather than the other way around. Murray (1993) compared women at high risk of depression before the birth with women at low risk. Mothers whose infants were irritable in the neo-natal period were significantly more likely to become depressed by six weeks postpartum than those with non-irritable infants. This was so regardless of the pre-natal risk of depression. However, this study has not followed the dyads on into the first year and beyond. Previous studies suggest that irritability in the infant changes for the better if the mother is responsive. They showed that the mother's responsiveness predicts the infant's later pattern of attachment to the mother. Thus, Hock *et al.* (1973) and Waters *et al.* (1980) demonstrated that irritability of a baby at birth did not predict later attachment anxiety at eleven months and one year respectively. Most revealing of all, Crockenberg (1981) measured infant irritability at five and ten days of age, maternal responsiveness at three months old, security of attachment of the child at age one year and the amount of social support the mother had throughout. Infant irritability changed according to maternal responsiveness which, in turn, was strongly influenced by social support. While it is plausible that maternal depression may sometimes be caused by an exceptionally difficult infant or by a particularly vulnerable mother giving birth to an infant with which she especially does not fit in interactional style, the evidence as it stands makes it seem unlikely that infant temperament accounts for much maternal depression. The balance of probabilities is that the implication of the six studies cited earlier (note 1) in which mothers attributed malign intentions to their offspring regardless of how difficult they were measured to be by independent observers, is correct: the mother's negative attributional system preceded the behaviour of her offspring.

Violent men attribute malevolence more than normal. So do depressed women. Do the latter's attributions not play a central role in causing the former's? Several mechanisms could be involved. It could be that violent men learn to expect the worst from others by witnessing their mothers doing so. It could also be that they identify emotionally with this characteristic, reproducing it in their own relationships. This would be Freud's (1900) 'identification with the aggressor', as opposed to the purely behaviourist learning of the pattern through reward and punishment. But there is another aspect of depressed mothers which could contribute: like violent men they are also extremely hostile and rejecting, and especially so in their dealings with intimates. That means offspring of depressed mothers are conduits for a great deal of negative criticism and malice. For the child who is the object of such persistent hostility *not* to subsequently attribute malevolence to others would require explanation – it is wholly expected. Together, the experiences of constantly having malign intents attributed to them and of being the actual object of maternal hostility, could go a long way to explaining the paranoia of aggressive boys and of the violent men they become.

HOSTILITY IN DEPRESSED WOMEN

Depression is most prevalent of all in mothers of young children, especially mothers with low incomes (Brown and Harris, 1978) – the sort of mothers violent men are most likely to have had, as suggested in chapter 3. It is a black, negative mood which encumbers all aspects of life (Weissman and Paykel,

1974). Either the victim feels so miserable that they are 'beyond tears', flat and without visible emotion, or they are palpably unhappy. Helplessness and hopelessness are common and the sense of worthlessness ranges from a vague, low self-esteem and the denigration of any accomplishments, to rampant feelings of failure, guilt and self-blame for real and imagined failings. Accompanying these negative states is a pervasive sense of fear and intense worry. There is a slowing down of the speed of thought, speech and movement which may alternate sporadically with manic phases of tense overactivity and agitation, a ceaseless pacing of rooms and quickfire, rambling locution. Sleep is disrupted, usually with night-sweats and insomnia, or at other times with a need for excessive amounts. To be feeling like this and responsible twenty-four hours of the day, 365 days of the year, for a baby is one of life's cruellest mental tortures. No wonder violence towards very small children is the only category in which women equal men (Geller and Ford-Somma, 1984).

Until the mid-seventies it was widely believed that depressed people are depressed because they are turning their aggression against themselves, as evident in the savage negativity they display towards themselves and, at its most extreme, in the physical attacks they make against their bodies – not just in suicide attempts, but in self-destructive illnesses such as the eating disorders bulimia nervosa and anorexia nervosa, both of which are more common among the depressed. The assumption was that outwardly-directed hostility must be reduced since it is all turned against the self. However, this view had to be modified after the publication of Weissman and Paykel's careful comparison of forty depressed women with forty non-depressed ones (Weissman and Paykel, 1974). It showed that depressed women are anything but unaggressive. They displayed 'significantly more overt interpersonal hostility in most relationships, and the intensity of these feelings ranged from resentment, general irritability, through arguments of increasing intensity, to physical encounters' (Weissman and Paykel, 1974). As in Patterson's studies, the brunt of this hostility was borne by their children, with whom they had twice as much friction as their spouses, although they were significantly more hostile to both of these than to their extended family members, friends and professional colleagues. In almost all their dealings they proved more hostile than the controls. Because of this marked viciousness towards intimates, Weissman was able to explain why researchers had not noticed the pattern before. Not being intimates the researchers doing the studies did not evoke it: 'The depressed patient's behaviour at interview is a poor sample of her actual behaviour outside. In the initial psychiatric interview she is cooperative, compliant and not hostile' (Weissman and Paykel, 1974).

It seems that depressed women not only attack themselves but direct more aggression outwards as well, especially to their intimates, seething with hostility towards their children. They are more aggressive in every direction. This is supported by numerous other studies. In general, they are more likely to behave in negative ways towards others (Biglan *et al.*, 1990), capable of being 'critical of other people to the point of delusion' (Philip, 1970). They are reported in six studies also to have a negative impact on others (Biglan *et al.*, 1990)[3] – causing mental illness and stress in marital partners – and are especially likely to show 'striking evidence of persistent hostility' (Paykel and Dienelt, 1971) if they are of the kind that attempt suicide. Four studies reveal that they display more aggression towards their spouses and have more conflict in their marriages than the undepressed[4] – significant when we recall the role of witnessing parental disharmony in the genesis of childhood aggression. Perhaps most significant of all for the causes of violence, they were markedly more hostile to their children in seven studies comparing the interactions of depressed mothers and children with undepressed couples[5], more likely to 'initiate hostile or rejecting exchanges' (Weissman and Paykel, 1974). If this is correct, then where it is present, maternal depression should cause aggression in boys (the best predictor of adult violence), since irritability (if anything, milder than hostility and rejection) in mothers is the single best explanation of the variance between aggressors and stealers. That aggression and depression go together in mothers was especially clear in a study by Altemeier (Altemeier *et al.*, 1982) which tested 1400 women prenatally, of whom twenty-three had abused their children within two years. The abusive women displayed significantly more 'aggressive tendencies' and 'felt grouchy' before the birth and at the same time had lower self-esteem and had felt depressed since the pregnancy began.

DEPRESSED MOTHERS ARE REJECTING; REJECTED SONS ARE AGGRESSIVE

A mother who is depressed, then, is especially likely to attribute malevolence to her children's deeds and to act hostile. Mothers who are like this can be legitimately characterized as rejecting since one of the effects of maternal depression from a child's point of view is to feel rejected. If boys who are rejected by their mothers are more aggressive than unrejected ones, and if maternal depression creates rejection, then it plays a significant role in causing violence in men.

The connection between rejecting mothers and aggressive boys has been known for a long time. Back in 1934, Newell's study of thirty-five rejecting mothers (Newell, 1934) concluded that their children were attention seeking and aggressively insecure as a result. Symonds's similar study in 1938 (Symonds, 1938) included a comparison group and found the rejected to be more rebellious and hostile. Wolberg described the character structure of the rejected child as low in self-esteem, full of rage and with a persistent sense of frustration (Wolberg, 1944). By 1968, Bandura was able to cite a long list of studies (Bandura and Walters, 1966) supporting his contention that 'the critical role of affectional deprivation and rejection in the formation of aggressive disorders has been demonstrated by numerous investigators . . . early and severe rejection, particularly maternal rejection, was predominant in the histories of aggressive children'. In his own thorough comparison of 26 aggressive boys with 26 un-aggressive boys he concluded: 'nonnurturance and rejection appear to be important preconditions of the development of antisocial aggression' (Bandura and Walters, 1966).

REJECTION AND 'ANXIOUS ATTACHMENT' IN CHILDREN

More recent work on rejection has mostly been channelled into study of two patterns of 'anxious attachment' – the avoidant and resistant-clinging – in young children (Ainsworth et al., 1978). Anxious attachment and aggressiveness as outcomes of rejection are, of course, not the same, but they are close relatives. Avoidant children aged six months to three years had 'primary caregivers' (in most cases, the mother) who were angry and rejecting towards them, the children reacting negatively on being separated or reunited as a result. In an experimental setting designed to test the theory, as well as through observations in the home, Ainsworth et al. (1978) and twelve subsequent studies[6] have reliably repeated the finding that angry rejection by the mother produces a rejecting, stand-offish child. The mothers 'more frequently had their positive feelings towards the infant overwhelmed by anger and irritation. They also expressed their rejection in terms of aversion to close bodily contact' (Ainsworth et al., 1978). Main (1977) found that the mother's rejection of contact and her angry behaviour correlated with a syndrome of specific behaviours in infants of only one year old. Normal infants when rejected in this manner avoided the mother rather than approach her after brief separations. This temporary reaction in normal infants is a permanent feature of rejected, avoidant infants who fail to approach friendly adults of all kinds, not just their mothers, and are also active in avoiding eye-contact or any other kind of direct communication. They act as if they could not care whether their mothers were there or not, pointedly giving them the cold shoulder. Above all, from our standpoint, Main's rejected infants hit and threatened to hit the mother, were actively disobedient to her and manifested a great deal of angry behaviour.

The resistant-clinging children can also be characterized as having been rejected, but in a different way. Their mothers have been psychologically unavailable, leaving the child emotionally abandoned, bereft and with mixed feelings. Experimentally separated, the children show distress and anger; on reunion they cling intensely yet resist attempts to make eye or emotional contact.

In their different ways, anxiously attached children display non-compliance and aggression to mothers who have rejected them whether by the direct expression of hostility or indirectly by not giving love. There are eight studies showing that rejection (in its broadest sense) causes anxious attachment[7], some of them exploring subtle distinctions in the form it takes. George and Main (1979) assumed that physically abused children may be taken as exemplars of the most rejected that a child can be, and compared attachment in ten victims thereof with ten normal one- to three-year-olds. The avoidant behaviour of the abused was significantly greater and they assaulted their caregivers and other children four times as often as the unabused. The explanation for this behaviour is suggested as a combination of imitation of the parent, attention seeking and sheer rage at having been attacked. Egeland (Egeland and Sroufe, 1981a, 1981b; Egeland *et al.*, 1983) followed a variety of samples of sixty-two maltreated children from birth to nearly five years of age, including twenty-four who had been abused, nineteen whose mothers were verbally hostile, and nineteen whose mothers were psychologically unavailable. The maltreated as a whole were significantly more anxiously attached, with the abused more resistant; the ones with psychologically unavailable mothers were more avoidant, angry and non-compliant; the hostile were liable to have elements of both patterns. The hostile mothers were 'Chronically verbally abusive . . . found fault with their children and criticized them in an extremely harsh fashion' (Egeland and Sroufe, 1981b), reminiscent of the depressive's critical, 'to the point of delusion', stance towards intimates, especially offspring. At the same time, another aspect of the depressive syndrome is evident in the psychologically unavailable mother's withdrawn, sad aspect. As noted above, depressed women can be principally outgoing and overtly hostile in their style of interaction or more silent and concealed in their anger, or a mixture of both. Egeland does not record the psychiatric status of these women but it is a fair bet that many of them were depressed.

The concept of anxious attachment is not of itself a direct measure of aggressiveness in children, although aggressive behaviour is part of its definition. Mawson (1980) has gone so far as to propose that much aggression should be understood as a species of attachment behaviour. He points out that the two have very similar determinants. Separation and rejection often precede both proximity seeking and violence; so do intense attachment behaviours like nagging, insults and threats; so, also, does stress. The targets of both violence and proximity seeking are often familiar people. The goal of violence is physical contact, often of a very extreme kind: Mawson suggests that the tendency for homicides to stab and penetrate the body of victims many times more than is necessary to kill indicates a potent need for contact for its own sake. Finally, he points to the fact that much violence indicates intense attachment-needs in the perpetrator, expressing feelings like jealousy and extreme dependence. It is worth quoting Mawson's conclusions in full:

> Starting with the observation that many victim–offender relationships in criminal violence involve intimates or familiars, the thesis of the present paper has been that much so-called aggressive, homicidal and assaultive behaviour is an intense expression of the tendency to seek proximity of familiar persons under conditions of stress, even when the individual toward whom the behaviour is directed is the source of stress. On this view, the injuries suffered by the victim in the course of the behaviour are the

unplanned and unintended consequences of the perpetrator's attempts to make strong contacts, albeit penetrating and sometimes lethal contact. It was further suggested that the stronger the offending individual's predisposition for attachment behaviour, the greater the probability that injury will be inflicted fortuitously in the course of seeking contact (Mawson, 1980).

Mawson might have added that violent men are much more likely to come from anxious-attachment-inducing childhood relationships and, therefore, are more likely to be engaged in proximity seeking of the kind he believes causes violence.

Certainly, there is abundant evidence that anxiously-attached children are more aggressive than the securely-attached. It can be indirectly inferred from the ten longitudinal studies of attachment listed above in note 6, but direct studies have also been made. Mention has already been made of George and Main's (1979) finding that their anxiously-attached, abused sample were four times as aggressive as the controls, but we should expect this of the abused anyway. To this can be added the studies by Egeland (Egeland and Sroufe, 1981a, 1981b; Egeland et al., 1983) which found that children who were anxiously-attached at twelve and eighteen months were significantly more likely to have 'behaviour problems', including 'acting out', at preschool ages of three to four. The avoidant were particularly aggressive; described as 'hostile', 'impulsive' and 'withdrawn'. Three other studies have similar findings.[8] It seems highly probable that most aggressive boys are anxiously-attached but that not all the anxiously-attached are aggressive.

A direct test of this idea with specific reference to the differences in the tendency to be a victimizer or a victim was conducted by Troy and Sroufe (1987). Their pattern of attachment having been assessed at ages one year to eighteen months, ten avoidantly- and ten resistantly-clingingly-attached and eighteen securely-attached four- to five-year-old children were observed. After six weeks together in a nursery school, the children were placed in dyads in a playroom and observed for fifteen minutes in seven play sessions on different days and the degree of victimization behaviour was measured. Victimization was only done by avoidant children – none of the secure or resistant-clinging children victimized, as previous studies have found (Erickson et al., 1985; Sroufe, 1983). There was victimization in every case where two anxiously-attached children were paired together. Resistant clingers were never victimizers and were liable to be victims, as two previous studies have shown (Pastor, 1981; Sroufe, 1983). Regarding the role of avoidant attachment in violence, Troy and Sroufe (1987) concluded that: 'Indisputably, as children, such individuals [the avoidantly-attached] learned both the role of abused and abuser. They later recreate that relationship by taking up the role of the latter.'

Unfortunately, Troy and Sroufe do not specify the genders of the different proportions in the dyads and different categories. The lack of differentiation between the genders in all the studies mentioned may conceal a major effect.

The fact that girls are much less aggressive and that women are less violent would lead logically to the conclusion that girls are more prone to a resistant-clinging pattern of anxious attachment than boys.

Nor do these studies discuss the psychiatric status of the mothers, but the behaviour of the mothers is consistent with what we know of the depressed. It seems highly probable that depression is a major cause of the rejecting (using the word in the broadest sense) patterns of mothering which cause anxious attachment and, indeed, direct proof of this hypothesis comes from five studies in which anxious attachment was more common in the children of depressed mothers, compared with controls.[9] The most impressive demonstration was by Radke-Yarrow et al. (1985) who compared attachment in fifty-six children of mothers with major depressive illnesses to thirty-one with normal mothers. Not only was there significantly more anxious attachment in the children of the depressed group, but the longer and more severe the mother's attack had been, the greater the likelihood of anxiety in the child. If the father was also depressed it made no significant difference to attachment. Taken with the other four studies, we can be confident that maternal depression, anxious attachment and increased childhood aggressiveness go together.

SO ARE THE SONS OF DEPRESSED MOTHERS MORE AGGRESSIVE?

To briefly recapitulate the argument so far, aggressive boys and violent men attribute malevolence more, as do depressed mothers. Perhaps such boys and men had depressed mothers from whom they acquired this cast of mind. Certainly, they come from the kinds of large, low income and poorly-supported families which are most likely to have depressed mothers. Depressed mothers are also malignantly hostile in general and are particularly so towards their children. For the child, not only would this feed the tendency to attribute malevolence, but also feel like rejection. Rejected boys are more aggressive than the non-rejected in the studies of twenty years ago, and more recent work on the anxiously-attached products of maternal rejection shows that they, too, are more aggressive. Since mothers of anxiously-attached children are more likely to be depressed it may be a major cause of anxious attachment, which correlates with aggression.

The final test of this argument is the evidence of studies directly addressing the question: are sons of depressed women more aggressive? Eleven investigations suggest that they are.[10] Patterson (1980), for example, compared the mothers of thirteen social aggressors and found them to be significantly more depressed than those of fifteen stealers. Weintraub et al. (1986) looked at teacher and peer ratings of the aggressiveness of 186 children of women with major affective illnesses and found they were judged to be significantly more aggressive than children with normal mothers. Richman et al.'s (1982) longitudinal study of ninety-three boys with behaviour problems such as 'temper tantrums', compared with ninety-one controls, found them significantly more likely to have a depressed mother. To these eleven studies can be added the more scattergun evidence of a further five[11] which recorded strong correlations between high maternal-depression scores on an inventory of psychiatric symptoms and aggressiveness in their children. The final source of direct evidence on this point comes from four[12] studies of abusive mothers. Since abused boys are significantly more likely to be aggressive than the non-abused; if their mothers are more likely to be depressed it follows that depressed mothers have more aggressive sons. In these studies, the mothers of the abused were, indeed, more likely to be depressed. Taken together, this body of evidence leaves little doubt that aggressive children are significantly more likely to have depressed mothers than unaggressive ones. It follows that violent men are more likely to have had depressed mothers since aggression in boys predicts adult violence, although no studies have tested this hypothesis directly, either prospectively or retrospectively, to my knowledge.

LIMITS TO THIS THEORY

There is an important caveat which must be acknowledged regarding the above argument: aggression is by no means the only consequence of having a depressed mother. At least nine studies have shown that it causes a variety of other symptoms including withdrawal, depression and anxiety in offspring and make no explicit mention of aggression as the outcome.[13] Several studies specifically found no increase in aggression (Rogers and Forehand, 1983, for example) and some have tested the theory that maternal depression actually reduces aggression in spouses and offspring by evoking pity and fear (Hineline, 1977). There are undoubtedly important and large differences in the ways children react to having a depressed mother and many factors, so far unestablished, affect this. Not least is the form the depression takes, which, as we have seen, varies considerably. It is tentatively known, for example, that a bipolar (manic-depressive) illness is associated with the avoidant pattern of attachment more than the others (Radke-Yarrow *et al.*, 1985) and that the psychologically unavailable mother (who is presumably more likely to suffer from unipolar, relentlessly sad and withdrawn symptoms) is more likely to produce children with resistant-clinging attachment (Egeland and Sroufe, 1981b). The intensity and longevity of the symptoms have also been shown to be significant, as we might expect (Radke-Yarrow *et al.*, 1985). Most significant factor of all in the different ways children react is their sex. In this chapter we have been forced to switch repeatedly between the words 'children' and 'boys' in describing the effects of depression because many of the studies reviewed make no distinction between the genders in reporting their results. Had they done so we suspect the results of many of them would have been far more clear-cut. Whereas boys are more likely to respond to all forms of parental disturbance with outwardly directed, destructive behaviour, girls tend to become self-destructive. If the studies had more clearly demarcated boys from girls, the boys' aggressive reactions might have come through more obviously; not masked by the girls' low aggression scores. It is with this difference that chapter 5 is concerned.

What we have seen in this chapter is that if mothers become helpless, angry and hopeless – depressed – it causes them to relate to their children in ways that increase aggression. If they get into a frame of mind where even the most innocent act seems like a persecution, it eventually rubs off on their children. The most visible manifestation of the way these mothers have related to their sons is that the boys imagine hostility ('What are you looking at?') that simply was never intended (just as their mothers did), before launching a physical attack – just as their mothers did. By this route, maternal depression may be a major contributor to the violence statistics.

WIDER IMPLICATIONS

What determines whether a mother becomes depressed, thereby – if the argument in this chapter is correct – increasing the likelihood of an aggressive son?

The mothers of aggressive children are conspicuously more critical and hostile because they are depressed. Their depression may, in some cases, be genetically inherited. However, the social and economic causes of depression in women caring for small children have been studied extensively in recent years and, as we shall see in chapter 3, are crucial. They are clearly different from any inborn impulsiveness in their offspring and, as discussed above, it is unlikely that inborn difficultness of the child is a major cause of maternal depression. Since women with low incomes are far more likely to be depressed than rich ones, they are concomitantly more likely to be providing the hostile, critical behaviour which is found in the homes of aggressive children. Since most violent men had a low-income mother, with the increased probability of being depressed that goes with this status, it may be a major factor in causing childhood aggression and adult violence: the more poor mothers, the more depressed mothers; the more depressed mothers, the more aggressive sons; the more aggressive sons, the more violent men.

One of the consequences of the increase from 19 per cent to 30 per cent in the number of low-income families since 1979 will almost certainly have been a concomitant increase in the numbers of depressed mothers. One of the consequences of that, if the argument of this chapter is correct, will be an increase in the number of specifically violent – not just criminal – men when these mothers' children grow up.

3 LOW INCOME VERSUS SINGLE PARENTING, LOW INTELLIGENCE AND THE UNDERCLASS CULTURE AS CAUSES OF PARENTAL ABUSE, DISHARMONY AND IRRITABILITY

> When I use the term 'underclass' I am indeed focussing on a certain type of poor person defined not by his condition – e.g. long term unemployed – but by his deplorable behaviour in response to that condition – e.g., unwilling to take on the jobs that are available to him.
>
> *Losing Ground*
> Charles Murray (1984)

INTRODUCTION

The large and soundly-based body of scientific evidence presented in chapters 1 and 2 strongly support the thesis that the difference between violent and non-violent men in technologically-developed nations is the way in which they were treated as children. In particular, severe and frequent physical punishment amounting to abuse, parental disharmony and irritability (especially in mothers) were identified as key variables. The evidence that these factors are significantly more common in families where the income is low is presented in this chapter and the fact that they co-vary so consistently strongly suggests that low income is a principal cause of violence-inducing parenting. However, three other factors which also co-vary with low income have also been offered as causal – single mothering, low intelligence scores and the underclass culture. These alternative explanations for why it is parents of low income who are most likely to act in a violence-inducing fashion are addressed in the second part of the chapter.

LOW INCOME, ABUSING, PARENTAL IRRITABILITY AND DISHARMONY

Do the three factors (abuse, irritability and disharmony) identified in chapters 1 and 2 to be decisive in determining whether a boy was aggressive or not and, by extension, whether he becomes a violent man, occur significantly more in families with a low income? If so, this fact more than any other may explain why most violence is perpetrated by men from poor backgrounds. The correlation is that if they happened as frequently in the homes of high-income males, they would be as violent.

Low Income and Abusing (as Part of a Severe Regime of Physical Punishment)

Low income, low educational attainment and lack of full-time employment have been shown to increase the likelihood of abuse by parents.

Evidence that the low-income parents abuse more comes from two main sources. The first is that of child abuse registers. The NSPCC survey for 1989–1990 revealed that nearly two-thirds of the fathers of children on at-risk registers were not in full-time employment, and NSPCC records have consistently found this to be so in previous years (NSPCC, 1990). Of those that were in work, most had manual jobs. An American survey of all 90,000 children on abuse registers in 1976–7 found that the lower the income, the greater the likelihood of abusing (Wilson et al., 1980). One half of all the families were subsisting on an income of less than $7000. Three other, smaller, surveys found similarly (Gelles and Hargreaves, 1981).

The limitation of this evidence is that it is likely that families on low income are much more likely to come to the attention of the welfare authoritites than the well-to-do. It is highly probable that there are many more middle-class abusers than these statistics suggest, although there is a limit to how much middle class parents could abuse their children without it coming to the attention of schools and neighbours, especially with the increase in recent years in awareness amongst teachers and other professionals of the possible significance of bruises and psychological disturbance in children. While there is a bias in the child register records towards discovery of low-class abuse, it may not account for such an overwhelming preponderance of poor families.

The second method – surveys of randomly selected, representative samples – does not suffer from these shortcomings. Straus's sample of 2143 American families found that abuse was significantly more common the lower the income, occupation and frequency of unemployment of the parents (Straus et al., 1980). Likewise, Gelles concluded: 'Those in the lowest income groups have two to three times greater rates of abuse than upper income families' (Gelles and Cornell, 1985). Several other studies have similar conclusions (Gray et al., 1979; Herrenkohl et al., 1984; Daniels et al., 1983; Green, A.H., 1979; Jason and Andereck, 1983), although one did find that neglect was more significantly associated with poverty than abuse (Gaines et al., 1978).

More equivocal is the evidence on the effect of unemployment alone on abusing, as opposed to low income, occupational status and lack of education. Steinberg (Steinberg et al., 1981) found significant correlations between welfare reports of abusing and rates of unemployment in two American communities over a thirty-month period. There were significantly more reports of abuse when the unemployment rate was high. Four reports find abusers to be more than averagely likely to be unemployed for members of their class (Madge, 1983; Straus *et al.*, 1980; Cater and Easton, 1980; Light, 1973). However, there are another four that find little relationship (Binns and Mars, 1984; McKee and Bell, 1985; Cantor and Land, 1985; Elder *et al.*, 1985). Being out of work not only means more money problems for the family, but it also puts the breadwinner in the company of the children more, increasing the opportunity to abuse. That it is not unequivocally correlated with abusing is puzzling.

As Patterson showed, the precursor to abuse is an inflated currency of physical punishment, escalating in frequency and intensity (Patterson, 1982). It is a well-established finding in numerous studies that severe physical measures to discipline children are significantly more common in low-class families than high-class ones. Words are employed less than deeds, and after the blows have been struck they are less likely to be explained as part of a consistent disciplinary regime. This was found in the 1950s and 1960s (Bronfenbrenner, 1958) and has been repeated many times since (Tonge *et al.*, 1975; Newson and Newson, 1976; Farrington, 1989b).

Common sense might suggest some of the reasons why there is more abuse in low-income families, and there have been numerous studies thereof attempting to specify the precise nature (Heady and Smyth, 1989; Kempson *et al.*, 1994). The pressures of constant money-worries, no car, no washing machine, no telephone or the other labour- and time-saving devices which the majority of families take for granted need no introduction. Run down, cold and cramped housing makes childcare more difficult. Not being able to afford holidays and the constant proximity to similarly placed families drains energy, strains goodwill and creates tension. The accumulation of these and numerous other factors, like the lower quality of educational and health services of the poor (British Medical Journal, 1994), conspire to make it far more likely that severe physical punishment, climaxing in abuse, occurs in poor homes: tempers fray under stress and the short-term advantages of clouting a child to get him to obey can become irresistible. However, such appeals to 'common sense' as to why low class causes abuse must be treated with all the scepticism they deserve.

For one thing, not all parents subject to these pressures become abusers and the question of why some poor parents do it and not others is attracting increasing attention. The fundamental point may be that poor parents are much more abusive; that as income increases the amount of abuse goes down, but the question of why some and not others, cannot be ignored. A few anthropological surveys suggest that low income may not be critical in all contexts. On a global scale, the majority of households do not have washing machines, cars and telephones, yet there is evidence, albeit of poor quality, that family violence is actually more common in technologically developed, wealthy nations than in the undeveloped world. Levinson (1983), for example, examined pooled ethnographic reports of wife beating and child abuse in forty-six small-scale/'folk' societies from around the world and concluded there were 'many' in which physical punishment was a rarity, compared with the 90 per cent of American parents that employ it. Gelles (Gelles and Cornell, 1985) has concluded that, although there is a lack of scientifically gathered evidence, descriptive and clinical data suggest that industrialized nations treat their children more harshly than non-industrialized ones. It is only a hypothesis, but, if true, it means we must not assume that merely lacking wealth is intrinsically stressful. The lack needs to be combined with the particular conditions of industrialized society. Factors such as heightened expectations, a competitive ethos and the isolation from communal support which is common among poorer people in cities may be crucial if low class is to activate the stress which causes abuse. It is possible that what causes abusing in one society does not do so in the differing cultural conditions of another, just as boys and girls react differently to a traumatic event such as sexual abuse (the boys growing into vengeful abusers much more frequently than the girls). Korbin (1981), for example, claims that many present-day Chinese who were abused by their parents do not become abusers themselves (although he offers no hard evidence to show that the proportion of abused Chinese who do not do so is higher than the 70 per cent or so of abused Americans who do not). Korbin also suggests that there are some generalizable factors which govern the incidence of abuse in all societies. If children are highly valued in a society for economic, religious, or psychological qualities (like innocence) they are less likely to be maltreated. If certain categories of children are arbitrarily deemed to be undesirable – being illegitimate, orphaned, a stepchild, female, retarded or deformed – they are likely to be abused. Perhaps most significant of all, if there is a network of concerned child-rearers beyond the biological parents this reduces the likelihood of abuse.

There is a more solidly-based body of evidence which contradicts this sketchy anthropological data. Support for the ubiquity of the correlation between low income and abusing comes from historical analysis. As we shall see in the next chapter, in general, as nations become wealthier they also become less violent. On the specific issue of the history of child abuse, the horrifying opening lines of Lloyd De Mause's book have been oft-quoted (De Mause, 1974): 'The history of childhood is a nightmare from which we have only recently begun to awake. The further back in history one goes, the lower the level of childcare and the more likely children are to be killed, abandoned, beaten, terrorized and sexually abused.' De Mause supplies such a wealth of evidence to support this initial paragraph that his book makes depressingly persuasive reading. Taken together, these historical data support the notion that wealthy and technologically-advanced societies are on the whole safer places to be if you are a child and, as a parent, that you are more likely to abuse your child if you live in low-class conditions - the closer to hunting and gathering and primate (animal) living you are, the more you are liable to destroy, beat or sexually exploit your offspring. The descriptive and clinical anthropological reports are misleading: while being poor may not increase the likelihood of abuse in all societies at all times, it rarely does not; in the industrialized nations with which this book is concerned, it does in every society - there are no developed nations in which the high-income families are more abusive than the low-income families. To avoid any risk of misinterpretation, unless otherwise specified, for the rest of this chapter whenever I refer to 'the poor' or to 'low class' I shall be meaning these groups 'within technologically-developed nations'.

Taken as a whole, the evidence leaves little room for doubt that abuse and the severe punishment that accompanies it are significantly more likely in families with low incomes, manual professional occupations and low educational attainment.

CLASS AND WITNESSING PARENTAL DISHARMONY

(PARTICULARLY PHYSICAL FIGHTING)

Gelles has asserted that: 'irrespective of the method, sample, or research design, studies of marital violence support the hypothesis that spousal violence is more likely to occur in low-income, low socioeconomic status families' (Gelles and Cornell, 1985). While the evidence does bear this statement out, it is mostly of rather poor quality. Four studies of battered women (Rounsaville, 1978; Gayford, 1975; Straus and Hotaling, 1980; Prescott and Letko, 1977), for example, show that their partners had higher than average rates of unemployment, but the methods by which the samples were selected make generalization hazardous. Straus's (1980) survey of 2143 families is more reliable and found significant correlations between low income and beating, but, surprisingly, the educational level of the men was not significant. Two similar surveys also found low income to be significant (Fagin and Little, 1984; Petersen, 1980).

Since money is frequently cited as the foremost bone of contention between partners, it would be logical if couples with little of it were more disharmonious than wealthy ones. In a reanalysis of Straus's sample, Sugarman found this to be so (Sugarman and Hotaling, 1986). Social class affects the likelihood of both marriage and divorce. High-class men are significantly more likely to get married in the course of their life and less likely to divorce, compared with the average (Haskey, 1983 and 1984). While it is obvious that many wealthy marriages are extremely disharmonious, money can ease the pain and reduce the direct impact on children through such factors as nannies, holidays and more spacious living accomodation.

CLASS AND PARENTAL IRRITABILITY, ESPECIALLY IN DEPRESSED
MOTHERS

As recently as 1974, Becker asserted that depression was most common in
middle-class women: 'High expectations leave a middle-class woman particularly vulnerable to feelings of disappointment with attendant feelings of guilt,
low self-esteem and depression. Since she is less able than a working-class
woman to explain her disappointment in terms of social deprivation she does
so in terms of personal failure' (Brown and Harris, 1978). A number of other
authorities shared this view, although what empirical evidence there was at
that time supplied a very different picture. In eight out of eleven studies in a
1974 review of surveys that had been conducted of randomly-selected women
in the community, depressive symptoms were found to be more common in
the lower classes (Dohrenwend and Dohrenwend, 1974). In the second half
of the 1970s, three large surveys found the same (Rutter and Quinton, 1977;
Warheit et al., 1976; Comstock and Helsing, 1976), culminating in the 1978
publication of Brown's highly influential study of 458 women in Camberwell,
London (Brown and Harris, 1978). This demonstrated large, statistically
significant class differences, with 23 per cent of the working-class women
seriously depressed compared to only 6 per cent of the middle-class women.
Without attempting a comprehensive review, since then there have been at
least nine further studies, from America and the continent as well as Britain,
which repeat Brown's findings. That being in a low class is a major cause of
depression in women in technologically-developed nations is one of the best
established and least disputed data of social psychiatry.

Granted that poor women are more likely to be depressed, it follows that
they are also more likely to be irritable, if the arguments and evidence of
chapter 2 are accepted. Weissman demonstrated that depressed women were
especially irritable and hostile in their dealings with offspring (Weissman and
Paykel, 1974). Watson also supplied detailed evidence for the co-variation of
irritability and depression in mothers (Watson and Tellegren, 1985), as did
Patterson (1982) and others from his research group (Wahler, 1980). It was
also shown in chapter 2 that children of depressed mothers are more
aggressive. Since aggressive boys from poor backgrounds tend to become
violent men, and since most violence is by men from poor backgrounds, it is
possible to trace a chain of causality:

from low income to maternal depression;
from maternal depression to maternal irritability;
from maternal irritability to childhood aggression;
from childhood aggression to adult violence.

These are the connecting links in the chain which shackles the high proportion (30 per cent) of poor mothers that have depressive symptoms to the more
than one-third of men from the same background who are violent.

ALTERNATIVE EXPLANATIONS FOR THE HIGHER INCIDENCE OF ABUSE, DISHARMONY AND IRRITABILITY OF PARENTS WITH LOW INCOMES

That parents with low incomes are more likely to be abusive, disharmonious and irritable than high-income parents does not prove conclusively that it is the low income per se which causes this pattern. It is possible that low income co-varies with other factors which cause violence-inducing parenting. Three main factors, all of them interlinked, have been put forward as alternative explanations for antisocial behaviour in general and, by extension, for violence, in sons of low-income families: single mothering and fatherlessness, low intelligence and the underclass culture.

FATHERLESSNESS AND SINGLE MOTHERING

There have been two main advocates of the view that single mothering and the consequent fatherlessness – both of which have substantially increased in the UK in recent years – significantly contribute to parenting that results in delinquent males. Neither theory specifically predicts violence as an outcome rather than antisocial behaviour in general, but the theories can be easily extended to include it. Whereas Dennis and Erdos (1992) focus on British single mothering, Charles Murray – the other advocate – concentrates on America, with special attention paid to black parents (who constitute 12 per cent of the nation, yet account for half of the US prison population, [Currie, 1985]).

The Arguments of Dennis and Erdos (1992)

Dennis bases his argument almost exclusively on the findings of two studies by Crellin *et al*. (1971) and Kolvin *et al*. (1990). According to Dennis, the studies demonstrate that the absence of a paternal authority and role model explains higher rates of aggression and violence (as well as other criminality) among children of unmarried parents and, more broadly, the rise in crime of 10 per cent per year since 1950.

The children with unmarried parents in Crellin's and Kolvin's studies were statistically significantly more likely to suffer all manner of problems, including heightened levels of 'maladjustment' and hostility towards adults and other children (which, as discussed in chapter 1, are strong predictors of later violence in adults). For Dennis, this is taken as clear proof that it is the absence of fathers that causes delinquency and violence. However, the maladjustment correlated with unmarried versus married (legitimate versus illegitimate); not with absence versus presence of father during childhood. This is a fundamental flaw in his analysis because the real test of Dennis's thesis is the latter.

The value of Crellin's study to the debate is somewhat diminished by the fact that it is twenty-two years old. In the early and mid-1960s when the children were studied, illegitimacy was still widely condemned and this must have profoundly affected the life of 'bastards' and their parents. Today it is widely acceptable and if present rates of change continue, will be the norm by the next millenium, as it already is in Sweden: the number of out-of-wedlock births rose from 12 per cent in 1979 to 30 per cent in 1992 (in the majority of cases – 70 per cent – there were two parents' signatures on the birth register, so the unmarried do not tend to be single parents [Kiernan and Estaugh, 1993]).

Crellin studied 600 children born illegitimately in 1958, of whom 160 were adopted. These were part of a larger sample of 17,000 legitimate children. When aged seven, detailed information about all aspects of the children were gathered. The key findings were: 24 per cent of the illegitimate were maladjusted compared with only 13 per cent of the legitimate; 28 per cent of the illegitimate from the bottom social classes were maladjusted compared with 19 per cent from the top.

However, single parenting did not cause maladjustment: children of lone mothers were actually less likely to be maladjusted than those with two parents. Strangely, this fact escaped Dennis's notice: in Crellin's report, father absence was not correlated with maladjustment. If the child was brought up by a lone parent it was not more likely to be maladjusted than if it was brought up in a traditional family. Contrary to Dennis's claims, Crellin (1971) commented that:

> One would expect a lower incidence of maladjustment among children who had since birth lived with both their natural parents since this is akin to the most typical family constellation in the population as a whole; or one might argue that the child in a one-parent family would be more likely to show maladjusted behaviour than one from a two-parent family, even if only one was his natural parent.
>
> However, suprisingly this proved not to be the case. Little difference was found between those living with their natural parents, those growing up in some other type of two parent family and those being brought up by their mother only. Indeed, there was a lower proportion of maladjusted children among those living alone with their mothers.

Thus, if anything, Crellin's study tells us that in the mid 1960s lone mothering was a protection against maladjustment in children, not a cause of it. Crellin's comments contrast sharply with Dennis's report of her study:

> The proportion of children found 'maladjusted' among the non-committed [i.e. unmarried] father sample was much higher than that among the other two groups. About two-thirds of both the committed-father and the adopted groups were 'stable' on Stott's test [of maladjustment]. This was true of under a half of the uncommitted father group . . . the non-commit-

ted father group contained a higher proportion of maladjusted children (Dennis and Erdos, 1992, p. 42).

It is hard to understand what Dennis based these conclusions on since the author of the study (who presumably is more to be trusted as to what her results were) came to the opposite one.

Dennis also makes extensive use of Kolvin's study (Kolvin *et al.*, 1990) in support of his argument. Three generations of families were studied over a thirty-year period. 847 children born in 1947 in Newcastle were followed up to see what had happened to them and their children.

The families were classified as 'non-deprived', 'deprived' and 'multiply deprived' using a variety of measures including parental illness, poor housing, poor mothering and marital instability (the inclusion of the latter introducing a tautological taint to the argument since marriages of this kind would obviously be more likely to suffer father absence). Families where the fathers were absent were statistically significantly more likely to be deprived than ones where the father was present. The more deprived the family, the more likely it was to breed criminals: by age thirty-three, 18 per cent of the non-deprived had been convicted of an offence – much less than the 49 per cent of the deprived and 66 per cent of the multiply deprived. Overall, the more the father was absent from the childhood home, the greater the likelihood that it was a 'deprived' one.

In later life, the more deprived the home, the greater the likelihood of its offspring being delinquent or criminal. So Dennis's argument runs that, since father absence and deprivation correlate . . . and since deprivation and criminality correlate . . . ergo father absence must be a cause of criminality. But this conclusion is far from the necessary one.

That the absence of a partner (and extra breadwinner) in a home makes it more likely to be a deprived one is not surprising – most studies (not just Kolvin's) show lone parent families are on average at least twice as poor as two-parent ones (Weitzman, 1986; Camara and Resnick, 1989; Fuchs, 1986; Brown, 1989; Hanushek, 1979). In America, for example, 80 per cent of never-married mothers have an annual income of less than $10,000. This is true of only 6–9 per cent of two-parent families (Hernandez, 1989). Money is a critical factor in the single-parent equation. There are no studies to my knowledge that demonstrate that wealthy single parents are more prone to depression, irritability and, consequently, to having aggressive sons than poor, two-parent families, for example.

Patterson's (1982) study of 146 recently separated single mothers with sons aged six to twelve demonstrated the causal chain and the independent role of low income very clearly. He followed them over a twelve-month period, soon after the mothers separated. Over half (55 per cent) were receiving state assistance and 40 per cent had depressed moods during the twelve months of the study. The chain ran from distress at the separation from the partner, to consequent incapacity to seek or accept social support, then to depression, heightened irritability and consequent aggression in the boys. At each stage the situation was greatly exacerbated by low income: this, more than any other variable, predicted the completion of the chain. Since all the factors by which Kolvin defines 'deprived' (bad housing, parental illness, and so on) are significantly more common in poor than in rich homes, the poverty resulting from there being only a single breadwinner – not the lack of a paternal role model and authority – is far more likely to explain why the children of the deprived were more likely to be criminal in his study.

An equally crucial problem with Dennis's reanalysis of the Kolvin (and Crellin) data is his avoidance of the role played by the direct and indirect (through its effect on parents) emotional effects of divorce or separation upon offspring. Much of what Dennis attributes to the absence of a paternal role-model and authority could be attributed to the distress caused to the child by the loss of a parent and the acrimony that almost invariably precedes parental breakup. It is not the absence of the authority or role model which disturbs, it is the presence of mourning and the preceding acrimony.

There are many good quality studies which prove that children of broken relationships are significantly more likely to be aggressive than intact ones (see Stevenson and Black, 1995, for a recent review of American evidence; see Burghes, 1994; Kiernan and Estaugh, 1993; Cockett and Tripp, 1994, for British studies). Half of the most deprived families in the Kolvin study had suffered divorce or separation. This, allied to the poverty of the deprived families, almost certainly accounts in the large part for their increased rates of delinquency and violence. In general, the finding that children of lone parents tend to be more delinquent than those with two is probably better explained by the trauma attendant on parental breakup than anything else.

That the father's absence is not critical in making divorce distressing to the child is suggested by the finding that they show as much delinquency in the years leading up to the split – while the acrimony is at its height – as in the years afterwards. Even more telling, when their mother gets together with another steady partner it does not change them for the better. A role model and authority figure are there but it does not help (Elliott and Richards, 1991).

No wonder, then, that delinquency rates are higher in studies of the children of single parents. Sixty per cent of them became single as a result of divorce or separation, thereby halving their income and creating severe emotional distress.

Murray (1984): Black Single Parenting

In North America there has been a positive epidemic of single parenting among young black people. It has been projected that nine in ten black children will spend part of their youth in a single-parent family (Hernandez, 1989). At present, only 43 per cent of American black children live with two parents compared with 81 per cent of whites. It is also true that blacks account for a disproportionate amount of that nation's high violence statistics, even when compared with whites of an equivalent class (Murray, 1984). Murray, a political scientist, has suggested a direct causal relationship between the high rates of black criminality and single parenting. He has suggested that it is this rather than low income which largely accounts for the difference between black and white rates. Like Dennis, he suggests that the effect of single parenting is partly that the fatherless boy has no adequate role-model and authority to discipline him, but he places even more emphasis on the effect on the father of not having a family, stating (in a newspaper article): 'men who do not support families find other ways to prove that they are men, which tend to take various destructive forms . . . marriage – meaning not just the wedding vows – is an indispensable civilizing force' (*Sunday Times Magazine* 26 November 1989). On another occasion (Murray, 1990), Murray placed illegitimacy so centrally in the causation of crime that he was moved to assert that 'single parenthood needs to be stigmatized as a morally unacceptable act'.

In Britain, 48 per cent of births to blacks born in the West Indies are illegitimate. However, as Murray accepts, since British blacks make up only a small proportion of the total population, this only accounts for a small minority of illegitimate births (Murray, 1989). He estimates that if you removed all black births from the British out-of-wedlock statistics, they would only drop by 1 per cent. Murray's argument is therefore less significant for Britain.

Murray makes no mention of the long-established fact that blacks have always been prone to illegitimacy as part of their familial structure. A review of the evidence concerning the black family in the Americas (Macdonald and Macdonald, 1978), for example, shows that the migratory work-patterns of the men – whether in Ecuador in South America, in the West Indies or in North America – mean that marriage is much rarer, and that they may father children with several women, sending money towards their upkeep as best they can. This does not mean the women lack social support, however, because the matriarchal nature of their social systems enables generations of women to help each other out, socially and economically (Wilson and Tolson, 1989; Sowell, 1979). On top of this, Murray takes no account of the role of divorce and of the consequent poverty attendant upon it (described above).

CONCLUSION

Neither Murray (1984) nor Dennis and Erdos (1992) are able to offer substantial evidence for supposing that fatherlessness and single mothering are key independent variables in causing the abuse, disharmony and irritability that are violence-inducing. Much of the effect that they attribute to fatherlessness is ultimately explicable by low income and divorce or separation.

LOW INTELLIGENCE

Wilson and Herrnstein (1985) and Herrnstein and Murray (1994) list several hundred studies showing that delinquent children score significantly lower than non-delinquent children on tests of intelligence. They go on to argue that low IQ is a major cause of delinquency and that it is more common in the lower classes, at least in part, through genetic inheritance. In support of this view, Moffitt and Henry's (1989) review of the evidence concluded that the reduced executive function implied in the low IQ score suggested greater difficulty in seeing means/ends consequences or difficulty in long-range planning.

However, longitudinal studies do not support the theory, as Patterson has pointed out (1994). Huesmann *et al.* (1987) assessed IQ and aggression in eight-year-old boys and again twenty years later. The impaired executive function hypothesis predicts that aggressiveness in childhood would lead to greater future risk of low IQ. However, childhood IQ was not correlated with increased adult aggression: in fact, the situation was just the reverse of that predicted by the executive function hypothesis; more in keeping with predictions from Patterson's coercion model (chapter 1). Here, antisocial behaviour is assumed to be one of the direct causes for lower levels of achievement and lower verbal (but not performance) IQ scores rather than the other way around (Patterson, 1982; Patterson *et al.*, 1992). The problem child's core non-compliance and abrasiveness make it extremely difficult for either parents or teachers to train the child. As shown in the study by De Baryshe *et al.* (1993), ineffective parental discipline and antisocial child behaviour make indirect contributions to later child achievement even after parental IQ is allowed for.

In a recent test of the Moffitt (1993) hypothesis, child IQ (WISC vocabulary) was included in a multivariate prediction of early onset arrest. The factors 'child antisocial' and 'family transitions' (divorce, and so on) made unique and significant contributions. In keeping with the coercion model, the contribution of child IQ was non-significant. The implication is that reduced achievement and lower verbal IQ scores are, in part, products of the coercion process.

A fundamental flaw in the low IQ–adult criminality thesis is that it is based on offenders who have been identified. These may well be a self-selected group of the least intelligent – the ones who got caught. There is no way of knowing whether there might not be, for example, two much more intelligent criminals or delinquents for every one that is apprehended. In general, criminals average eight points less than non-criminals and are especially lower in their verbal skills in some studies (Wilson and Herrnstein, 1985). However, most studies of the question reveal no statistical difference in the IQ scores of delinquents and non-delinquents from the same class. It very much remains to be proven that the IQ differences are not merely caused by social class differences, since criminals tend to come from low classes and low classes reliably score at least eight points less on this middle-class invention. As Herrnstein and Murray (1994) acknowledge, verbal IQ scores contain an in-built bias in favour of the white and the middle class.

Regarding differences between types of criminal, those committing crimes such as forgery, bribery and embezzlement and tend to have slightly (but not statistically significantly) higher IQ scores than violent criminals (Wilson and Herrnstein, 1985). Again, this could be purely a matter of class, fraud and suchlike tending to be white-collar crimes; violence tending to be committed by those in manual professions. The idea that low IQ is a significant factor either in making adults more criminal in general or violent in particular – or that it makes parents more likely to act in violence-inducing ways to their children – is not much supported by this evidence.

Perhaps the most striking counter-evidence to the theory – studiously ignored by Herrnstein – is the fact that although boys with XYY (an extra male) chromosomes are significantly less intelligent than controls, they are not more violent. This is notable since Herrnstein is the most eager proponent of the Social Darwinist, genetic explanation for why the poor are more likely to be criminal. The assumption is that they are a self-selected group of genetically vulnerable individuals, heirs to a biological legacy of low intelligence, mental illness and antisocial tendencies which they pass on to their children. As Herrnstein himself told me (in May 1990 at the Centre For Policy Studies conference in London, reported in the *The Independent*, 21 May 1990): 'there are different genes for different classes'. To fully substantiate this claim beyond dispute, Herrnstein would need to supply evidence that the actual genes – the DNA and RNA – of the poor differ from those of the higher classes. At present, no such evidence exists, although there is evidence that intelligence is at least partly heritable (Plomin and Mcleary, 1993). There is also some evidence (see chapter 6) that stealing may be influenced by genes but, at present, there is no reason to suppose that this genetic propensity is more common in the lower classes: forced to live in poor conditions, just as high a proportion of wealthy people might turn to crime as existing poor people do at present. As Box has suggested (Box, 1983), the wealthy may anyway be every bit as criminal as the poor but their crimes are detected less. Above all, even if the propensity for property crime is inherited to a large degree, we should not forget that the evidence suggesting it is (the twin- and adoption-studies described in chapter 6) proves equally that violence is not.

As noted above, poor people are more likely to suffer most kinds of mental and physical ailment, both of which may increase their likelihood of marital disharmony and abusing (Mirowsky and Ross, 1989). These higher probabilities are very likely to be due to low income more than any other single variable; even ailments like schizophrenia that are believed to be substantially heritable (Plomin and McCleary, 1994) can be triggered by the stress of certain family relationship styles (Brown *et al.*, 1972; Kuipers and Bebbington, 1988;

Johnstone, 1993) which are liable, in turn, to be worsened by low income. If 10,000 babies born to poor parents were swapped at birth with 10,000 babies from rich parents, it is highly likely that the rates and types of antisocial behaviour, illness and so forth, would reflect class of adoption, not of origin. There are many high-income people with low IQs, but there is no evidence that they are more likely to commit crimes or to parent in a violence-inducing way than people of equivalent wealth with high IQs. At present, the weight of the evidence is that some people may be born more genetically susceptible to criminality than others, but social conditions determine whether the potential is fulfilled.

In conclusion, the evidence does not support the claim that low IQ is a major cause of delinquency in general, of violent behaviour in particular, or of violence-inducing parenting practices.

THE UNDERCLASS CULTURE

A final alternative to low income as the main cause of abuse, disharmony and irritability is culture. Recently, the theory has been advanced that it is the special characteristics of the culture of a segment of the poor, rather than their financial circumstances, which is critical in causing criminality in them and their children (Murray, 1984, 1989). This group is characterized as a lawless, antisocial 'underclass' of dropouts. By opting out of employment and adopting a culture akin to that of the 1960s 'counterculture', it has been claimed, these people (many of them allegedly single parents) become voluntary refugees from the conventional world of work (Murray, 1989).

Strictly speaking, the very word under*class* is misleading if the phenomenon it purports to define is principally a cultural one, as it is by Murray. Class, as in class of socioeconomic status, refers primarily to an occupational and income group, not to a set of cultural attitudes. 'Underculture' would be a more appropriate word for Murray's underclass, although even that is questionable in that the prefix 'under' is value laden and assumes that persons participating in this culture are in some way inferior to, or below, other people of different ones (who should presumably be termed the 'overclass').

In contrast to Murray, Field defines the underclass primarily by their economic circumstances – a group who are permanently in and out of employment; in most cases, more out than in (Field, 1989). He stresses the danger of confusing effect with cause in the matter of the role of culture in causing an underclass. After many years of low-income underemployment, Field's underclass develop a culture appropriate to their circumstances, a culture described by Dahrendorf (Field, 1989) as including: 'a lifestyle of laid-back sloppiness, association in changing groups or gangs, congregation around discos or the like, hostility to middle-class society, particular habits of dress, hairstyle, often drugs or at least alcohol – a style, in other words which has little in common with the values of the work society around'.

Neither definition of underclass is sufficiently precise as to be testable: it is far from clear whether a new social phenomenon has emerged at all. The lack of a scientific, operational definition of the concept makes it a convenient political football, easily kicked in economic or cultural directions depending on the polemical impulses of the individual player. Regarding Field's underclass, there have been a large sector of poor people who have remained so across several generations throughout the twentieth century and in some cases probably stretching all the way back to the start of the industrial revolution. What is new about the group Field claims to have identified – in what significant respects are they different from the Registrar General's lowest class, Social Class V? Was the alleged new group there all along or did it emerge for the first time during the 1980s? Regarding Murray's underculture, there is more than a suspicion that its ambiguity enables him and his supporters to use it to express moral, racial and political prejudices unhampered by the need for scientific evidence.

Murray argues that the emergence of a welfare state since the Second World War removed the incentive from the lowest classes to better themselves and made them dependent on a 'nanny state' (Murray, 1984). His central claim that young blacks in America (or Britain) do not want employment has never been tested by offering a sample of them well paid employment with middle-class career prospects. It may be true that young people in general, and blacks in particular, have become choosier about what work they are prepared to accept, and what they regard as fair pay for it, as part of a more general rise in expectations. The last forty years have seen a considerable increase in prosperity in the technologically-developed world and expectations have risen accordingly. Inevitably, they fluctuate with the business cycle. When times are hard people will accept less, when times are good they expect more. Murray has not demonstrated that anything new has happened beyond these predictable trends; ones that have been with us for as long as paid labour has existed.

A fundamental criticism of Murray's thesis is that there is no evidence that wealthy single parents (such as the mother of our future king) with poor mental health, low intelligence and so on, abuse their children as much as their poor equivalents. They can get a real nanny to help them out, take advantage of expensive sanatoria if they have severe mental problems, and are not penalized if they lack intelligence by having to do menial, repetitive and stressful work. They are cushioned from the effect of these problems by money. To suggest that it is the culture rather than the economic circumstances of low class people which causes their increased abusing, disharmony and depression does not accord with these facts. Where the cultural and individual psychological factors upon which the underclass argument relies might be relevant is in addressing the question of why some parents react to low income with violence-inducing childcare and not others.

SOCIAL SUPPORT AND 'LOSS OF VIRTUE' AMONG MOTHERS

In Brown's 1978 report (Brown and Harris, 1978), low income was only one of several predictors of the maternal depression which, as discussed in chapter 2, is a significant correlate of aggression in boys and, by extension, of subsequent violence in men. The others were caring for three or more children, loss of a parent before the age of fourteen and lack of social support. Studies exploring the causes and effects of lack of social support have tested the hypothesis that vulnerability to depression is increased by lack of social support only if preceded or accompanied by a major stress, such as a bereavement or marital crisis. In at least eleven studies it has proved to be correct (listed in Henderson and Brown, 1988). What emerges is that women who have few or no 'very close' relationships are significantly more vulnerable to depression when stresses hit them. It has also been shown that mothers are more rejecting the less social support they have (Colletta, 1981). This in turn predicts that their sons will be more aggressive (Crockenberg, 1981; Patterson, 1990; Wahler, 1980; also, see chapter 2). Why some women are less able to form close relationships and to benefit from potential sources of support is the next question for research in this field. At present, Brown has proposed that differences in the early childcare experiences of the women may be critical (Henderson and Brown, 1988; Wilson, 1984; Dornbusch *et al.*, 1985; Kellam *et al.*, 1982; Mcadoo, 1978).

An alternative interpretation of the difficulties suffered by women on low incomes is offered by Anderson (1993) in a paper entitled 'Domestic Economy: Improvidence and Irresponsibility in the Low-Income Home', part of a book decrying a 'loss of virtue'. It addresses the question of why some families on low incomes manage their affairs better than others, given the same low income. He reviews a number of small-scale studies of household management, concluding that 'ignorance' of value-for-money due to lack of 'shopping skills' is an underconsidered factor in causing poverty.

> There is little sign that most (housewives on low incomes) take much time and trouble to shop well or to cook well, though clearly they are not short of time. They buy expensive convenience foods designed for people who do not have time . . . in psychological language they are unmotivated, in moral language, possibly demoralized or lazy, certainly incompetent . . . (Anderson, 1993).

Anderson goes on to criticize their 'incompetence with money'. None of these assertions are supported by statistical evidence from the studies cited. For example, there is no indication of what proportion of families – if any – buys convenience foods rather than unprepared raw materials.

In explaining the alleged behaviour, Anderson offers 'badly formed or unstable' families, although he offers no scientific evidence that there are differences in domestic management between intact and broken, or single, families. He also suggests that state welfare that is not conditional on changes in behaviour (often described as 'welfare dependency') is an explanation, even though this could never explain why some mothers depending on state benefit were 'incompetent', but not others. In short, Anderson's paper adds nothing at all of any scientific value in addressing the question of why some women on low incomes survive better than others. The same can be said of Murray's work.

WIDER IMPLICATIONS

The body of evidence suggesting that low income is the principal cause of the abuse, disharmony and irritability which cause violence is substantial. It seems unlikely that single mothering, low IQ or underclass culture individually or together explain more than a small part, at most, of the variance in the amount of violent behaviour between high- and low-income families.

The implication is simple and clear: the more families there are living on low incomes within a given social group, the more aggressive boys it will contain and, a few years later, violent men. However, by no means can all violence against the person be explained in this way. As we see in the next chapter, the structure and culture of a society also affect males directly once they are grown up and, when understood in the context of inequality, play a significant part in determining how violent the society is.

4 INEQUALITY: THE DIRECT EFFECT OF ECONOMICS AND CULTURE ON THE PREVALENCE OF ADULT MALE VIOLENCE

A family is poor if it can't afford to eat.

Keith Joseph

The position outlined so far is that low income causes violence indirectly, through its effects on parental care. Low- rather than high-income families are more likely to care for sons in the violence-inducing ways identified in chapters 1 and 2. However, there are a great many possible factors other than childcare which could account for the large differences in the prevalence of violence against the person between classes, and even more emerge when the canvas is broadened to include differences between nations, historical eras and anthropological cultures. By no means does low income only cause violence indirectly – it has a direct effect once boys have grown up as well. While the factors described in chapters 1 and 2 can account for the great majority of the variance in answering the question 'why are some men from low-income homes in technologically-developed nations in the late twentieth-century more violent than others?', they account for less of the variance in answering the question 'why are men from low- rather than high-income families more likely to act violently?' – even when the effects of low-income parenting are acknowledged – and even less still if we ask 'why are men from different societies or eras more or less violent?'. As will be discussed in chapter 6, biological factors are unlikely to account for much of the variance in answering any of these questions, although I suggest in chapter 5 that biological differences between the genders may play a part in making men so much more violent than women. However, there are clearly many social and cultural factors associated with low-income men, unconnected with their childcare, which also account for their greater violence. What follows is a commentary rather than a comprehensive review of the arguments and literatures, starting with the most general issues.

VIOLENCE AND PROSPERITY: HISTORICAL, ANTHROPOLOGICAL AND CROSS-NATIONAL

A number of objections are commonly made to the suggestion that low income is a major causal factor in violence, whether through childcare or directly.

1 If being poor makes people violent, why have the British become more, rather than less, violent during the last forty years? In this period they became several times richer, not poorer.
2 Why are not all Third World nations always violent to the same degree that they are poorer than technologically developed nations?
3 What about prior to the twentieth century, when the vast majority of the population were living in what would seem like abject poverty by today's (developed nation) standards - were they that much more violent?
4 Why should being poor in itself make men go out and hit people, and how is it that many poor people are never violent?
5 How are we to define 'low income', 'being poor' and so on? Can a solicitor on £30,000 a year, who perhaps longs to be a millionaire or who has recently begun to pay alimony, not feel poorer than someone who's never expected to earn more than £10,000? In which case, how is it that solicitors very rarely act violently? And if it is argued that poverty is absolute, then surely no one in Britain need be poor (hungry or without a bed for the night) and, therefore, none of us should be violent if poverty is a major cause of violence?

The short answer to all these questions is that, overall, the more socio-economically inequitable a nation and the poorer a social class or a family within a social class, the more violent. It is inequality, not low income in itself, which directly causes violence.

There is no absolute living standard below which violence becomes inevitable, there is no invariable set of material conditions under which all men infallibly become violent in their behaviour. In terms of the power to purchase goods, the poorest inhabitants of New York are wealthier than those of Calcutta. If you transferred the New Yorkers to the streets of Calcutta even the few dollars they possessed would make them able to afford a great deal more. Yet the average poor New Yorker is as violent as the average Calcuttan (Gurr *et al.*, 1977): the effect of low income always partly depends on the cultural, social and political context. Prior to the revolutions of 1989, Eastern European nations were the least violent in the world (measured by homicide rates, although there is some debate about the way statistics were gathered under these Communist regimes), yet they were by no means the poorest. Within the European Community there are considerable variations in the degree of violence within poor classes with identically low incomes in different nations.

Despite all these exceptions, the historical and cross-national comparative evidence that prosperity leads to a decrease in violence and, above all, that socio-economic inequality is the crucial variable is compelling.

A Short History of Violence: As Nations Became More Prosperous They Also Became Less Violent

An analysis of violence since 1800 in four cities (London, Sydney, Stockholm and Calcutta) concluded that, with the exception of Calcutta, there was: 'a declining trend during the second half of the nineteenth century and into the early decades of the twentieth century' (Gurr *et al.*, 1977). By 1920, a Londoner was eight times less likely to be the victim of attempted murder or an assault than in 1840.

There seems little doubt that life before the industrial revolution was more violent than after it. Parish records stretching back to the thirteenth century exist for English homicides revealing that there was ten to twenty times as much violence in medieval England compared with the present day (Gurr, 1989). As the industrial revolution got underway, violence may have increased temporarily in some cities caused by the drastic disruptions which threw millions off the land and into cities without livelihood, income or the traditional supports and restraints of family and local community. But then, in most cases, violence decreased. In much of Europe, and even the United States, it declined in the late nineteenth century as the displaced were gradually, more-or-less successfully, integrated into stable occupational and communal roles in the industrial order and granted broader access to education and political participation (Inciardi and Faupel, 1980; Hewitt and Hoover, 1982).

It is only very recently, in historical terms, that violence has begun to rise in the technologically-developed world – since about 1950. The scale of this rise is considerable: by the early 1970s Londoners were ten times as likely to be assaulted compared with 1940 (Gurr, 1989). As we shall see, the principal reason for this is the form of modern socio-economic inequality.

Today's Rich Nations Are Less Violent Than Today's Poor Nations

Comparison of contemporary nations supports this generalization, with some interesting exceptions.

Overall, there is twice as much assault in the Third World compared with technologically-developed nations (Wolfgang, 1981). Wolfgang also compared the incidence of homicide per 100,000 between 1970 and 1975 in the main regions of the world. The league table was as follows:

Homicides per 100,000 population	
Latin America	8.2
Caribbean	6.7
North Africa/Middle East	4.7
Asia	2.3
Western Europe/North America	2.1
Eastern Europe	0.7

These figures clearly reveal a positive correlation between poverty and homicide, but some of the exceptions are so telling that it makes the generalization of limited value. Asia was nearly four times less homicidal than Latin America without being four times poorer and it was only a fraction more homicidal than Western Europe/North America which is many times richer. Taken alongside the figure for pre-1989 Eastern Europe, which is poorer than Western Europe/North America yet half as homicidal, this shows that wealth alone does not simply explain the incidence of homicide. Anyway, there are many reservations that can be made as to whether the statistics in Wolfgang's cross-national analysis are a true basis for comparison.

A more precise comparison was made by Messner (1982a). In a study of fifty countries, he demonstrated that economic development, measured by the growth of Gross National Product per capita, is associated with declining rates of homicide. His explanation was that, in the long run, economic development reduces inequality. He concluded: 'the more developed societies do not exhibit especially high levels of homicide, in part because the greater equality in the distribution of income accompanying development serves to deflate the homicide rate'.

INEQUALITY: THE EXPLANATION FOR DIFFERENCES IN RATES OF VIOLENCE BETWEEN NATIONS

America is one of the richest nations on earth, yet it is also by far the most violent among the technologically developed. The American criminologist Elliott Currie (1985) has offered a detailed explanation of why this is the case; his argument is summarized as follows (p. 171-2):

It isn't accidental that among developed countries, the United States is afflicted simultaneously with the worst rates of violent crime, the widest spread of income inequality, and the most severe public policies towards the disadvantaged. The industrial societies that have escaped our extremes of criminal violence tend either to have highly developed public sectors with fairly generous systems of income support, relatively well-developed employment policies and other buffers against the 'forces of the market', or (like Japan) to accomplish much the same ends through private institutions backed by an ethos of social obligation and mutual responsibility. By any measure we can construct, these countries have been less plagued by the extremes of inequality and economic insecurity. Our [American] pattern of development into an advanced industrial nation, on the other hand, has been unusually harsh and disruptive of the conditions that inhibit interpersonal violence.

During the period of rapid economic growth which followed the end of the Second World War, American governments were much less prepared than those in Europe to minimize inequality through job protection and welfare intervention. They created no active labour-market policy to maintain full employment through substantial job-retraining and public job-creation. Unlike Sweden, Norway or West Germany, America developed no comprehensive apprenticeship system to guide the young from school into steady work; unlike Austria, it adopted no commitment to economic planning to anticipate the disruptive impact of technological change. Such measures were largely responsible for keeping jobless rates in many Western European countries below 3 per cent throughout most of the the 1970s, and holding rates of youth unemployment at levels often lower than the rates for American adults (Currie, 1985). In America it was believed that the quantity and quality of employment should be left to market forces – with clear-cut effects on their violence statistics. Countries that developed employment policies had both much lower unemployment and less crime throughout the post-war period. As Krohn (1976) demonstrated in a comparison of twenty-four nations, between 1959 and 1976 the average unemployment rate in America was nearly double that of its nearest European counterparts, Italy and Britain, and between three and four times the average rate in countries like West Germany, Sweden, Norway, Austria and Japan. The American homicide rate ranged up to more than ten times that of these countries. Perhaps even more significant – given the strong correlation between low income and violence-inducing parenting established in chapter 3 – Americans are far more violent towards their children than Europeans. One study showed that an American child aged between one and four years was eleven times more likely to die of injuries 'purposely inflicted by another person' than a Dutch child (Christoffel and Kiang, 1983).

When all the indicators of inequality are taken into account its central role in causing violence is clear. Around the world, at every level of economic development, increasing equality goes hand in hand with lower risks of homicide. Thus, in a careful analysis of murder rates in thirty-one countries, Braithwaite and Braithwaite (1980) concluded that higher homicide rates were associated with a broader gap between high and low wages, large disparities in income between workers in different sectors of industry and low per capita consumption of protein. Messner (1982b) arrived at similar conclusions from a study of thirty-nine countries. Income inequality explained 35 per cent of the differences in homicide among these countries, even when population density, degree of urbanization and level of economic development had been taken into account.

On top of America's higher rates of unemployment, it also did far less than European nations to meet the needs of its poor through health and welfare programmes. Studies comparing different states within America (whose state benefits vary considerably), showed a strong correlation between the extent of provision and rates of violence. Currie (1985) demonstrated that in Texas in 1980, where welfare payments are some of the lowest and there is an extreme avowal of 'market forces', the average monthly payment was $109 compared with $366 in Wisconsin, whose citizens are more protected than in almost any other state. With three times the population and nearly five times the number of poor people, Texas had almost the same number of families receiving benefit. As predicted, the homicide rate in Texas in 1980 was six times that of Wisconsin. In a nationwide survey correlating levels of state aid to families with children and crime rates, DeFronzo (1983) found that higher rates of aid had a clear and consistent negative effect on rates of homicide, burglary and rape. DeFronzo calculated that increasing the state payment by $10 a month for each member of a welfare family would reduce the murder rate by about one per 100,000.

Some authors have interpreted these findings differently. Davies (1983) argued that the rising crime rates since 1950 in all developed nations except Switzerland and Japan prove that equality *causes* crime; that the rates are the result of the 'corrosive ethic of socialist egalitarianism'. This is argued to have replaced the 'sense of personal moral responsibility'. In addition, he argues (as does Murray, 1984) that the growth of public welfare actually eroded family stablity by encouraging divorce and single mothering and that it actually destroyed the work ethic by creating welfare dependency.

By this argument, those societies with greater commitment to a welfare state should suffer more crime. The evidence is precisely the opposite. The industrial societies that have done the most to blunt the inequalities produced by the market system have low rates of crimes. As OECD figures prove (1978), during the 1960s and 1970s America had the widest spread of income inequality of any developed nation. The narrowest spread was in Holland where the share of total income going to the poorest fifth of the population was more than double that in America. During the same period, according to Archer (1978) the homicide rate in America averaged more than thirteen times the Dutch rate. In Denmark, where public expenditure amounted to about half of the Gross National Product compared with one-third in America (where so much more of the public expenditure is devoted to defence [Currie, 1985]), the homicide rate in the late 1970s ranged between one-tenth and one-nineteenth of the American rate.

Relative equality also partly explains the dramatically low levels of crime in Japan and Switzerland which, until recently, had seen no rises since 1950. The Japanese are exceeded only by Holland, Sweden and Norway in the extent to which they have narrowed the range of income inequality, and by Holland and Sweden alone in the proportion of personal income that goes to the bottom fifth of the population. Elaborate provisions for job security and other private cushions against the impact of the market in Japan make it far closer to the welfare states of Western Europe than to America, which is uniquely lacking in the mechanisms of reciprocity and mutual obligation that have been developed in other industrial societies. Likewise, the Swiss have a relatively narrow spread of income inequality and low rates of unemployment which minimize the impact of national affluence (Clinard, 1975). Their economic development was far more decentralized than that in most other countries, based on local self-government with less disruption to communities resulting from industrialization. Like the Japanese (Dore, 1958), strong networks of personal ties still bind them together.

Cross-national comparison of proportions of GDP spent on social service programmes to ensure the well-being of the workforce - compensation and benefits paid to the unemployed, children, the aged, the handicapped - further supports the role of inequality in causing violence, as Reich's (1983) study demonstrates. America spent just 14 per cent of its GDP on these programmes. Sweden spent 33.8 per cent, West Germany 30.6 per cent, Holland 27.7 per cent and France 22 per cent. Once the exceptional welfare role of employers in Japan was taken into account, Japan's 17 per cent was similar. Regarding these figures, Currie (1985, p. 168-9) commented:

> What these figures represent is a historical commitment - often achieved through long and painful struggle - to shift the moral balance of these societies towards greater concern for social solidarity and mutual support. The United States is the industrial country whose cultural and political traditions have been least favorable to that kind of commitment, the country in which the 'forces of the market' have been least cushioned and regulated in the name of the wellbeing of its people. Can it be merely coincidental that it is also the country most torn by interpersonal violence?

CULTURE VERSUS POLITICO-ECONOMIC STRUCTURE IN EXPLAINING THE RISE IN VIOLENCE IN TECHNOLOGICALLY DEVELOPED NATIONS SINCE 1950

Violence has risen by an average 9-10 per cent per year since 1950 in Britain and throughout much of the developed world, and the lowest income groups are most responsible for it. The effect of class within technologically-developed nations on criminality in general, including theft and other non-violent crime, has been the subject of much debate (Tittle et al., 1973), but there is little doubt that the poorer classes commit the most violent crimes. Wolfgang et al. (1982) analysed the amount of crime committed by the 10,000 boys born in 1945 in the city of Philadelphia. The lower the class of the boy, the significantly greater was the likelihood that he would commit violent crimes. This was still true after race was removed from the equation; black boys in all classes being more likely than whites to offend. It can be objected that poorer boys are more likely than rich ones to be caught because they spend more leisure time in the kind of public places where police and witnesses abound; also, once apprehended, that their parents are able to afford less effective legal representation. However, it is improbable that these factors could account for the magnitude of the differences in the rates of conviction in Wolfgang's study. Where such considerations may have a major effect on the official statistics is in the reporting of sexual abuse, child physical abuse and wife beating – domestic violence. Poorer people are much more likely to be 'known' to the relevant authorities (police; welfare agencies). State schools are more likely than private ones to report suspicions to state officials. The higher density housing of the poor makes it harder to conceal rows and abuses and, once accused, the poor are less able to pay the fees of skilled advocates to put their case. These types of factors make it impossible to assert with any confidence that sexual abuse is more common in poorer homes than wealthy ones.

Steven Box (1983) has offered persuasive reasons to believe that the rich may be just as criminal as the poor, in general. He points out that the definition of a crime is defined by the powerful rather than the weak and that far more resources are devoted to detecting and prosecuting the crimes of the latter rather than the former: 'The process of law enforcement . . . operates in such a way as to *conceal* crimes of the powerful against the powerless, but to *reveal* and *exaggerate* crimes of the powerless against "everyone"' (Box, 1983). In support of this argument, he stresses the scale and damaging consequences of corporate and police crime. That the total resources devoted by the police to violent crime or to petty theft – both of which are committed more by people from poor backgrounds – are far greater than those available for the much more middle-class crimes like computer theft or tax evasion, seems indisputable. The reason given for this distribution of resources is that the crimes of the poor are more 'serious'. This is certainly debatable.

However, when Box addresses the issue of violent crime in particular, his argument seems shakier:

> . . . Definitions of murder, rape, robbery, assault, theft and other serious crimes are so constructed as to exclude many similar and in important respects identical acts and these are just the acts likely to be committed more frequently by powerful individuals.
>
> Thus the criminal law defines only some types of avoidable killing as murder: it excludes, for example, deaths resulting from acts of negligence such as employers' failure to maintain safe working conditions in factories and mines . . . (Box, 1983).

Box adds to this list of hidden avoidable 'murders' those resulting from inadequate safety standards, failure by governments to give 'adequate' warnings of environmental health risks, aggressive marketing campaigns by drugs companies of inadequately-researched drug products, dangerous drugs which reach the market because of 'bribes' to Health Authorities, car manufacturers who fail to recall thousands of faulty vehicles, and deaths due to reckless or drunken driving. The list, he claims, 'could go on and on . . . we are encouraged to see murder as a particular act involving a very limited range of stereotypical actors, instruments, situations and motives. Other types of avoidable killing are either defined as a less serious crime than murder, or as events beyond the justifiable boundaries of state interference.' To persuade us that these categories are legitimate the state employs 'skilled machiavellian orators' with 'silver tongues', and if these do not defend its definitions it has at its disposal, in the last resort, 'the iron fist of police and military physical violence' (Box, 1983).

Whatever view you take of the merits of this theory, it does nothing to challenge the evidence that men from low-income families are far more likely than wealthy men to hit, stab or otherwise physically attack. The link between non-domestic violence and low income holds for all developed nations where studies have been done. Even in Denmark, which has one of the lowest rates of criminal violence and fewer poor people than almost all other European nations, the few violent criminals come from the poorest sector of society (Anderson, 1984). Whilst Box may (or may not) be right that the powerful are indirectly responsible for just as many fatal physical injuries, the fact remains that they are much less directly violent, face to face.

Thus, while caution is needed in the matter of class and domestic violence, it can be confidently asserted that assault outside the home – which accounts for most recorded violent crime – is largely a low-class phenomenon. What is more, a further reliable finding is that within poor classes, the poorer the family, the more violent it is.

411 English boys followed from the age of eight to thirty-two by Farrington (1989a) were drawn from the bottom three social classes. Although class alone did not predict violence, one of the most powerful predictors was how poor the boys' families were. Despite the fact that all the families in the study came from the lower social classes, how poor they were was still highly significant. Economic deprivation was measured not just according to low income but also poor housing and family size. Of the ninety-three boys who came from the poorest families of all, 42 per cent had been seriously aggressive at some stage by the age of thirty-two. This was a statistically significantly higher proportion than the boys from better-off homes. The cross-sectional study by Wolfgang et al. (1982) in North America supports this finding. There seems little doubt that, at the lower end of the class scale, the less wealthy a family is compared with others from the same class, the more likely it is to produce violent male offspring.

The fact that low classes and the poorest families within them are the most violent does not in itself explain why developed nations have become more rather than less violent since 1950. Currie (1985) argues that economic development within the market system tends to undermine traditional institutions of support and mutual obligation which help to foster close ties:

> Such relationships are important bulwarks against interpersonal violence both because they provide a fundamental sense of belonging to a larger supportive community and because they provide the setting in which informal social sanctions against aggression and crime can operate effectively. And this helps explain what has gone wrong in those countries where growth has, if anything, brought intensified interpersonal violence. Economic development within the market system tends to undermine traditional institutions of support and mutual obligation; what is most crucial in influencing the pattern of violence and crime is the extent to which these traditional supports manage to survive in the face of that disruption (recall Japan's private mechanisms of social obligation) or are supplanted by new ones (Western Europe's welfare state). Where this happens the overall effect is to decrease interpersonal violence over time. Where it fails to happen, economic growth may weaken or destroy the supportive relations that existed in more traditional communities without putting anything substantial in their place. The result is an impoverished rural and urban underclass deprived of respectable livelihoods, torn away from personal attachments and informal controls, and dependent on an often inadequate labour market as the exclusive provider of social integration, material welfare and self-esteem.

Currie maintains that these processes are most in evidence in Third World nations that have experienced a wrenching transformation to unregulated economic development. Community life is destroyed by urbanization and at the same time there rapidly emerges a 'small but glittering sector of extravagent affluence with which the displaced poor must compare themselves'. This is offered as explanation for the high levels of violence in Brazil, the Philippines, the Caribbean and parts of Africa. It is also, he argues, why, in the late 1960s – when there was great public concern, as today, with rising crime in industrialized nations – Mexico's homicide rate was twenty-six times that of Holland; Trinidad and Tobago's was eighty-eight times that of New Zealand, and Manila's about twenty-seven times that of Vienna. Where social integration remains intact in the Third World, violence is conspicuously low. Thus, America's per capita income is many times more than in China, yet homicide is far less common in Peking than in Washington. The state-imposed familial and locally-organized networks of monitoring and reciprocal control make it extremely hard for violent acts to occur undetected and unpunished in China. Clinard and Abbott's (1973) study of crime in two poor neighbourhoods in Kampala, Uganda, showed that the neighbourhoods with more cohesiveness, greater participation in local organizations, less geographical mobility and more frequent visiting between neighbours had considerably less crime, despite having slightly worse material conditions. Hartjen (1982) found low levels of juvenile crime in India, despite widespread poverty: 'Indians are immersed in a network of role relationships that involve a variety of obligations towards kin, subcaste and community. Children and youths are included in almost all forms of social activity, including work, especially agriculture but even in non-agricultural commercial enterprises, children are working: filling tyres with air, packing groceries in the tiny shops along the streets or working with their parents on construction and highway crews.' There is no pretence that anyone can be high caste so the average Indian is not encouraged to feel that he is a 'loser' because he has failed in a supposedly open system, as is the case of blacks and Hispanics in America. The status of Indians is not dependent on economic performance. 'Regardless of one's position in the economic structure, one still belongs to the larger social system in terms of family and community membership. An Indian may be low in the membership hierarchy but he or she is still a member' (Hartjen, 1982).

Crucial to Currie's argument as to why technologically-developed nations have tended to become more violent since the affluence of the post-1950s is the collapse of communities that industrialization often brings with it, but he also follows many other observers (most notably Wolfgang and Ferracuti, 1967) in pointing up the role of the subculture that can develop in its wake. Originally developed to explain gang culture among youths in developed nations, the 'subculture of violence' specifically addressed the reasons for the development of alienation and violence in the midst of the unprecedented economic abundance of the 1950s and 1960s. The argument was that the subcultures stressed toughness and predatory behaviour in place of legitimate achievement. This was a response to the fact that some groups (such as unacademic poor whites; blacks) were blocked from achieving the goals of status and material well-being encouraged by the dominant culture. More important than the sheer material impact of absolute deprivation was the social psychological wound of relative deprivation, of being hindered from attaining what others were able to attain. The theory was advanced to account for the fact that not all poor groups in developed societies were as likely to act violently as others. Thus, for example, young black American men are significantly more likely than their white counterparts of the same class to commit, or be the victim of, violent crimes (Wolfgang et al., 1982; Blaus and Blaus, 1982). Blaus and Blaus found strong associations between economic inequality and homicide rates, but even stronger ones with racial inequality. Poverty alone was a less powerful explanation for homicide than inequality. They concluded that the strongest predictor of violence was not sheer absence of material goods but attitudes of alienation and hopelessness produced by inequalities seen as unjust. Great inequalities of any kind caused corresponding alienation at the bottom but, in professedly democratic, allegedly equal societies, to be excluded from opportunities on the basis of race was particularly alienating – blacks feel that, despite the official view, not anyone can be President of the United States of America. According to Blaus and Blaus, violence results, 'not so much from lack of advantages as being taken advantage of'.

One difficulty with this theory is to disentangle subcultural effects of race and inequality from structural poverty, since those who experience inequality and its attendant subcultures are very often the poorest. Where attempts have been made to separate the effects, structural factors such as low income and poor education account for the great majority of the variance between nations or subgroups – the culture follows the structure (Loftin and Hill, 1974; Parker and Smith, 1979; Blaus and Blaus, 1982).

QUALITY OF EMPLOYMENT AND CRIMINALITY

Studies of the relationship between employment and crime give a valuable insight into the structure–culture relationship. Downes (1993) points out that several studies show no link between unemployment and crime per se (for example, Carr-Hill and Stern, 1979) although others claim a clear causal link (Hakim, 1990, for instance). It is only when the type of work, the dynamics of the local labour market and the wider social and economic infrastructure are analysed that the links become unambiguous. He summarizes three types of approach: cross-sectional, relating crime and unemployment rates across areas at the same point in time; trend data, using time series for one or more countries or other geographical bases; and individually based data, comparing the behaviour of a particular person when in and out of work. All three approaches find some unemployment–crime links, though not consistently.

An example of the cross-sectional approach was Box's (1983) analysis of English records, demonstrating a strong correlation between unemployment rates and both burglary and violence against the person. By contrast, Field's (1990) time series found striking differences between property and personal crimes in relation to consumption growth (rather than unemployment) in the business cycle. During periods of rapid personal consumption growth, property crime tends to grow relatively slowly, or even fall, whilst crimes against the person grow relatively quickly, and vice versa. For example, rising consumption, drinking in pubs and clubs, and violence are plausibly strong correlates. Personal consumption emerges as a better measure of crime than unemployment, making it clearer why full employment is no panacea for preventing violence – why the 1960s as well as the the 1930s were periods of rising crime. Farrington et al. (1986) exemplifies the third approach: analysis of individual cases. Data from the early 1970s showed that youths were significantly more delinquent when out of work even in a time of full employment. Dropping in and out of work was a more voluntary activity then than in more recent times of endemically high rates of youth unemployment, which could be more criminogenic largely as a result of increased drug use. Parker et al. (1988) and Pearson (1987) documented the rise in drug use in the most socially deprived areas of Britain in the late 1980s. Parker identified a 'new to crime' group whose need to finance their habits, combined with prolonged criminal careers of already delinquent users, accounted for higher rates of property crime. The 'extra' crime that the Wirral in Liverpool experienced in the early 1980s appears to be closely related to the community's heroin 'epidemic'. Their rates of crime rose by 113 per cent in the period from 1979 to 1986, compared with 40 per cent for Liverpool as a whole and 46 per cent for the whole of Britain. Since surveys reveal that 87 per cent of heroin users fund their habit with burglary and theft from cars (Downes, 1993), this probably accounts for much of the Wirral's greater crime rate. The ten townships in the Wirral with the highest rates of known opioid use had a mean unemployment rate of 20 per cent. The nine with a zero opioid problem had a rate of 6 per cent.

Any remaining ambiguity in these findings disappears when studies take into account the quality of employment and its relation to the wider labour market. Jobs may be dead-end and badly paid; they can flow from explosive commercial and industrial developments which strain communities. Unemployment may be short-, medium- or long-term, voluntary or enforced, and it may hide considerable activity in the black economy. Currie (1985), Mcgahey (1986) and Sullivan (1984, 1989) suggest that links are strongest when length and quality are considered. Downes (1993) suggests a triple effect of unemployment on crime: First, high rates of long-term unemployment, in particular, undermine and destabilize communities, weakening informal social controls against crime; second, desistance from crime is strongly associated with finding stable jobs of sufficient income and quality to support a family, and unemployment adversely affects all these processes; and finally, unemployment opens up a void in people's lives that facilitates a drift into delinquency and drug use, which in turn demoralizes communities further.

Allan and Steffensmeier (1989) made a telling demonstration of the effect of job quality on crime. Labour market effects on arrest rates were different for juveniles than they were for young adults. The availability of employment produced strong effects on juvenile arrest rates: full-time employment was associated with low rates; unemployment with high rates. In the case of young adults, however, high arrest rates were associated with low-quality employment as measured by inadequate pay and hours. The implication is that for juveniles aged fourteen to seventeen, for whom work is part-time and voluntary and provides them with recreational goods and services (pocket money), any job will do. However, by the age of eighteen to twenty-four, work of some quality is the main requirement for self-support, let alone that of a family.

The difference between holding a succession of dead-end, secondary labour-market jobs and having a stable, primary labour-market job is a principal reason for the imperfect relationship between crime and unemployment. Mcgahey (1986) showed that white youths in Brooklyn, New York, had access to work in primary labour-markets through family contacts. Lacking family members with such contacts, black and Hispanic youths lost out in the competition for high-quality employment. As a consequence, the delinquent careers of the white youths were shorter lived and less predatory than those of the non-whites, who resorted more frequently to robbery and drug-dealing for income support.

While informal networks may help determine who gets which jobs, they do not generate more jobs. Moreover, although better and more employment may be a precondition for lasting community crime reduction, it is not the whole story. Especially in the worst-hit areas, which have tipped from moderate to severe levels of crime, the erosion of stable employment of any sort not only promotes but is exacerbated by the weakening of key social institutions. The reality and fear of crime can drain communities of jobs through the loss of retail shops, small firms and the impoverishment of services, as Sullivan (1984, 1989) describes in the Brooklyn area of New York. In a review of federally sponsored programmes to prevent violent juvenile crime in a number of high crime, inner-city areas across America, Fagan (1987) concluded that social and institutional factors were as crucial as economic ones in three (out of six) areas where violence was reduced.

WIDER IMPLICATIONS

It is abundantly clear from the many studies cited above that inequality in incomes combined with false promises of equality of opportunity, American-style lack of welfare support for the disadvantaged and poor job-quality are major causes of violence in developing and developed nations alike. From 1979 onwards in Britain, all three of these patterns were adopted as a deliberate government policy: the gap between rich and poor increased to pre-war levels; the amount and kind of state support for the disadvantaged was reduced dramatically; the quality of jobs available to young men decreased after union power to guarantee minimum wages and conditions of work was removed. These changes coincided with an unprecedented increase in violence against the person from 1987. In chapter 7 I suggest that, alongside the large increase in the proportion of boys raised in low-income families, these three changes in our structure since 1979 were a substantial cause of this rise in violence.

5 GENDER: THE OUTWARDLY-DIRECTED VIOLENCE OF DEPRESSED MEN AND THE INWARDLY DIRECTED VIOLENCE OF DEPRESSED WOMEN

> Yet each man kills the thing he loves,
> By each let this be heard,
> Some do it with a bitter look,
> Some with a flattering word.
> The coward does it with a kiss
> The brave man with a sword!
>> *The Ballad Of Reading Gaol*
>> Oscar Wilde

> Nobody kills himself who had not intended
> to kill someone else.
>> *The Psychopathology of Neurosis*
>> Otto Fenichel

One of the greatest mysteries about violent behaviour is that 20-50 per cent of boys respond to abusive, disharmonious and irritable parenting by becoming violent, but their sisters – subject to exactly the same experiences – do not.

More than by anything else, violence is caused by not being female. A cross-national survey of rates of female arrests showed that, at most (in the West Indies), women account for 21 per cent of arrestees and, at the least, 2 per cent (Brunei). The average is 10-13 per cent (Simon and Sharma, 1979); in Britain the proportion of all cautions or convictions that were female rose from 10 per cent, from 1980 to 1987, to 15 per cent, from 1987 to 1993. In virtually all times and places men commit the vast majority of violence; there has probably never been a society in which women were more physically violent than men. This does not mean that women have had less cause to feel frustration and anger, only that the way they express these feelings is indisputably and predictably different: women – worldwide – display depressive symptoms twice as much as men. And just as the sexes differ, so do classes, rural and urban communities, age groups and nations, in a rule-governed manner. The fact that these patterns are so fixed and enduring suggests there are reliable causal mechanisms operating. The most fundamental of these is the way humans channel aggression. Before considering the details of how and why men and women in particular channel aggression, this needs to be introduced.

THE AGGRESSION-DEPRESSION HYPOTHESIS

To the layperson a relationship between aggression and depression is not intuitive. A man smashing his fist into another man's face does not immediately bring to mind the image of a woman sitting haggard and bowed in a curtained room, sobbing with melancholy. The two appear poles apart yet, psychologically, they are close blood-relatives. The woman is paralysed by a self-loathing which is distinguishable from the man's in its hatred and anger only by its target. If she takes a razor blade to her wrist she is launching an assault whose motive may be identical to her brother's, as he wields one taken from the same packet, but put to a different use, at a football match. That he is slashing another person, whereas she attacks herself, should not distract from the identity of psychological purpose in the two acts: destructiveness. Someone who feels frustration and anger can direct these feelings outwards or inwards. The cause of the unpleasantness can be taken to be external and, having attributed blame, an attack launched. Alternatively, the frustrating stimulus may be taken to be one's self and the anger directed inwards in a stream of self criticism. Statistically, two columns can be drawn up representing the average direction in which aggression is directed in comparison between various groupings:

Inward Directed	Outward Directed
Women	Men
The Higher Classes	The Lower Classes
Elderly Men	Young Men
Young women	Middle Aged Women
European Men	North American Men

HOMICIDE FOLLOWED BY SUICIDE

The most compelling evidence for a close relationship between aggression and depression comes from the surprising fact that men who commit homicide are far more likely than the general population to subsequently kill themselves. Press coverage of prison suicides highlights it as a perennial problem of incarceration – especially of those on remand – but among violent men it is most likely of all.

Those convicted of homicide are much more at risk than other kinds of offenders of ending their own lives. The homicide-followed-by-suicide (or, 'murder–suicide') is seen at its most transparent in the case of the 'spree' mass-killer – rare in Britain (such as Michael Ryan in Hungerford) but a common occurrence in America. Having randomly discharged his firearms at the general public, he is inevitably cornered by the authorities. At this point, in only a tiny proportion of cases does he not either shoot, or deliberately make a target of, himself. Like the surviving party of the first stage of a suicide pact who has killed his partner, when the spree is over he wants only to die himself.

Different nations channel their frustration and anger differently. Coid cites some seventeen studies of murder–suicide which reveal large variations in its prevalence between nations.[1] In England and Wales in one study, between one-quarter and one-third of convicted killers subsequently killed themselves (West, 1966). This is many times greater than the figure for the USA (2–4 per cent) where murder is an everyday part of life and may be much less a cause for guilt and self-hate (in Denmark it is 42 per cent and in Australia, 22 per cent). Whereas British killers of all kinds are liable to suicide, it is mainly restricted in the USA to men who have killed a lover or spouse and are feeling remorse (71 per cent of one survey [Allen, 1983]).

Regardless of nationality, there are many studies revealing that the suicidal are significantly more aggressive than the non-suicidal (Paykel and Dienelt, 1971), suggesting that attacks on others are but a step away from attacks upon the self.

THE RELATIONSHIP BETWEEN HOMICIDE AND SUICIDE

The notion that aggression and depression are two sides of the same coin, although no longer a fashionable one, operated as the basic unit of intellectual currency for over a century in the study of violence. The core hypothesis is that depression is caused by the inhibition of aggressive responses to frustration (Kendell, 1970). The most widespread method for testing it has been to examine the relationship between homicide and suicide statistics. It is hypothesized that, on a national scale, if aggression is being inhibited then suicide rates should be high and homicide rates low, but if being expressed, homicide rises and suicide falls. Since homicide reflects the most extreme eruption of outwardly directed aggression (violence) and suicide can be regarded as a similar index of the inwardly directed variety (depression); since there are good records for both dating back into the last century in many nations, and since there are the least of all possible definitional problems with these indices compared to such categories as assault and depression, they have been used in a number of studies, internationally, to study the ebb and flow of aggression and depression.

In 1830, Guerry showed that in France, as suicide rates rose so those for homicide fell (Guerry, 1833). Studies in 1860 and 1879 (Maury, 1860; Morselli, 1879) demonstrated similar correlations elsewhere in Europe. Although sceptical of the relationship, the French sociologist Durkheim, in his classic text on suicide, established a whole series of such connections (Durkheim, 1952):

- Between 1826 and 1880 in France, Prussia, England, Italy and Austria, homicide fell when suicide rose, and vice versa.
- In more detailed analyses of different provinces in France and Austria, the same relations obtained.
- The countries with the lowest suicide rates (Spain, Ireland and Italy) were also the ones with the most homicide.
- During times of war, when aggression was nationally directed outwards, suicide rates fell in France and Prussia.
- The Catholic countries, in which aggression was held to be more outward directed, had lower suicide rates than the Protestant ones, who were supposed to be more inward looking.

Similar co-relationships were still being mapped in 1970 when it was reported that of forty-eight surveyed, (Kendell, 1970), the most homicidal nations were also the least suicidal (Mexico and Guatemala). Suicide was more common in the higher classes and rose as steadily with age as homicide dropped. Depression was invariably found more commonly in low-status, relatively powerless groups like women and old men.

In a wide variety of nations, war heralded drops in the suicide rate and on cessation, homicide rates rose. A 110-nation survey (Archer and Gartner, 1976) of homicide rates in relation to war between 1900 and 1976 showed this correlation. On a smaller scale, Lyons (1972) showed that suicide halved when homicide rose in Ulster in 1970 at the start of the present 'Troubles', and that these trends were most pronounced in the parts of Belfast most affected by the violence, compared with rural areas. Six other studies showed similar correlations.[2]

Until the early 1970s most research on the subject found aggression and depression to be linked in this way, but since then the relationship has become less and less straightforward on this massive cross-national scale, compared with the era considered by Durkheim. Henry, for example, persuasively showed the business cycle and homicide/suicide prevalences to be correlated between 1929 and 1949 (Henry and Short, 1954). In times of prosperity, suicide fell, being a predominantly high-class activity of those brought up to suppress aggressive impulses. When hard times came, it rose, as the pressures and frustrations for the rich grew. By contrast, homicide rose with prosperity, Henry believed, because, it being the poor man's way to express anger, the feeling of envy and frustration at not being able to participate in the increased wealth was exacerbated at such times. From about 1964 this relationship has ceased to fit the facts, possibly because the cultural differences between rich and poor are less extreme. In addition, the rapid erosion of the differences in upbringing between nations, classes and sexes and the rise in permissive values means aggression is increasingly less compartmentalized into different sociological groups.

None the less, the basic mechanism seems not to have changed: frustration and anger can be directed inwards or outwards. In one survey (Humphrey, 1977), the factors influencing the occurrence of sixty-two homicides compared with ninety-six suicides were compared. The suicidal tended to have been people who had functioned quite well and then lost social status. They were more likely to have lost a job or become divorced than a control group of non-violent neurotics, for example. This sense of loss overrode any urge to attack. By contrast, the homicidal came from deprived, abusive backgrounds and had never had much to lose in the way of social status (although there are more recent studies reporting a heightened risk of childhood abuse in the histories of completed suicides (for example, Shafii *et al.*, 1985). It made them more likely to lash out when pressurized. So the study supports the aggression–depression hypothesis but demonstrates some of the complexities involved.

The psychoanalyst Glaser (1983) drew a distinction between 'self-preservative' and 'malicious' violence and related this to the fight–flight mechanism found throughout the animal kingdom. Danger mobilized aggression which could be used for either. Given that threat for humans in technologically-developed societies was no longer physical in most situations, in the main the flight had become a psychological one – that of emotional withdrawal and depression. Threat need not be external at all: it could be one part of the self, criticizing or attacking another part. In extremes, this produced a physical assault upon the self – suicide. Interesting though this may be, it takes the debate into untestable domains.

AGGRESSIVE, VIOLENT MEN; DEPRESSED, VIOLENTLY SELF-DESTRUCTIVE WOMEN

The basic facts of how violence and depression are distributed between men and women are straightforward. Females are much more subject to depression; outward directed aggression is much more common in males. Why this should be so is the cause of heated debate, but that it is so, is not. It starts in childhood.

DEPRESSION AND AGGRESSION IN BOYS AND GIRLS

'Virtually all the evidence indicates that boys . . . are more impulsive and more aggressive and that they get into quarrels and fights more often than girls', states one reviewer of the evidence (Gove, 1979). Aged from five to nine, boys are more often referred for treatment for psychiatric ailments, especially 'conduct disorders' and 'attention deficit/impulsivity', but ten years later the situation is reversed. In the specific case of depression, girls outnumber boys from puberty onwards, it being rare in either sex before the age of ten. Kandel and Davies's (1982) large survey of 8206 children aged from fourteen to eighteen found this, and in Rutter's (1986) surveys, although the ratio of depressed boys to girls was two-to-one before puberty, this was reversed in post-pubescence. Whatever the reason, by adolescence boys are directing aggression outwards and girls are less self-assertive. As Sears (1961) concluded after following up 160 children from age five to age twelve: 'Girls are more fearful, more passive and more conforming to social norms; boys are more violent, rougher and more destructive.' The girls were significantly more prosocial in their aggression and anxious about being aggressive compared to the boys, whose aggression was significantly more antisocial. This is the consensus of dozens of similar studies (Kellam, 1990).

DEPRESSION AND AGGRESSION IN MEN AND WOMEN

By adulthood, in all but one of thirty-five studies of the subject, women were being treated for mental illness more often than men.[3] Specifically with regard to the prevalence of symptoms of depression, on average the ratio of women to men was two-to-one in a meta-analysis of forty-nine international studies (Weissman and Klerman, 1977). The same was found in two other more recent reviews (Bebbington, 1988; Hirschfield and Cross, 1982). Likewise, attempted suicide, which is normally accompanied by depression, is twice as common in women as men (in twenty-eight studies) (Weissman and Klerman, 1977). At just the age when men begin to commit violent crimes in large numbers and at a frequency about seven times greater than women, women become twice as likely as men both to be depressed and to launch physical attacks on their bodies.

DEPRESSION AND AGGRESSION IN MEN AND WOMEN OF DIFFERENT CLASSES

Depressive symptoms are significantly more common in the poorest classes for both sexes (Kaplan *et al.*, 1987) although there is some debate as to whether severe manic-depressive and unipolar depressive illnesses are class linked (Bebbington, 1988). Beyond doubt, depressive symptoms (as opposed to full-scale depressive illnesses) are most prevalent among women with low incomes, three or more small children and little social support (Brown and Harris, 1978). Women with these characteristics are at least six times more likely to have depressed symptoms than well-to-do men and three times more likely than well-to-do wives (Weissman and Myers, 1978). As many as one-third of young women in low-income homes have depressive symptoms. At precisely the time when this proportion of their sisters are succumbing to depression, at least the same proportion of young men are becoming violent. In Farrington's study of men from poor homes (Farrington, 1989a), 42 per cent of those from the poorest homes were seriously violent by the age of thirty-two.

DEPRESSION AND AGGRESSION IN MEN AND WOMEN AT DIFFERENT AGES

Depressive symptoms are most prevalent in women before the age of thirty-five; least so then for men, who become increasingly depressive from the age of fifty-five onwards, peaking at the age of sixty-five (Weissman and Myers, 1978; Bebbington, 1988; Hops *et al.*, 1990). Women gradually catch up to men in their seventies after a relatively undepressed middle-age. As men enter their mid-thirties they become dramatically less violent (Tarling, 1993). Thus, just when they express their aggression less through violence, their rate of depressive symptoms climbs.

Can it really be coincidental that male depression peaks at the point when they become home based and no longer part of the work force; in the same position as mothers without paid jobs – the group with the highest depression rates? It is of more than passing interest that it coincides with the point when they suddenly, on retirement, undergo this massive diminution in power, status and income. It is very tempting to suggest that when men become socio-economic women they become depressed (they also become depressed if unemployed).

After childbirth, women's bodies are changed in shape – often irrevocably – from the form that is held to be most sexually valued by advertisers. Given the extent to which women are still valued according to appearance, this has no small significance for how they are reacted to and for their actual personal powers. Seventy per cent of women with children under the age of two do not work (19 per cent work part-time, 11 per cent full-time (Kiernan and Wicks, 1990) and so, like the retired man, they lose their breadwinning status and independent spending power if they give up a job to become a mother. For the retiring man and the new mother there is a dramatic loss of power, status and wealth accompanying these life events; this is also the time when they are most at risk of depression.

The idea that aggression (caused by frustration and anger) can be channelled inwards or outwards certainly makes sense of much of the evidence considered so far. Homicidal men are often on the brink of attacking themselves shortly before they kill others, and in England up to one-third eventually do commit suicide (West, 1965). These perpetrators of the most extreme violence of all towards others are also the single most self-destructive group in the community. We have also seen that boys direct aggression outwards; girls inhibit theirs by comparison. As adults, frustrated and angry men from poor backgrounds become violent to others, whereas their sisters attack their own bodies, have low self-esteem, and become depressive. When ejected by unemployment or retirement from the workplace, an arena in which they can direct their aggression outwards, men, too, become depressive. Lack of opportunity to externalize frustration and anger, causing it to turn inwards, seems a plausible explanation of the differences between the sexes.

Weissman and Paykel's (1974) study of the depressed woman showed her not only to be more self-critical than normal, but also seething with outward directed hostility and criticism – only expressed towards intimates. To strangers or acquaintances, she is passive and unaggressive. Only when relations with family members were examined did the aggression become apparent. It shows that she is, above all, an angry person; usually without adequate means for controlling the causes of her frustration and without the option of the impersonal world of work as a vehicle for expressing her need to feel effective and valued and, insofar as this is part-and-parcel of all workplaces, for expressing her destructive impulses constructively. Overriding and even destroying the plans of others and executing successful alternatives is, after all, a significant portion of the satisfaction of much work.

It might be said, therefore, that depression is the most common form that female violence takes. But we are still some way from answering our central question: boys who are brutalized in their childhood homes become violent; many of their sisters are subjected to exactly the same, or even greater, levels of abuse – why do they not become violent, too, instead of depressed? According to Bach-Y-Rita and Veno (1974a): 'More men enter the criminal justice system than enter the mental health system.' One of the reasons this answer is inadequate, taken on its own, is because the opposite argument of 'female depression is inward directed violence' works just as well: male violence can be viewed as outward directed depression.

MALE VIOLENCE AS MASKED DEPRESSION

There is substantial evidence that violent men feel depressed but use violence as a way of coping with it; that depressed poor young men drink beer and turn nasty, and their sisters take antidepressants and withdraw, but both are depressed. There is a significant correlation between high alcohol-consumption and depression in many studies (Weissman and Myers, 1978) as well as between drinking and violence (Tuck, 1989). The majority of violent crimes take place under the influence of alcohol and the reason for the drinking in the first place is depression, as Weissman has suggested (Weissman and Klerman, 1977): 'Depression and alcoholism are different but equivalent disorders. Women get depressed. Men are reluctant to admit being depressed and accept treatment. Instead, they tend to drink alcohol. Thus, men self-prescribe alcohol as a psychopharmacological treatment for depression.' The claim is that not only are violent men violent but they are depressed, too. In fact, they are violent *because* they are depressed. If this is so, there should be

abundant evidence of depression in studies of violent offenders compared
with non-violent ones – which there is.

DEPRESSION IN VIOLENT MEN

Given that homicidal men are so suicidal, and given that suicide is caused
primarily by depression, it is reasonable to suppose that non-homicidal, but
violent, men will be depressed and suicidal, too, compared with other
criminals. Nine studies directly found this to be so.[4] In one entitled 'Aggressive
behaviour as a means of avoiding depression', Burks and Harrison (1962)
reported that, as therapy with aggressive boys progressed, the aggressive
behaviour gradually gave way to sadness and acute depression. Violence was
an attempt to avoid depression and they cited Bowlby's (1944) comments on
the subject as interpretation: 'It is my belief that the (violent) affectionless
character is intimately associated with depression and may perhaps be
fruitfully looked upon as chronic depression of a very early origin.' Burks and
Harrison (1962) concluded that: 'Among older children 'acting out' and
sociopathic manifestations are more likely to mask underlying depression.
These may take the form of disobedience, temper tantrums, truancy and
running away.'

Lesse's (1968) study of 121 juvenile delinquents supports this view. The
half who were depressed were also significantly more likely to have committed violent rather than other kinds of offences. Fighting and destructive
behaviour were seen as an attempt to contain depressive symptoms which
were in danger of erupting to the surface. In treatment, and stripped of the
gang culture which had helped to sustain their battle against depression, they
were immobilized by feelings of inadequacy, hopelessness and overt depression. Anthony's (1968) survey of 197 prisoners, of whom thirty had committed
violent crimes, used a battery of tests including a physical one of psychomotor
reactions. The violent sample were significantly more depressed. Likewise, in
a sample of eighty-one hospitalized patients (Rosenbaum and Bennett, 1986)
there was a significant correlation between the amount of violence they
displayed, their likelihood of having attempted suicide and their depressive-
ness. Patterson (1990) found that his antisocial boys were more depressed
than controls, and that if the parents were depressed then these aggressive
boys were significantly more likely to be so as well. Two other studies
(Bach-Y-Rita and Veno, 1974a; Climent and Ervin, 1972) recorded the significantly greater likelihood of suicidal thoughts and suicide attempts in large
samples of violent criminals compared with non-violent ones. In one Bach-Y-
Rita and Veno study, 42 per cent had scars from acts of self-mutilation and half
had engaged in serious self-destructive acts, a rate six times higher than the
prison population as a whole. Taken with the evidence for suicidal behaviour
in the homicidal, these studies leave little doubt that violent criminals are more

depressive and suicidal than non-violent ones, and are far more so than men
in the community generally.

ABUSED CHILDREN ARE MORE DEPRESSED THAN NON-ABUSED ONES

There is overwhelming evidence that physically abused boys are more
aggressive than non-abused ones, as we saw in chapter 1. Can they also be
more depressed? If so, since abuse is one of the main causes of adult violence,
it would follow that the aggression could be a defence against depression.
Eight studies[5] of samples of abused children report them as suffering depressive symptoms such as suicidal thoughts and attempts, withdrawal, passivity
and low self esteem, compared with various control groups. Green, for
example, conducted two studies (Green, 1978a) of twenty and sixty abused
children aged five to twelve, and compared them with both neglected and
normal samples, finding that: 'abused children commonly exhibited overt
types of self-destructive behaviour such as suicide attempts, gestures, threats
and various forms of self-mutilation'. He explained that: 'self-destructive
behaviour represented the child's compliance with parental wishes for his
destruction and/or disappearance . . . [self-destructive behaviour] may also be
conceived as the transformation of feelings of low self esteem and self hatred
in action' – the acting-out of depression. Galdston (Galdston, 1965) compared
the same three categories of child, but at a younger age (average eighteen
months). He described the abused sample as resembling 'cases of shell shock
in adults . . . they sit or lie motionless, devoid of facial expression'. Whereas
studies of the clinical treatment of aggressive juveniles (see Burks and
Harrison, 1962, described above) show them moving from an aggressive
condition to a depressive one during treatment, Galdston's treatment, starting
so much younger, produced the opposite. As they came out of their shells the
eighteen-month-olds became 'offensive'. Indeed, psychotherapists confirm a
more general finding among non-violent patient populations that the depressed have difficulty expressing assertive, aggressive impulses, whereas the
aggressive patient is unable to stay with depressive affects for long (Menninger, 1942). As the symptoms are treated the depressed may enter an angry,
aggressive phase whilst for the aggressive it is the opposite.

It seems that very early abuse produces a withdrawal that conceals
aggression whilst later aggressiveness may cover depression. There are three
studies which support the suggestion that the later the abuse starts, the more
aggressive the child; the earlier it starts, the more depressive or passive-
aggressive the child (Kinard, 1978; Rohner, 1975; Sears, 1961). Another factor
affecting direction of aggression after abuse is how often it is repeated. In two
studies (Kagan, 1977), the children who were abused as a matter of routine
were significantly more docile, passive and withdrawn – battered into submission and hopelessness, it might be said. Thus, repeated early abuse creates a
bias towards depressive symptoms for more of the time, since violent

aggression may occur as well at other times, whereas intermittent, middle-childhood abuse predicts predominant aggressiveness and suppressed, occasionally experienced, depression.

CAN THEY BE AGGRESSIVE AND DEPRESSIVE AT THE SAME TIME?

Abused boys and violent men are more aggressive than comparison groups; they are also more depressed. Depressed women are more hostile and malevolent to their intimates than undepressed women. On the one hand, it is argued that men are aggressive as a defence against feeling depressed and, on the other, that female depression is a defence against directing aggression outwards. Can both things be true?

The original proposition was that frustration and anger create aggression which can go inwards or outwards. Anthony developed the idea as follows (Anthony, 1968): 'The frustrations inevitable in life and exaggerated by civilization may be met by impulsive aggression, by withdrawal, depression, and apathy, by Brer Fox cunning and strategy, by charm, magic, persuasion, or by patient scientific study and action.' There are a great variety of ways to cope with frustration and they are not mutually exclusive. A comparison (Timberlake, 1981) of two groups of fifty-six maltreated foster children aged six to seven, one group physically abused, the other neglected, illustrates this. The abused were significantly more aggressive but both had high incidences of depression. Criticizing those who have argued that aggression and depression in children only occur singly or alternately – never simultaneously – the author explained their coexistence in her abused sample as 'a third pattern of maladaptive coping of aggressive impulse and depressive process . . . a pattern of simultaneous manifestation of depression and aggression' (Timberlake, 1981). The abused felt depressed but acted aggressive at the same time. She went on to explain why the abused were more aggressive and how 'a lifestyle of externalized aggression' develops into adult violence, rather than depression: 'By way of cumulative effect of social learning, of identification with the aggressor (i.e. with abusive parents), of repetitive use of aggression to avoid painful effect and the self image projected onto them, the overt aggressive mechanisms of the 6 and 7 year old physically abused child become the more violent mechanisms of the delinquent adult' (Timberlake, 1981).

It seems perfectly feasible that children respond to abuse with both aggression and depression and that both can be a way of keeping the other at bay. A depressed housewife could also be – as Weissman (Weissman and Paykel, 1974) has shown she is – filled with an anger and hostility that is expressed frequently towards intimates but not towards others. Likewise, her abundantly violent husband or brother could also feel intense self-hate but be unable to tolerate it for more than minutes at a time; the less depressed he is capable of being, the more violent.

Kandel and Davies's (1982) study of depressive mood in a very large (4204) sample of fourteen- to eighteen-year-olds and their parents provides another building block in this argument. There was significantly more depression in the girls compared with the boys and the boys were more delinquent, as all the studies find. But Kandel and Davies took the research a step further in an attempt to explain why these sex differences occur: they tested the hypothesis that 'antisocial behaviour is the equivalent among boys of depressive mood among girls'; a 'substitution of behaviours or masked depression'. The simple method was to add together the numbers of boys who were depressed or delinquent and to see if they equalled the number of depressed or delinquent girls. If delinquency and depression could be regarded as interchangeable ways of expressing the same emotional needs, and if these needs are generated in children of both sexes in equal amounts, then the amounts would be similar. And so they were; almost identical: there were as many more delinquent boys than girls as there were more depressed girls than boys; overall, the sum totals matched. The result perfectly fits the theory that in any group of adolescents there are a proportion of both sexes who are frustrated and angry (as a result of such experiences as abuse and neglect), but the genders express these feelings in different ways. If the study had substituted 'violence' for 'delinquency' as a measure (delinquency includes a good deal of non-violent behaviour), the result might have been even more decisively supportive of the hypothesis. None the less, this study is powerful evidence (especially so, given the size of Kandel's sample) that boys' delinquency and girls' depression are, psychologically speaking, functional equivalents and that on being abused they would react differently.

The final strand to this theory is to add a third alternative to directing frustration and anger inwards or outwards: projection of the emotions onto others – paranoia. As noted in chapter 2, experimental and observational studies have demonstrated that aggressive boys (Dodge, 1980) and violent men (Blackburn and Lee-Evans, 1985; Blackburn, 1986) and the depressed (Weissman and Paykel, 1974) are significantly more likely than controls to attribute malign intentions to the neutral actions of others. Thus, paranoid ideation is a feature of both the depressed and the violent. Quiggle *et al.* (1992) explored this factor in a comprehensive study. They measured the depression and aggression of 220 boys and girls (104 boys, 112 girls) but, in addition, their patterns of social information processing were also tested by asking them to make inferences about motives in six stories which they were read by the experimenter. As with other studies, depression was significantly more common in girls than boys, aggression more common in boys. Both aggressive and depressive children showed a significant general bias towards attributing negative intentions and to focusing on negative aspects of the stories. The aggressive were more likely to identify others as the cause of negative events whereas the depressive attributed negative situations to internal or global causes. Children who were both depressive and aggressive had the attributional patterns of both types. This is potent evidence that paranoid, depressive and aggressive ideation are close relatives and that all three can coexist in one person.

However, it does not explain why boys are more aggressive and girls more depressive.

FURTHER DIFFERENCES BETWEEN THE SEXES

The strongest clue as to why boys turn their aggression outwards, and girls inwards, comes from studies of the different ways they react to parental disharmony. Emery (1982, p. 316) cites ten which show that boys are more sensitive to both divorce and disharmony than girls. Boys with overtly warring, hostile parents displayed significantly more behaviour problems than girls, in another study of sixty-four disturbed children (Porter and O'Leary, 1980). Likewise, where 102 children with mothers in battered-women refuges were compared with ninety-six normal families, the boys were significantly more aggressive than the girls (Wolfe *et al.*, 1985). Twenty-four preschool boys showed more aggression than twenty-four girls of divorced parents two years after the separation in a further prospective study (Hetherington *et al.*,1979). It is beyond doubt that, at the time, boys display more signs of overt aggression. However, this does not mean that girls are unaffected. Emery concluded his review: 'girls are just as likely to be troubled by marital turmoil as boys are, but they may demonstrate their feelings in a manner more appropriate to their sex role, namely by becoming anxious, withdrawn, or perhaps very well-behaved' (Emery, 1982). Two studies especially support this conclusion.

Forehand *et al.* (1989) compared nineteen adolescents from families with parents with low levels of conflict with twenty from high-conflict families. The boys in the distressed families were significantly more aggressive, 'externalizing' their aggression. By contrast, the girls in the high-conflict families were actually better behaved than those in the low-conflict ones. It was concluded that when parental storms gather, girls try to pacify by being good. Block *et al.* (1986) offered strong evidence that this is so. Children from 110 families were given a battery of tests at ages three, four, five, seven, eleven and fourteen. By the age of fourteen, the parents in forty-one of the 110 families were separated or divorced. Looking back at what the children of the broken families had been like compared with the intact ones, the boys had been significantly more disturbed as much as eleven years before the marital breakdown compared to the boys whose parents were still together. They were 'under-controlled' in their impulses, aggressive and over-energetic. But the girls from broken homes were quite different. They were 'goody-goodies', displaying such traits as setting high performance standards for themselves in their conduct, high achievement at school and being easily provoked to feel guilt. Block concluded that pressure to conform to socially prescribed expectations of how little boys and girls should behave was the most plausible explanation. Boys could be seen as well as heard protesting if they were distressed by their parents' behaviour; girls exercised diplomacy.

The most significant proof of all that something of this kind was going on came from three further studies which show that the girls' responses are at a psychological price and that it cannot be argued that they simply are not as upset as their brothers. Carlson (Carlson, 1983) confirmed the finding that girls appear less disturbed at the time of marital conflicts, but when they were followed up as adults they recorded significantly higher indices of mental illness and family problems – such as disharmony in their own marriages – than women from intact families. Hetherington (Hetherington, 1972) reported similar findings in another, similar, study, with the women from broken homes particularly prone to distressing and dissatisfying relationships with men in later life. Reporting on a British study of 5362 children born in the same week in 1946, Kiernan (1986) showed that, along with many other adverse effects, increased likelihood of marital breakdown and neuroticism were significantly more likely as long-term effects on girls of divorced parents. Thus, while boys may show it at the time and girls may act the goody-goody, there are real and enduring disturbances taking place in the girls.

EXPLAINING THE DIFFERENCES BETWEEN THE SEXES: CHILDCARE

Adult men and women are exposed to radically different social conditions, with different rates of pay, expected social roles and all the other major discrepancies of which feminism has made us aware. But, long before all these influences come to bear, as children they receive very different treatment. There is a large body of evidence proving that adults respond very differently to boys and girls from birth onwards. It is beyond the ambition of this text to review all the relevant evidence, but I shall make a brief summary of the most significant findings here:

1 At all ages in childhood, parents react differently to different-sexed off-spring, encouraging sex-typical behaviour and discouraging behaviour expected of the opposite sex.
2 From infancy, boys get more reactions from both parents, both positive and negative.
3 Boys are given toys that require active problem-solving and parental involvement. Girls' toys give less opportunity for innovation, adult involvement and initiative.
4 Boys are encouraged to explore and play more, and to do so alone. Girls are kept within mothers' eyesight, making them more used to having to conform to adult expectations.
5 Fathers play rougher with boy infants than girl infants and insist on higher, achievement-orientated standards from their sons. They encourage dependent, passive behaviour in daughters by comparison.

6 Mothers respond to requests from sons for help with problems, but with criticism of daughters making the same requests.

7 Fathers encourage assertiveness and directness in sons and react, like mothers, with criticism to daughters, by comparison.

8 Both parents interrupt and talk across daughters more than sons, who get listened to.

9 Studies of teachers show they are liable to presuppose aggressiveness in boys and social co-operation in girls even if they do the opposite.

10 From as soon as they are mobile, children form groups according to gender and are encouraged to do so. This limits their experience of peer pressure to behave other than as their sex is meant to.

One author summed it up thus: 'Girls, compared to boys, receive encouragement to display dependency, affectionate behaviour and express tender affectionate emotions' (Hops *et al.*, 1990).

EXPLAINING THE DIFFERENCES BETWEEN THE SEXES: SOCIOLOGICAL FACTORS

There have been many studies suggesting that societies encourage a definition of masculinity which contains within it the seeds of violence (see Gornick and Moran, 1971; Miedzian, 1992; Campbell, 1993; Jukes, 1993; Chodorow, 1994). Several theoretical attempts have been made to establish the extent to which societies are merely mirroring biological differences in this or whether these differences are fashioned to suit patriarchal systems (for a digest of some of the best, see Mitchell, 1974). The most sophisticated recent empirical work has been by Hagan *et al.* (1987) whose power-control theory of gender and delinquency incorporates the differential effect of class and job as well as gender on domestic role-playing. Hagan hypothesized that traditional ('patriarchal') families (mother at home, father at work) would exercise greater control over daughters and encourage risk-taking in them less, resulting in lower levels of delinquency than in non-traditional ('egalitarian') families in which the female's occupational status was as great as, or greater than, that of the male. It was assumed that occupational roles would impact on power relations within the home. Parents of 463 students were interviewed. Patriarchal families did indeed discourage risk-taking among daughters compared with sons and delinquency was much more gender-linked in them than in egalitarian families. Girls were more delinquent the higher the status of the mother's occupation in relation to the father, or in homes that were female headed. Hagan concluded that: 'The implication is that daughters are freest to be delinquent in families in which mothers either share power equally with fathers or do not share power with fathers at all' (Hagan *et al.*, 1987).

TOWARDS MORE DEPRESSED MEN, MORE VIOLENT WOMEN?

There is no need to labour a point of which everyone has extensive first-hand experience: boys and girls are encouraged in different directions from the start and we live in societies that institutionalize these differences in every aspect of adult life. The test of whether girls can really be behavioural boys and vice versa has yet to be made, for even the most ardently feminist mother, scrupulously avoiding sex stereotypes, cannot help expressing them despite herself and cannot inoculate her offspring from the influence of the 'sexist' wider society portrayed on television and in other mass media. Only after several generations of female emancipation will it become clear to what degree the violent expression of aggression is genetically antithetical to the gender which for so long was assumed to have a 'maternal instinct' – an idea now disputed by many (Badinter, 1980). If women are not genetically prone to depression, then, as the restraints on their expression of aggression are lifted, so their rates of depression should drop to those found currently in men. Likewise, if men are not genetically prone to violent externalizations of frustration, as their role changes and if the much heralded 'New Man' ceases to be a myth, their rates of violence should drop and, of depression, rise proportionately. Although females have increased from 10 per cent to 15 per cent of all people cautioned or convicted of violence against the person since 1987, it is hard to determine how much this is reflected in the overall figures recorded by the police. Nor is there yet any unequivocal contemporary evidence that depression in men is on the increase – although the rise in suicide by young men may be a sign of this – or that depression in women is declining.

That men overtake women in the depression and attempted-suicide stakes once they approach retirement age and become socio-economic women is no coincidence. For when women undergo a similar demotion in status and retire to the home to become mothers, their depression rates also rise to the highest of their gender. A link between social status and depressive symptoms seems undeniable. However, it must be said that as yet there are few signs that female criminal violence or male depression have increased since the 1960s at the rate we might have expected given the huge changes in sex roles that have gradually come about, so to date the possibility that there are indeed some powerful genetic differences at work cannot be discounted. Back in 1977, Weissman wrote: 'As behaviours between the sexes become more similar, females may begin to employ modes of coping with stress that are similar to men' (Weissman and Klerman, 1977). Thirteen years and a generation of feminist-influenced mothers later, there is little support for the thesis. Perhaps we shall have to wait and see how the children of the children of the children of the 1960s behave before the position is clearer. Perhaps these changes only occur very gradually.

In the meantime, it is evident that no definitive answer exists to the central

common than normal in populations of violent individuals. It is true that the genetics of specific populations of violent types, such as paedophiles, have never been studied and, therefore, it is theoretically possible that heritable forms could be uncovered among these rare individuals.

CHROMOSOMAL ABNORMALITIES

Considerable research and debate resulted from Jacobs's 1965 report (Jacobs *et al.*, 1965) of a higher than normal incidence of men with an extra Y (male) chromosome in a prison population. As a result, a number of samples of XYY boys were followed prospectively over many years to see if they were more aggressive (Ratcliffe and Paul, 1986). They were not. Their behaviour was well within the normal range, although they had slightly lower intelligence and tended to be slightly less emotionally developed. In some of the studies the XYY boys were more criminal than comparison groups but their crimes were not violent. These prospective studies dispel the myth of the XYY man as a hyperaggressive, supermasculine sociopath. They also pose a strong challenge to the theories of Wilson and Herrnstein (1985) and Herrnstein and Murray (1994), as noted in chapter 3. These authors point to the fact that low intelligence is a powerful predictor of criminality in general (although the association with violence in particular is much less robust). They also stress the evidence that there is a strong heritable element in intelligence differences. Studies of 4672 pairs of identical twins do indeed reveal a 40–50 per cent heritability (Plomin *et al.*, 1994). Making the further, socio-biological, assumption that those in a society with the 'fittest' genes will rise to the wealthiest, highest status and most powerful echelons, and that those at the bottom will be least fit genetically, they argue that the higher prevalence of criminality among low-income men reflects their lower intelligence – particularly verbal intelligence scores on IQ tests, which have been associated in some studies with greater aggression in boys. The weakest link in this chain is the assumption that low intelligence is in some way causal of either criminality or violence. As Patterson (1994) has shown, the key variable is much more likely to be the kind of social information processing, caused by dysfunctional coercive family processes. If there is a genetic effect, it is more likely to be on impulsivity or hyperactivity, although the evidence that these traits are significantly affected by genes is based on small samples (Plomin, 1994). That genetically-inherited low intelligence accounts for a significant amount of the variance in differences in violence remains a plausible hypothesis which is not supported by the evidence.

INHERITED VIOLENT PERSONALITY TRAITS

There are two methods employed to test if violence could be an enduring feature of personality or psychopathology; part of a man's make-up, like introversion or exceptional creativeness. In twin studies, the degree of difference/similarity of genetically-identical individuals is compared with that between fraternal (non-identical) twins. If the identical twins were more similar in a particular characteristic such as intelligence or aggressiveness than the fraternal ones, then genes may explain the variance. The second method is to compare adopted children with their biological parents. If the biological father of an adopted boy were violent and the boy's adoptive parents were not, it would be strong support for the genetic hypothesis if the boy were also violent.

Twin and adoption studies have provided evidence that a variety of personality and psychopathological characteristics may have a significant genetic component (Plomin *et al.*, 1994), including extraversion (0.51 average heritability in a total of 9887 pairs), neuroticism (0.46 heritability in a total of 9902 pairs) and adolescent scholastic achievement (0.38 heritability in 1300 pairs). Many of the studies have been criticized on methodological grounds, especially the earlier ones, such as those by Kallman in the 1950s (Marshall, 1984). The studies suggest that adult, and to a lesser extent juvenile, delinquency have a significant hereditary component alongside the well-established environmental factors, such as being brought up in a low-income family. But delinquency is not the same as violence and only three samples – all of them Scandinavian – provide direct evidence specifically on violence.

Mednick (Hutchings and Mednick, 1975) identified 1145 male adoptees aged thirty to forty-four in Denmark (where state records are easily accessed and comprehensive) and compared their rates of registered criminality and psychiatric illness with those of a matched sample of non-adoptees. The adoptees were twice as criminal as the non-adoptees and, since the biological fathers were three times more criminal than either the adoptive or control fathers, this strongly suggests inheritance as the main explicator of the variance. Furthermore, adoptees' criminality correlated with that of their biological fathers: those whose fathers were criminal were significantly more likely to be criminal themselves than those adoptees with law-abiding biological fathers. Mednick (Mednick *et al.*, 1984) went on to expand the study by looking at the adoption records for the entire Danish nation over an extended time period – some 14,000 adoptees – although this time without a control group. The results replicated the finding that biological-father and adoptive-son criminality were correlated. However, when we look at the precise types of crime that correlated, there is a crucial finding: only the biological father's property crimes predicted adoptive criminality; adopted sons of fathers who committed violent crimes were no more likely to be convicted of violent crimes themselves than adopted sons whose fathers were law abiding or engaged in robbery. Thus, to the extent that Mednick's work proves stealing is inherited, it also proves that violence is not.

The second study was of 2324 Swedish adoptees by Bohman (Bohman, 1978). Unlike Mednick's, this found no correlation between biological and adoptive criminality, although there were oddities of sampling which may have accounted for it. Not one of the adoptive parents was criminal whereas the biological parents had a higher than normal rate of criminality. The only finding of relevance to the study of violence was that the biological father's rate of criminal violence better predicted alcoholism in the adopted son than criminality. This suggested a lukewarm genetic connection between paternal violence and sons' alcoholism. Again, it should be noted that a negative correlation in a study of this kind is as strong evidence against a genetic contribution to violence as a positive one would have been for it: paternal violence and sons' violence did not correlate.

The final relevant study was another Danish one; of twins (Cloninger and Gottesman, 1987). They identified all twins born between 1880 and 1910 and, where both members survived to the age of fifteen, traced the twins through police records and penal registers. If one of the identical twins was criminal, the other one was significantly more likely to be so as well, compared with the concordance rates for the fraternal twins. There were many problems with the methods employed in the study which biased the results (8-9) and reduced their ability to be generalized but a reanalysis was conducted addressing the issue of violent hereditability in particular. They revealed no significant correlation for violence. In fact, there was a strong tendency for the behaviour of siblings to be similar whether fraternal or identical, suggesting that 'family factors' were a decisive consideration.

All three of these studies suffered weaknesses (Carey, 1989). They relied solely on official records for their measures of violent behaviour, and the legal definitions thereof probably concealed some violence that would have come to light in American legal definitions. For example, what would be registered as an assault in America might be called 'disturbing the peace' in Scandinavia. Despite these and other reservations, Carey points out that: 'the fact that twin concordance is significant ensures that the record classification is not totally unreliable' (Carey, 1989). He concludes: 'Together the data do not suggest a strong role for heredity in violence . . . the failure in both adoption studies to detect a significant effect between violent offending and other indices of crime in separated relatives is evidence that any putative genetic factor is weak.'

As a whole, the evidence of research into genetic causes of violence is helpful in that it clearly reveals the central role of social and psychological, rather than genetic, factors, as, indeed, do all behavioural genetic studies of twins (Plomin and Daniels, 1987). Studies like that of Mednick make it doubtful that there is some hitherto unforeseen hidden genetic variable at work.

DO VIOLENT MEN HAVE DIFFERENT PHYSIOLOGIES FROM NON-VIOLENT MEN?

For every physiological study that suggests violent men are physically different in some respect from the non-violent, there is at least one that shows they are not. Even if there were a consensus finding that, for example, violent men have different patterns of electrical activity in their brains from non-violent men, it would not tell us why. It might be because they inherited genetically an abnormal limbic system or a tendency towards hyperactivity; but equally it could be that men who have been subjected to abusive environments as children have different brainwaves as a result. A good deal of the physiological evidence is of this kind.

THE LIMBIC SYSTEM

Located in the upper brain stem and lower cerebrum, the limbic system has been linked to emotional and sexual states. In experimental animal studies, some rats and cats have become aggressive when the system was electrically stimulated (Bandler, 1982). In humans, such procedures have produced fear as often as aggression (Sian, 1985). There have been clinical reports of aggressive individuals who had tumours in these parts of the brain (Mark, 1978). Surgical removal of small parts of the limbic system in 128 violent men produced very varied results (Balasubramaniam *et al.*, 1972). Only nine ceased 'destructive rage' altogether, forty-four showed some improvement and the remaining majority showed none. It has not been proven that violent men have different limbic systems and, even if it had been, the question of cause remains open.

EPILEPSY AND EEG STUDIES

Evidence that epileptics are aggressive during seizures is thin; that they are more likely to be so in between them is equally weak (Sian, 1985). It is largely based on electroencephalographs (EEGs) of the brains of epileptics – in themselves a weak measure of epilepsy since about one-fifth of the most severely afflicted (with *grand mal*) have EEGs that are indistinguishable from normal populations (Jones, 1965). Some studies have shown that children with behaviour problems have different EEGs from normal ones, but the results are inconsistent and even a principal proponent of that theory concluded that, 'at best the EEG has very little prognostic value in regard to aggressive behaviour' (Moyer, 1976). Even if it were to be shown that the aggressive or violent have differing EEGs, what would it tell us of the causes of violence?

HEAD INJURIES

A number of studies have shown that aggressive boys and men are more likely to have suffered minor and major head injuries than the unaggressive (Lewis and Santok, 1977). It has been hypothesized that they suffered brain damage which subsequently makes them more impulsive. However, in sustaining these injuries they were experiencing abuse, which is itself a clear cause of aggression. The fact that males who were abused without suffering serious head injuries become aggressive suggests that it is the emotional experience, rather than the neurological consequences, which are most significant.

SKIN CONDUCTANCE IN PSYCHOPATHS

Some (but by no means all) studies have found samples of psychopaths to be less responsive to stresses like loud noises, as measured by their skin conductivity. It was hypothesized that they were less fearful of adverse consequences from danger signals and, therefore, less affected by attempts to punish them. This accounted for their lack of conscience and their prepared- ness to act violently (Mednick *et al.*, 1982). Unfortunately, the definitions of 'psychopath' vary widely so that it is far from clear whether the studies are of the same populations (Blackburn, 1988). It is also the case that 'psychopaths' have not been shown to be more aggressive than other psychiatric types or normals (Heilbrun, 1979). Finally, the links in the theoretical chain from a low conductivity reading on hearing a loud noise to a violent act are tenuous and unproven.

BIOCHEMISTRY

Numerous atttempts to correlate quantities of the male hormone, testoster- one, with aggressiveness have produced only contradictory findings (Olweus, 1986). There is no straightforward relationship because the rates at which it is secreted depend a great deal upon context and age of the subject. If violent men were to be shown to have higher levels, the question of why would still remain crucial – it could be a consequence of upbringing.

Other studies have examined the effects of 'brain poisons', like ampheta- mine or alcohol. Since it has been demonstrated that diabetics experience mood swings when blood sugar levels drop very low (Moyer, 1976), other toxic chemical changes could have similar short-term effects. While the association between drinking and violence is beyond doubt, there is no evidence that the one causes the other in the sense of acting directly on the brain to induce violence: clearly, not everyone who has several drinks becomes violent as a result – half of drinkers are women (who are very rarely violent, whether sober or drunk), and of men, most are non-violent whether under the influence or not. All these considerations apply to the effects of amphetamine.

Another hypothesis is that diet influences criminality. Gesch (1990) reports a pilot study of this theory, claiming that 'biochemical tests have revealed metabolic abnormalities that appear to be directly proportional to the severity of the individual's criminal behaviour'. Gesch supplies some anecdotal evi- dence supporting this claim. He does not, however, offer any evidence that violent men differ in their diets from non-violent men of the same class. Since most young men from low-income homes are used to diets that are high in additives, saturated fat, sugars, processed meat and cheese and carbohydrate and low in fresh vegetables and fresh meat, this is crucial.

Finally, links have been demonstrated between violence and certain chemical transmitters in the neural pathways, most notably serotonin. Linnoila *et al.* (1983) found lower levels of the major metabolite of serotonin in the cerebrospinal fluid of impulsive compared with non-impulsive violent offenders. Other studies have shown a link between low levels and suicide attempts, depressive moods, alcoholism, impulsive firesetting and homicide (Virkunnen *et al.*, 1989). Antidepressant medications which reduce the re-uptake of serotonin from the synapse have been proven to reduce depression (*Drugs Supplement*, 1992). Together, these studies implicate serotonin as a key neurotransmitter in both depression and aggression which are, as we have seen (chapter 5), intimately related states. However, none of these studies tell us anything about the cause of the lower levels of serotonin. While genetics could play a part, animal studies have shown that serotonin levels in rats vary according to environmental stimuli. Thus, rats who were successful in staged fights had higher serotonin levels after their victories while the levels of losers fell (Mischzek, 1993). If the same pattern were found in humans it would suggest a precise environmental explanation for the lower serotonin levels in violent men. They are more likely to have been the object of physical abuse as children. Repeated experience of physical abuse could lead to permanently lowered serotonin levels and the use of violence against others as a method for raising levels.

WIDER IMPLICATIONS

If genetic factors play as little part in causing violent behaviour as presently seems to be the case, the social implications are far reaching. In theory it means that if the environmental causes of violence can be identified and if they are of a kind that can be influenced by social and economic policies, then a society in which violence is largely nonexistent is feasible. Property crime emerges from this survey as having a genetic component and it should follow that it will be less affected by social policies. However, it seems improbable that any genetic propensity to steal could account for the huge national and cross-national variations in rates of theft. The tendency to steal is almost certainly largely determined by environmental conditions – such as not having much money. Studies of the relationship between the business cycle and rates of stealing, such as that by Field (1990), show that rates of this crime are sensitive to environmental influences.

From the standpoint of this book, the crucial point is that genetics play little or no part in causing individual differences in violence.

7 EXPLAINING THE UNPRECEDENTED RISE IN VIOLENCE AGAINST THE PERSON SINCE 1987

Society had sinned, not directly against them [criminals] but against their parents and forbears.

Resurrection
Leo Tolsoy

There is no such thing as Society.
Margaret Thatcher

We come to the main object of this book, the explanation of the unprecedented rise in violence against the person since 1987.

First, recall the precise extent of this rise. In 1950 there were 6000 crimes of violence against the person recorded by the police. With average rises of 10 per cent during that decade and of 9 per cent in the 1960s and 1970s, this had become 95,000 crimes by 1979. The rise in the early 1980s was relatively low – an average of 5 per cent per year to 1986 – then began the unprecedented increase. For three years the figures rose 12 per cent annually, taking the total from 125,000 in 1986 to 177,000 in 1989 and broke the 200,000 barrier (205,000) in 1993. An average yearly increase of 3000 crimes between 1950 and 1986 became 12,000 per year from 1987 onwards. Of course, these increases might have been mere artefacts of the way statistics are gathered or reported, but Appendix 1 contains the evidence that there is every likelihood that they reflected actual behaviour in the real world.

INCREASED INEQUALITY AS AN EXPLANATION

In chapter 4 we suggested that inequality is the single most important factor in predicting variations in the amount of violence within and between nations across time and cultures. Since 1979, inequalities of all kinds have increased dramatically in Britain. These have impacted on the violence-against-the-person statistics since 1987 in two principal ways, indirectly and directly:

- The increase in the number of boys being raised in low-income families has led to a substantial increase in the number of ten- to sixteen-year-olds cautioned or found guilty of violence against the person.
- The direct effect of increased inequality on young men, particularly the twenty-one-and-over age group.

THE IMPACT ON JUVENILE VIOLENCE

The increase in low-income families can be seen in the statistics produced by the Department of Social Security until 1985 (continued by the independent Institute for Fiscal Studies until 1987, when the series was discontinued [Oppenheim, 1990]). They reveal that in 1979, 19 per cent of all children (under sixteen years old) were being brought up in a family living on a low income, defining this as a net income below 140 per cent of supplementary benefit. From 1981 onwards this figure was 30 per cent or above (Oppenheim, 1990). The raw numbers of children living in a family with a low income were as follows:

1979	2,380,000
1981	3,580,000
1983	3,880,000
1985	3,560,000
1987	3,610,000

Thus, from 1981 onwards there has been an average of about 1,300,000 more children than in 1979 living in low income families at any one time – 650,000 boys.

Proof that the proportion of boys in low-income homes stayed at the 30 per cent-plus level after 1987 comes from a second source of evidence, the annual *Households Below Average Income* government survey which uses 50 per cent of average income as the measure for low income. In 1979, 1.4 million of all children (10 per cent) were living in a low-income family by this measure (after housing costs had been taken into consideration). By 1991–2, this had grown to 4.1 million, or 32 per cent (*Households Below Average Income* 1993, HMSO).

It is possible to estimate the raw numbers of extra-violent men that the increase in boys from low-income families has caused if we assume that about 40 per cent of such boys become seriously aggressive at some stage before the age of thirty-two. West and Farrington found that among their low-class sample (411), the poorer the family, the greater the likelihood of producing a violent man (West, 1969). Of the ninety-three boys from the poorest families (defined in the study as an income of £15 a week or less in 1961 money, which would be worth £156 in 1991) that they followed from the ages of eight to thirty-two, 42 per cent had been seriously aggressive by the age of thirty-two (Farrington, 1989a). If the percentages in Farrington's study were replicated precisely, 273,000 (42 per cent of the extra 650,000 boys in low-income families revealed by the Low Income Families survey) more boys will become violent men as a result of the increase in the numbers of boys brought up in low-income families since 1979. Of course, not all these boys will become violent men at the same time since their ages ranged from birth to fifteen-years-old in 1981. Distributed fairly evenly across the range, they will have been reaching the age of sixteen at an average rate of about 17,000 per year (one-sixteenth of 273,000) since 1981 and will continue to do so until the number of low income families decreases.

Inevitably this is an approximate and theoretical figure. We cannot be more precise or certain because there are three crucial facts about which there is insufficiently detailed evidence: the length of time the families of these boys had low incomes; the extent to which the families were the same ones from year to year; and the exact ages of the boys when these things occurred. We cannot tell, for example, what proportion of the 3,580,000 children in low income families in 1981 were still in such families in 1983 and made up the 3,880,000 of that year. It is known that much of the increase between 1979 and 1987 was caused by the rise in unemployment in the early 1980s (Layard and Nickell, 1989) and that most of the families which were relying on supplementary benefit did so for a minimum of three months (Johnson and Webb, 1990). Of all unemployed persons at the end of 1985, 40 per cent (or 1.5 million) had been so for more than one year and a further 20 per cent had been on the register for between six months and one year (Tuck, 1989). Exact figures for parents floating in and out of low incomes (rather than on and off supplementary benefit) are not available. This issue is important since the longer a boy's parents were subject to the stress of low income, the greater their likelihood of abusing, becoming disharmonious and of the mother becoming depressed and irritable – the violence-inducing family processes. In general, the younger the age of the boy when the family became of low income, the greater the likely effect (Maccoby, 1989).

The figure of 1,300,000 extra children in low-income families (with its corollaries of 650,000 boys and 273,000 extra-violent men at a rate of 17,000 per year) is conservative in that a great many more children than this must have been in families which drifted into the low-income band during the whole period from 1979 to 1987, but it assumes that many of them will only have remained there a short time – too short to produce the kind of family processes which cause violence. Balancing out this conservative assumption is another that is less so: a boy's family does not need to be violence-inducing for the whole of his childhood in order to make him violent, and the age at which it begins to be so is assumed to be as late as fourteen. For example, it is assumed in this model that some fourteen-year-old-boys' families may have become low income for the first time in 1980 and that this was sufficient in some cases to have turned an otherwise non-violent boy into a violent man. If the model relied heavily on this assumption it would be considerably weakened, but in fact only a small minority of our 17,000 a year are assumed to fall into this category. The great majority will have been in violence-inducing families for longer than a year, and from a considerably younger age than fourteen.

Another way of being more conservative would be to assume that it is only before a younger age than fourteen – such as ten years old – that violence-inducing family processes make a violent man out of an otherwise non-violent boy. Taking the age of ten as the latest age, and starting in 1981, the first extra-violent men would not reach the age of sixteen before 1987. Even more conservative would be to choose age five, in which case the first extra-violent man would not be sixteen until 1992. Whichever model is chosen, sooner or later there will be many thousands more violent men per year coming through. By choosing the average increase for the whole period (1.3 million, 1981–1987) I hope to have identified a bare minimum of extra-violence-inducing families producing extra-violent men.

Another consideration is that not all 17,000 extra men per year will become violent immediately they turn sixteen. Serious violence tends to start at a later age than property crime (Tarling, 1993). Sixteen would be too old an age to use as our starting point if we were considering property crime, since the median age-range of arrest for the thrill-seeking crimes like shoplifting and auto-theft is fourteen to sixteen. It is not until the ages of sixteen to eighteen that arrests for violent crimes like aggravated assault and rape become common; eighteen being the peak in the rate per 100,000 for 'violence against the person'. Domestic violence, such as wife- and child-beating, is most prevalent at even older ages – between twenty-five and thirty (Turner et al., 1981). Thus, a few boys will already have been criminally violent before their sixteenth birthday and many will not become violent for a number of years after it.

So what did actually happen? Appendix 2 makes a detailed analysis of the criminal statistics for male juveniles cautioned or found guilty (all courts) of crimes since 1980. It reveals the following:

1 Between 1987 and 1993 the rate per 100,000 of male juvenile violence against the person has increased by 40.5 per cent in striking contrast to a 26 per cent decrease for all juvenile offences. The number of recorded violent juveniles increased by 34 per cent – despite the 31 per cent decrease in raw numbers for all offences.
2 Another striking contrast is between the amount of juvenile violence between 1980 and 1987 compared with 1987–93. Between 1980 and 1987, the rate of juvenile violent-offending rose by only 2 per cent and the number fell by 15.5 per cent. As noted in 1. above, the equivalent figures for 1987–93 were plus-40.5 per cent and plus-34 per cent respectively.

3 Comparison of the figures for juvenile violence with those for theft and handling stolen goods further highlights the extent of the increase in violence: between 1987 and 1993 theft/handling decreased by over 40 per cent – about as much as the increase in violence.

4 The proportion of juvenile crime that is violent as a proportion of all juvenile crimes has increased significantly since 1987, suggesting that they have become more violent as a group. By contrast, the proportion of crime that is violent in older age groups (seventeen-to-twenty years old and twenty-one and over) has not changed significantly.

Individually and in sum, these findings strongly suggest that 1993's cohort of ten- to sixteen-year-olds are dramatically more violent than the cohort of 1986. From 1987 onwards they suddenly started committing more crimes at a higher rate per 100,000, and the proportion of crimes that were violent increased substantially. While there are many caveats which must be borne in mind (considered in detail in Appendix 2), these figures are wholly consistent with the thesis that the increase in the number of boys raised in low-income homes since 1979 has caused an increase in violence among ten- to sixteen-year-olds since 1987. Juvenile crime as a whole – most notably theft and handling stolen goods – was declining sharply between 1987 and 1993; the increase in violence against the person ran flat against this trend.

How much of the unprecedented increase of 12,000 crimes of violence against the person recorded by the police since 1987 was caused by juveniles is the subject of Appendix 2. Unfortunately, this is almost impossible to estimate accurately because the age (and gender) of offenders does not come to light unless the crime results in a court conviction or a police caution, and only one-quarter to one-third of recorded acts of violence against the person have this outcome every year (in 1993, for example, 63,000 cautions/convictions out of 205,000 recorded). When police record an act of violence against the person, they may not even know the age or gender of the assailant. Many factors determine whether the act leads to a caution/conviction (discussed in detail in Appendix 2) and so multiple are these that it is highly probable that the demographic profile of those convicted/cautioned and those recorded but not acted against by the police, are significantly different. Ten- to sixteen-year-olds accounted for 17 per cent of cautions/convictions for violence against the person in 1993, but we cannot assume they accounted for the same proportion of all violence against the person recorded.

None the less, the fact that the rate of violent offending per 100,000 juveniles increased by 40.5 per cent since 1987 (against all other juvenile crime trends) suggests they will have made a significant contribution to the 12,000 per year overall increase in recorded violence. It is reasonable to conclude that the 17,000 extra violent males per year created by the rise in low-income families has played a substantial role in swelling the recorded violence statistics.

THE IMPACT ON ADULT VIOLENCE

As we saw in chapter 4, there is compelling evidence that the prevalence of violence in a society is strongly associated with the degree of inequality therein. In a number of cross-national comparisons, the extent of the gap in income earnings, employment opportunities and the extent of welfare provisions and public services (health, education, housing) for those on low incomes in a given society all correlated strongly with the number of homicides per capita. There have been profound changes in the equality of Britain since 1979 and there is every reason to suppose that they have directly affected how violently British men have behaved since 1987 (Joseph Rowntree Foundation, 1995). Thus, *Households Below Average Income* (1994, HMSO) reveals that 25 per cent of Britons were living with an income less than half the average in 1991–2, compared with 9 per cent in 1979. The real income of the poorest 10 per cent of Britons fell by 17 per cent during this period compared with a 62 per cent rise in real income for the wealthiest 10 per cent. Only the top 30 per cent of the population (ranked by income) achieved above-average growth in their incomes. Whereas 80,000 Britons earned more than £700 per week in 1979, 1.1 million did so in 1991–2. The conclusion is that Britain is more unequal today than it was before the Second World War.

Regarding welfare provision for the lowest income sectors, benefits for the unemployed or the young have been reduced in real terms. The trend away from state provision of cheap housing by councils to private renting has also affected rates of homelessness. Perhaps most telling of all, the effect on health of the new inequality has been dramatic. The *British Medical Journal* (1994) devoted an issue to the subject, with several papers showing unambiguous correlations between inequality and poor health in comparing European nations. Regarding Britain, an editorial summarized their view as follows:

'Growing socioeconomic divisions are likely to be an important part of the reason why average life expectancy in Britain slipped from 12th to 17th position among the 24 nations belonging to the Organization to Economic Cooperation and Development between 1979 and 1990 . . . Once it seemed possible health was best served by faster economic growth, which was incompatible with greater equity. Among the rich nations, however, little or no relation exists between growth and the rate of fall in mortality: the problem is relative not absolute deprivation. Indeed there is evidence to suggest that national infant mortality rises if the rich get richer while the real incomes of the poor remain constant.' (*British Medical Journal*, 1994)

Given the inequality–violence association demonstrated in chapter 4; and the large increase in inequality in Britain since 1979, it should come as no surprise that violence against the person has increased unprecedentedly. It would have been a sharp rebuff to the inequality–violence thesis if anything else had happened. Unfortunately, for reasons mentioned above (and in Appendix 2), we have no way of estimating how much the increase in recorded crime as opposed to cautions/convictions has been caused by men as opposed to juveniles.

A question that demands attention in considering the possible impact of the increased inequality since 1987 is why it was that the unprecedented increase in recorded violence against the person only began then – why did it not occur in 1986, or 1985, or before, when inequality was already considerable?

The answer could be that it took this long for the governmental policies which led to the inequality to fully impact on the psychology and culture of the nation (Joseph Rowntree Foundation, 1995). The shift from a society in which 9 per cent were living on less than half the average income to one in which 25 per cent were doing so happened steadily throughout the 1980s. As the material well-being of millions gradually changed, so might their culture and their attitude. It may be a good example of Currie's (1985) thesis that low income or simple lack of material well-being do not in themselves cause violence; they must always be seen in full cultural and economic context. Thus, while it is true that unemployment increased rapidly after 1979 and that many of the policies which were to lead to the lessening in welfare provision for those on low incomes were being implemented from the early 1980s onwards, it may be that their full effect was not felt until the late 1980s. In particular, the culture which accompanied the new status quo did not emerge fully until the mid-1980s, with its films, television programmes, 'sex'n'shopping' novels and tabloid newspaper stories, all describing glittering wealth on the one hand and a despised underclass on the other. It may be that it was not until then that the low income began to be translated into a sense of unreasonable and provocative inequality with no light at the end of the tunnel (see Appendix 3 for a more detailed discussion of this necessarily speculative issue).

CONCLUSION

It is unfortunate that we cannot even estimate the contribution of juveniles rather than adults to the increase in recorded violence against the person since 1987. However, the analysis in Appendix 2 of the statistics for juveniles cautioned/convicted for violence demonstrates that they have become considerably more violent and give convincing reason to believe that their contribution was substantial.

The precise impact of the increase in inequality since 1979 on adult male violence is also incalculable. However, given the evidence that increased inequality increases the prevalence of violence, and given the size of the increase in inequality since 1979 in Britain, it is highly probable that it also played a major role in the increase in violence since 1987.

ALTERNATIVE EXPLANATIONS FOR THE RISE IN RECORDED VIOLENCE

SHORT-TERM FACTORS

If the increase in recorded violence since 1987 was a real one, there are still many alternative factors that could have contributed to it other than those discussed thus far. I have divided them into short-, medium- and long-term factors.

By short-term factors influencing the violence statistics I mean ones that have their influence in a 0–4-year timescale. They include events as diverse as wars, changes in the business cycle and methods of gathering statistics.

I have addressed a first short-term factor – and fundamental objection to my theory – in Appendix 1; namely, that the rise was not real at all and were due to changes in the way statistics were reported in recent years. I conclude that there were solid grounds for largely rejecting this view. Another theory that could wholly or partly displace my own is an economic one:

Short-term effects of the business cycle

A Home Office report by Field (1990) demonstrated that combined rates of recorded violence against the person and sexual violence track increases and decreases in 'real personal consumption per capita' – the amount people actually have to spend. Since 1950, when spending power has increased, so has the amount of violence; when spending decreases, so does violence. Since consumption growth climbed to one of its periodic peaks in the years 1987 and 1988, the fact that the violence statistics also rose in these years is consistent with Field's theory. For further corroboration he advances the fact that the previous two consumption growth peaks in 1971–73 and 1977–79 were also accompanied by increases in violence against the person. His principal explanation for these correlations between spending power and violence is uncomplicated and practical: when people have more money to spend they pass more time outside their homes, and therefore are available in greater numbers to get involved in violence, whether as victims or perpetrators.

While there seems little doubt that, overall, Field is right that consumption growth and violence do correlate, there is considerable doubt as to how much increases in violence should be attributed to consumption growth and how precise the correlation is. Field's citation of the periods 1971–73 and 1977–79 as evidence for his thesis are good examples of these caveats. The average rate of annual growth in violence against the person during the 1970s was 9 per cent so an increase of 27 per cent would be expected every three years. The rise of 27 per cent which he cites for 1971–3 looks less impressive in this context – it was merely the exact average rise for the decade. Furthermore, the rise of 14 per cent for the period 1977–79 is actually less than the decade average – actually contradicting, not supporting, his thesis. Furthermore, had Field cited the period which immediately preceded the consumption growth peak of 1971–73 he would have had to explain how there could have been an even higher percentage increase in violence against the person between 1969 and 1971 (of 50 per cent, as against the 27 per cent of 1971–73 (Field, 1990), well before the consumption peak.

If we apply his theory to the period 1987–88, it holds water only in very general terms and is immediately contradicted if we extend the period to include 1989, when the violence rate should have been dropping and not continuing at the 12 per cent of the previous two years, since the consumption peak had been passed. Nor can Field's theory account for the sheer magnitude of the increase in violence from 1987, in which an average rise of 5000 crimes per year (1970–86) (or 4000 from 1980 to 86, depending which period you choose) became one of 15,000 (1987–90). While it is wholly plausible that the amount people go out (especially to pubs and clubs) would affect the amount that violence occurs in general (he offers some evidence from telephone polls to support this view), Field would need to show that they went out a very great deal more than usual between 1987 and 1989, even for a time of high consumption growth, to account for an increase in the annual average as large as that from 5000 (or 4000) to 15,000 crimes. This he does not do, and although a reasonable supposition, he does not offer scientific evidence that people actually do spend more time out of the home in high consumption growth periods compared to low ones. In short, the peaking of the business cycle in 1988 may possibly explain a small proportion of the increase since 1987 but it seems unlikely to explain the extent of the change: to 15,000 more crimes a year.

Finally, it is possible that there is a further interpretation to be added to Field's (already outlined in chapter 3). Suppose we accept that recorded crimes of violence generally rise and fall with the business cycle, and that when there is less wealth about, people go out less and are therefore less available either as victims or perpetrators. When the nation as a whole is poorer in the short term, there is less public violence recorded. If this is correct, then it follows that the greater time spent in the home during periods of recession should lead to more domestic violence, including the abuse of children and fighting between parents – major violence-inducing family processes. Since such a small proportion of domestic violence is ever re- corded, official statistics cannot be used to test the theory out, but it is a plausible one with an important implication: if recession does increase child- and wife-abuse by keeping male partners at home then it would also lead to more violence when the children grow up. The effect of recession may be a cut in the amount of public violence in the short term, but an increase in it in the long term. It would be of considerable interest to rework Field's data to see if the rises and falls he presents might be explicable by the lagged effects of increases in low-income families a few years before.

Other short-term factors

Field shows two further correlations (Field, 1990): between high rates of beer (as opposed to other alcoholic beverage) drinking and violence against the person (to be expected since both are primarily working-class phenomena); and between high rates of violence against the person and unemployment growth in the previous year. He points out that these two trends will tend to counter each other. Beer drinking depends on wealth, so it will rise as spending power does, whereas unemployment growth in the previous year should reduce spending power (and therefore beer drinking) occurring at times of relative economic recession. Neither of these factors or their interaction can account for the specific increase in violence in the period 1987–93 which is the concern of this book.

Of the other short-term factors known to affect rates of violence against the person, none are obvious candidates for explaining the increase. There were no wars likely to have affected rates of violence (the Gulf War did not affect the vast majority of the population directly) or other extreme political factors like widespread strikes or social unrest, for example.

In conclusion, changes in police reporting and the peaking of consumption growth in 1988 may have accounted for a few of the percentage points in the increase since 1987 but the great majority of the increase is not explicable by short-term factors.

MEDIUM-TERM FACTORS

Medium-term factors operate over a five- to fifty- year timescale. They are social trends, like rates of divorce and single parenting; cultural factors like the emergence of an 'opting out' (underclass) culture or the winner–loser business culture; lifestyle patterns, such as in the use of alcohol and illegal drugs; changes in broad mores and their interaction with aspects of popular culture such as levels of violence in feature films, on television and in the tabloid press; and government economic and social policies. Whereas short-term causes directly affect the behaviour of the fifteen- to twenty-five- year-old men most likely to be violent, medium-term causes are indirect and lagged. The argument that the rise in violence since 1987 is due to family processes caused by increased numbers of low-income families five to ten years earlier is an example: a change several years before is held to affect the violence statistics of the present. As Skogan (1989) describes it: 'We will see the effects of the current state of the [American] family perhaps fifteen years from today.'

Government social and economic policies

Since 1979 the British government has pursued policies radically different from those of governments in the preceding twenty years. State subsidies for unprofitable public industries were reduced, causing large reductions in their workforces and mass unemployment. The power of unions to increase the pay of their members was substantially reduced and the number of low-paid workers rose. The abolition of restrictive union practices in many industries made it easier for employers to keep staff levels as low as they wished and to employ more on short-term contracts. While these changes were intended to increase entrepreneurial incentives, they also increased the numbers of low-income families – both through unemployment and by strengthening the employers' hand in pay negotiations (Layard and Nickell, 1989; Brown, 1989). This increase in the number of low-income families is, of course, what I claim to be primarily responsible for the increased violence against the person since 1987. Medium-term government social and economic policies, therefore, have been the primary cause of the increased rate in the rise in recorded violence since 1987, according to this view.

Whether or not these policies were the 'right' ones (economically or socially) is, of course, another matter which will no doubt tax political economists for many a year to come. It is not within the scope of this book or the competence of the author to answer such a question.

Social trends

At any one time there are changes occurring at a steady rate in the social behaviour of the population, such as the divorce rate. For one of these to affect such a large rise in violence against the person as the one since 1987 there would need to have been a rapid acceleration in the trend in the years immediately preceding the rise.

One trend that did change its trajectory dramatically in the 1980s was that of single parenting. However, its role as a significant cause of violence has already been rejected in chapter 3. It was argued that its main proponents (Murray 1984; Dennis and Erdos, 1993) confounded the effects of divorce and of low income with those of fatherlessness.

The divorce rate did not markedly increase the speed of its rise in the early 1980s (Brown, 1989) and therefore is unlikely to be associated with the rise in violence at the end of the decade. However, it can be argued that government policies did lessen the income of single parents, thereby indirectly affecting the violence statistics by increasing the number of resultant families with low incomes. Three-quarters of all the children living in a low-income family in 1987 were cared for by a single parent rather than a couple (Oppenheim, 1990). Insofar as single parenthood is a cause of low income, and insofar as low income increases the likelihood of violence-inducing family processes, it forms part of my overall argument and is an important cause of the rise in violence. But it is the low income rather than the single parental status which is critical. Wealthy single parents are much less likely to suffer the stresses which cause violence-inducing family processes. It seems very possible that the government's response (or lack of response) to the trend meant that a great many extra boys were brought up in a family whose low income was largely due to its head being a single parent (Brown, 1989). That single parenthood does not necessarily lead to low income is demonstrated by comparison with other nations. Out-of-wedlock births in Denmark (44 per cent) and Sweden (50 per cent) are a long-standing tradition and the state support for unmarried mothers is so extensive that most do not have low incomes as a direct consequence of single parenthood (Kiernan and Wicks, 1990). If these Scandinavian policies had been adopted in Britain it is certain that single parenthood as such would be less impoverishing. Again, the question of whether this would have been a desirable course for the welfare of the economy is beyond the ambit of this book, but there can be no question that such measures would have had this effect.

The emergence of an 'underclass'

Another possible root cause of the increase in low-income families during the 1980s is the alleged emergence of a class of lawless, antisocial drop-outs, the 'underclass' or underculture. In chapter 3, I offered substantial reason to doubt that any new cultural or economic phenomenon exists. Empirical evidence that a special section of the Registrar General's Social Class V has become less eager to accept work is lacking. There is also no empirical evidence that this alleged group grew since 1987 or that it was more prone to act violently than other members of that class.

Changes in patterns of intoxicant use

In America, the emergence of the cocaine derivative known as 'crack' has been offered as an explanation for increased violence in some inner cities. In 1988, for example, the city of Washington DC suffered one homicide per day – much of it attributed to crack dealing and the reduced tolerance of frustration that it induces. Thus far, crack has not become widely available in Britain and has therefore had no effect on the violence statistics. Earlier in the 1980s there was an epidemic of heroin use in many technologically-developed nations which brought in its wake a great deal of related crime. By 1987 this was increasingly less of a problem in Britain and it barely affected the violence statistics, unlike America (Wagstaff and Maynard, 1988). While drug use, crime and inequality are clearly correlated in Britain (Parker et al., 1988), there is no reason to suppose that the association has particularly increased since 1987.

Another trend which could have affected the violence statistics was the ever-more-youthful age at which teenagers began drinking alcohol and the rise of lager beers and the 'lager lout' during the 1980s. But this factor was nothing like substantial enough to explain the extent of the rise in violence since 1987, nor did it specifically accelerate between 1987 and 1993 (Tuck, 1989).

Changes in patterns of intoxicant use cannot explain the sharp rise in violence since 1987.

Changes in mores and their interaction with popular culture

The massive shift in values that occurred during the 1960s undoubtedly led to a reduction in the respect shown by youth to authority – at home, in school and when confronted by police (Rutter, 1979). At the same time, popular culture has become unimaginably less censored than it was thirty years ago. Explicit sex is a staple of feature films and the limits to what forms of violence may be portrayed continue to be pushed ever further. While these, and related trends too numerous to mention, may have played a decisive part in the overall rise in crimes of all kinds in the last forty years in the technologically-developed world (with the exceptions of Switzerland and Japan), there is no evidence that they accelerated at an especially rapid rate between 1987 and 1993 and, therefore, are unlikely to have been responsible for the sharp rise in violence.

In conclusion, medium-term factors do account for a significant portion of the rise in violence against the person between 1987 and 1993. Government economic and social policies caused the increase in the numbers of low-income families which, in turn, accounted for the increased numbers of violent juveniles starting five years later, and they created a large increase in the number of unemployed or low-income males. Insofar as they also succeeded in creating a winner–loser culture, this may have exacerbated the malevolence of the potentially violent at the decade's end (see Appendix 3).

Long-Term Factors

These are fundamental social and economic changes usually taking place over a century or more. The industrial revolution in nineteenth-century Britain transformed an agrarian nation into a principally urban, manufacturing state with a complex division of labour. The traditional rural society had been glued together by a 'mechanical' solidarity, in which each villager subscribed to the same basic world-view and religion (Durkheim, 1933). This was rapidly supplanted during the industrial revolution by a diversity of belief systems and far looser family and clan ties in the cities. The 'glue' became economic obligation (Durkheim's 'organic solidarity') expressed in legal contracts and enforced, in the last resort, by burgeoning courts and police forces. The sheer smallness of the village had made it logistically difficult to get away with crime, and shame and ostracism from family and those upon whom physical survival depended were potent disincentives. None of this applied in the city. There, social controls had to be imposed through impersonal state agents, like the police and magistrates (Gurr, 1989).

When fundamental changes like these take place gradually over decades or a century they do not account for short-term rises and falls in the criminal statistics. In some developing countries they have occurred in remarkably short periods and, as Currie (1985) suggests, when they do, the effect on the violence rates is immediate. But while the pace of social change continued to accelerate during the 1980s, none of these deep, long-term trends climaxed in Britain (unlike Eastern Europe) at the end of the 1980s.

CONCLUSION AND IMPLICATIONS

It was beyond the scope of this book to test the lagged theory of violence in detail cross-nationally. Wolfgang (personal communication) has suggested that it is an eminently testable theory in that there are several nations in which records are available for medium-sized communities both for the proportion of families with low incomes and rates of crime of all sorts. Thus, it would be possible in America to identify towns which suffered sudden and lasting increases in unemployment and a consequent rise in families on low income. Rates of violence over the next five to fifteen years could be compared with those in matched communities which suffered no employment changes in the same period. Similar studies could be carried out in Scandinavian nations with relative ease.

In the meantime, the conclusion of this book is that, while variations in the business cycle and changes in the reporting of violent crime may have caused a small proportion of the increase since 1987, they are insignificant compared with the medium-term factor, government economic and social policies during the 1980s. They caused the increase in low-income families which created the rise in juvenile violence after 1987. They also created a winner-loser culture which may well have been influential in encouraging young men to interpret and express the new inequality in a violent manner.

The implication of the evidence of this book is that every year there are a great many more British boys turning into violent juveniles and men as a result of inequitable government policies since 1979 and that this will continue for at least a decade, even if new, more equitable, policies and cultures are introduced immediately. Since 1979 we have become shaped economically like America and have become clothed in that culture. It may be no coincidence that our violence statistics have become more like America's as well.

APPENDIX 1

DOES THE UNPRECEDENTED INCREASE IN VIOLENCE AGAINST THE PERSON SINCE 1987 REFLECT WHAT HAS ACTUALLY HAPPENED IN THE REAL WORLD?

It is an undeniable fact that the number of notifiable offences of violence against the person recorded by the police has increased at an unprecedented rate since 1987. More debatable is whether this increase reflects an actual increase either in the number of males committing violent crimes or in the rate of offending. No student of crime assumes that the official figures and the actual numbers of crimes are one and the same. There are two main reasons for questioning whether more men and boys are actually acting violently since 1987.

One is that the rate of increase in the official statistics is not matched by the rate reported by respondents in British crime surveys, the regular surveys of victims of crime funded by the Home Office. This has led some authors to suggest that the recorded increase is not a real one.

The other reason is that the number and rate of all indictable offences for which juveniles (ten- to sixteen-year-olds) were cautioned or found guilty has actually decreased in recent years. This flatly contradicts the thesis that the increase in the number of low-income parents has led to an increase in violence among young men . . . and an increase in the violence-against-the-person statistics since 1987. If the thesis were correct, the number of violent young offenders should have increased substantially. I demonstrate in Appendix 2 that this is in fact what has happened: whilst recorded juvenile crime as a whole has decreased, recorded violence against the person on the part of ten- to sixteen-year-olds has risen substantially. Furthermore, the fact that the number of young people (fourteen- to twenty-year-olds) has dropped by 20 per cent since 1987 gives good grounds for believing that, if anything, young men have become even more violent than the increase in the amount of recorded violence against the person suggest. This leaves the matter of changes in the reporting and recording of statistics.

CHANGES IN REPORTING AND RECORDING OF STATISTICS, 1987–93

It has been argued that the increase in recorded violence against the person during the 1980s reflects a change in the way police have recorded violent behaviour and preparedness to report it, not the actual amount of violence that has occurred (Davidoff and Dowds, 1990).

Fluctuations in violence statistics are difficult to interpret because they can reflect changes in public tolerance of violence and in police responses, rather than actual increases. Witnesses to crimes, and victims thereof, may vary in their willingness to report incidents; the police may vary in their definition and recording of incidents reported to them as criminal, and the police may be more or less energetic or effective in uncovering crime.

One scientific scheme to get a truer picture of the actual – as opposed to recorded – amount of crime has been the British Crime Survey (BCS). Large representative samples of members of the public are asked to describe their experience as victims of all crimes suffered during the previous twelve months, whether they reported the incidents to the police or not. In almost every category the surveys discover a great deal of crime that has not been reported to the police. However, there is a large discrepancy between the rate of increase in violence against the person recorded by the police and the increase in the amount of violence that the BCS respondents report. The BCS shows an increase of 24 per cent in the total number of incidents of violence against the person reported by their respondent victims between 1981 and 1991 (Mayhew et al., 1993). This is almost three times less than the 69 per cent total increase recorded by the police during the same period.

Davidoff and Dowds (1990) specifically analysed the disparity in increases between 1981 and 1987 (also more than threefold: 12 per cent BCS versus 40 per cent recorded by police) and concluded that while a 'real' increase in the actual amount of violence could not be ruled out as the reason for the police's higher figures, it was more likely to be due to a change in police recording practices and procedures and to an increased preparedness on the part of women to report domestic violence. The authors themselves admit that this conclusion is based on flawed evidence and it is a highly debatable one.

They base their conclusion on a reanalysis of police statistics from twenty-eight forces between 1985 and 1987. But they only have full responses for both years from six of the forces, thereby drastically reducing the size of their sample, and even more seriously, they report that in asking the police to reclassify their records, the police 'were not provided with detailed instructions as to how to apply the descriptive classification' (Davidoff and Dowds, 1990, p. 12). This means that very significant differences could have occurred in interpretation of the researchers' categories and, for example, crucially for their thesis concerning the way police recorded domestic incidents; what one force chose to regard as a 'street- or pub-brawl' another may have registered as a 'domestic'.

Their thesis is seriously undermined by the findings of the latest BCS, published in 1993. Davidoff and Dowds made much of the fact that the proportion of BCS women respondents who had reported domestic assaults to the police had risen from 20 per cent in 1981 to 50 per cent in 1987. This could have accounted for most or all of the much larger increase in violence against the person recorded by the police during those years. However, the 1992 BCS flatly contradicted this finding: only 21 per cent of women respondents reported domestic assaults upon them to the police. As the 1992

BCS stated: 'Figures from the 1992 survey, however, suggest that the level of reporting (by women of domestic assaults) in 1987 was unusually high' (Mayhew *et al.*, 1993).

If increased reporting of domestic assaults does not account for the disparity, police recording procedures would have to have undergone a very radical change starting in 1987 to have accounted for such large differences. The authors do not demonstrate that this occurred, nor are there any hard facts to suggest that it might have done. They ignore altogether the contrary evidence that Home Office circulars in 1978, 1985 and 1990 have led to a decrease in recording of juvenile crime and an increase in cautioning (Hagell and Newburn, 1994) and informal cautioning. Above all, they do not consider the most obvious alternative explanation: that the 1988 BCS, whilst effective for many categories of crime, failed in some way to gather a true picture of the amount of this kind of violence.

A close inspection of the 1988 BCS data suggests this may be so. The great majority of violence against the person is perpetrated by sixteen- to twenty-nine-year-old men from the lowest socio-economic classes in inner cities, and their victims are also mostly of their own gender, class and age group (Tarling, 1993). It so happens that the 1988 BCS sample was least representative in this particular age group and, therefore, may not have had a large enough number of potential victims of violence against the person in the sample to truly reflect the incidence of this crime. As the authors of the British Crime Survey of 1988 themselves stated (Mayhew *et al.*, 1989, p. 94): 'In general, the represent-ativeness of the core sample was sound. However, as regards age, there was a slight shortfall among men and women in the 16–29 age group . . . '. Closer inspection of the data shows that in practice this meant 11.8 per cent rather than 14.1 per cent (which would have been representative) of the 10,392 respondents were men aged sixteen to twenty-nine, a total of 1226. In a nationally representative sample of this age group, (depending on definitions) about 300 of them would be from the lowest socio-economic families. Of these, a proportion would be from rural communities and at lower risk of being victims. Given that violence against the person is a rare offence even among young men from poor backgrounds, the likelihood of any 200–250 having been the victim of violence in any given twelve month period is low. Such a sample size may be too small to accurately reflect the real amount of violence against the person, hence a disparity between the figures of the survey and those recorded by police. Indeed, it could be argued that even if the survey had had the truly representative proportion of 14.1 per cent, once this is reduced further by the need to allow for class and the rural–urban divide, it would still be too small a subsample. Thus, while it is always possible in theory that recording practices and public preparedness to report have played a part in the recorded rise in violence since 1987, it is also very possible that they were not a significant factor at all, and that the BCS's findings regarding violence against the person can be largely discounted. Indeed, since Davidoff and Dowds's paper, the latest BCS report (Mayhew *et al.*, 1993) has made explicit recognition of the fact that BCS estimates of violent behaviour cannot be relied upon: 'The BCS count of violence is unlikely to be a full one; for a number of reasons many incidents will go unmentioned in the interview. Offences between non-strangers are particularly likely to be undercounted (p. xi). Later in the report the point is reiterated: '. . . the BCS cannot be taken as providing hard and fast figures on the extent of different types of violence (p. 80)'.

Thus, while it is always conceivable that there were some hitherto undiscovered reporting factors which led, or at least contributed to, the sudden meteoric increase in reported violence against the person in 1987, there is no firm evidence that this is so. As far as we can tell, there was – in reality as well as on paper – a very substantial rise in violence against the person between 1987 and 1993.

APPENDIX 2

HOW MUCH OF THE INCREASE IN VIOLENCE AGAINST THE PERSON SINCE 1987 IS EXPLAINED BY JUVENILES?

Official statistics for juvenile crime have been falling steadily for a decade (Table 1). *Criminal Statistics* (1980–93) reveal that the rate per 100,000 of ten- to thirteen-year-olds found guilty or cautioned at all courts fell by 45 per cent (from 3075 to 1678) and by 23 per cent among fourteen -to sixteen-year-olds (from 7585 to 5872), between 1980 and 1993. Similarly, the number of juvenile offenders fell by 54 per cent (from 48,900 to 22,200) among ten- to thirteen-year-olds and by 45 per cent (from 95,200 to 52,600) among fourteen- to sixteen-year-olds in the same period.

Table 1 Rates per 100,000 and numbers of offenders cautioned or found guilty (all courts), boys aged 10–13 and 14–16, 1980, 1987 and 1993, all offences.

	Rate per 100,000		Number of offenders	
	10–13	*14–16*	*10–13*	*14–16*
1980	3075	7585	48,900	95,200
1987	2477	7473	30,400	82,200
1993	1678	5872	22,200	52,600
Changes:				
1980–87, %	–19%	–2%	–38%	–14%
1987–1993, %	–32%	–22%	–27%	–35%
1980–1993, %	–45%	–23%	–54%	–45%

(Figures for 1993 from table 5.25 of 1993 *Criminal Statistics*; for 1987 from Table 5.23 of 1992 *Criminal Statistics*; and for 1980 from Table 5.18 of 1980 *Criminal Statistics*.)

Doubts have been cast on the degree to which these figures reflect the actual amount of criminal behaviour among juveniles. These doubts were considered in some detail by a Home Affairs Committee investigation of juvenile offenders (HAC, 1992). While it was generally accepted that there had been a fall in the number of juvenile offenders since 1981, several sources disputed that the rate of offending had dropped.

It was argued that there may have been a significant rise in informal cautions by the police. These are not recorded as a part of the official criminal statistics and they could substantially deflate the figures. The Association of Chief Police Officers, for example, submitted to the committee that when this was taken into account, along with the fall in the numbers of fourteen- to twenty-year-olds, there had been an estimated 54 per cent increase in juvenile crime between 1980 and 1990, not a fall in the official statistics.

Whatever the truth of these and other speculations advanced to the Home Affairs Committee (discussed further at the end of this Appendix), little regard seems to have been paid to a critical point: while the number of recorded juvenile offenders as a whole has fallen, recorded violence against the person has risen.

THE RISE IN RECORDED JUVENILE VIOLENCE AGAINST THE PERSON: AN ANALYSIS

Summary

The analysis of official criminal statistics which follows is strongly consistent with the thesis that the cohort of juveniles raised in the early 1980s is more violent than the preceding cohort. The findings are summarized as follows:

1 Between 1987 and 1993 the rate per 100,000 of recorded juvenile violence against the person has increased by 40.5 per cent – despite the 26 per cent decrease for all juvenile offences – and the number of recorded violent juveniles increased by 34 per cent – despite the 31 per cent decrease for all offences.
2 Between 1980 and 1987, the rate of juvenile violent offending rose by only 2 per cent and the number of offenders fell by 15.5 per cent: on the face of it, juveniles have been significantly more violent since 1987 compared with the period from 1980 to 1987.
3 Comparison of the figures for juvenile violence with those for theft and handling stolen goods highlights the extent of the increase in violence: Between 1987 and 1993 theft/handling decreased by over 40 per cent, about as much as the increase in violence.
4 The proportion of juvenile crime that is violent as a proportion of all juvenile crimes has increased significantly since 1987, suggesting that they have become more violent as a group. By contrast, the proportion of crime that is violent in older age groups (seventeen to twenty, and twenty-one and over) has not changed significantly.

THE RISE IN JUVENILE VIOLENCE

Table 2 shows that the rate of offending for violence against the person per 100,000 among ten- to thirteen-year-olds increased by 52 per cent between 1987 and 1993 and the number of offenders by 64 per cent. Among fourteen- to sixteen-year-olds, the rises were 29 per cent and 4 per cent. Combined, the rate of violent offending by ten- to sixteen-year-olds rose by 40.5 per cent, between 1987 and 1993, and the numbers of offenders by 34 per cent. Of particular significance for the thesis of this book, we find a very different

̇pattern when we compare these figures with those for 1980-87. The rate of juvenile violent offending rose in this period by only 2 per cent (compared with 40.5 per cent between 1987 and 1993) and the number of offenders actually fell - by 15.5 per cent (compared with the 34 per cent rise between 1987 and 1993). That this should have been so, strongly supports the thesis that the cohort of boys raised after the increase in low-income families in the early 1980s are more violent than the preceding cohort.

Table 2 Rates per 100,000 and numbers of offenders cautioned or found guilty (all courts), boys aged 10-13 and 14-16, 1980, 1987 and 1993, violence against the person.

	Rate per 100,000		Number of offenders	
	10-13	14-16	10-13	14-16
1980	92.3	606.8	1,467	7,616
1987	99.1	590.8	1,216	6,576
1993	151	763.4	1,998	6,838
Changes:				
1980-87, %	+7%	-3%	-17%	-14%
1987-93, %	+52%	+29%	+64%	+4%
1980-1993, %	+39%	+20%	+27%	+10%

(Rate per 100,000 for 1987 and 1993 calculated by dividing the rate per 100,000 for all offences by the percentage for the year in that age group in Table 5.12 of *Criminal Statistics* 1987 and 1993 that were crimes of violence against the person. Percentages for the age groups in 1980 (3 per cent ten to thirteen, 8 per cent fourteen to sixteen, 14 per cent seventeen to twenty) derived from Tables 5.4 and 5.2 of *Criminal Statistics* 1980; rate per 100,000 for all offences in 1980 in Table 5.18 of *Criminal Statistics* 1980.)

The degree to which the figures recorded for juvenile violence against the person run against the trend for juvenile recorded statistics as a whole is highlighted by comparison with the figures for theft and handling stolen goods (Table 3) - the most common category of juvenile crime. The theft/handling rate of offending fell by 39 per cent between 1987 and 1993 (compared with the 40.5 per cent rise in violence) and the number of offenders fell by 42.5 per cent (compared with the 34 per cent increase in violence).

There is little reason to suppose that the size of the disparities between these changes, from 1987 to 1993, in juvenile violence compared with theft and handling stolen goods or all offences are explicable by changes in police recording practices. There is no evidence, for example, that in 1987 the police suddenly ceased informal cautioning for juvenile violent offences (as opposed to other crimes) and began to record more of these as official cautions. To affect the figures this would have had to have occurred nationwide and to have been part of an official directive from the Home Office, for which there is no evidence. However, in the Home Affairs Committee on juvenile offenders

Table 3 Rates per 100,000 and numbers of offenders cautioned or found guilty (all courts), boys aged 10–13 and 14–16, 1980, 1987 and 1993, theft and handling stolen goods.

	Rate per 100,000		Number of offenders	
	10–13	14–16	10–13	14–16
1980	2060	4399	32,763	55,216
1987	1709	4559	20,976	50,142
1993	1024	2818	13,542	25,248
Changes:				
1980–1987, %	–17%	+4%	–36%	–9%
1987–1993, %	–40%	–38%	–35%	–50%
1980–1993, %	–50%	–36%	–59%	–54%

(Rate per 100,000 calculated by dividing the rate per 100,000 for all offences by the percentage for the year in that age group in Table 5.12, *Criminal Statistics* 1987 and 1993 and Table 5.18 in *Criminal Statistics* 1980 that were crimes of theft and handling stolen goods.)

there were several witnesses who specifically argued that informal cautioning for theft/handling had greatly increased in recent years, and if these claims are correct they could partly account for the large size of the decrease in its recording.

As summarized in Table 4, the figures suggest that juveniles became significantly more violent between 1987 and 1993, despite the broader picture of declining recorded juvenile crime.

Table 4 Rates per 100,000 and numbers of offenders cautioned or found guilty (all courts), boys aged 10–13 and 14–16, 1980, 1987 and 1993, violence against the person, theft and handling stolen goods, and all offences compared, percentage changes 1987–93.

	Rate per 100,000		Number of offenders	
	10–13	14–16	10–13	14–16
% Change, 1987–93:				
Violence against person	+52%	+29%	+64%	+4%
Theft/handling goods	–40%	–38%	–35%	–50%
All offences	–32%	–22%	–27%	–35%

Still further evidence that recorded juvenile violence has increased against the trend is the change in the proportion of the crime that is violent in that age group. Table 5 provides these figures and those for theft and handling stolen goods as comparison.

Whereas violence was only 4 per cent of all recorded crime committed by ten- to thirteen-year-olds in 1987, it was more than twice as much – 9 per cent – in 1993. It rose from 8 per cent of all crime committed by fourteen- to sixteen-year olds in 1987 to 13 per cent in 1993. This contrasts with little or no change in the proportions from 1980 to 1987. These figures are highly supportive of the thesis that the youth cohort raised in the early 1980s are more violent than their predecessors. It is also interesting to note that among seventeen- to twenty-year-olds, and twenty-one and older, the proportions have changed little or not at all, again strongly supportive of the thesis.

Table 5 Offenders found guilty or cautioned (all courts) as percentage of all offences by type of offence and age, boys aged 10–13 and 14–16, and men aged 17–20 and 21+, 1980, 1987 and 1993 compared, violence against the person, and theft and handling stolen goods.

	10–13	14–16	17–20	21+
Violence against person as % of offences in age range				
1980	3%	8%	14%	13%
1987	4%	8%	13%	14%
1993	9%	13%	11%	14%
Theft/handling goods as % of offences in age range				
1980	67%	58%	48%	46%
1987	69%	61%	47%	42%
1993	61%	48%	38%	39%
Change 1980–87:				
Violence against person	+1%	0%	–1%	+1%
Theft/handling	+2%	+3%	–1%	–4%
Change 1987–93:				
Violence against person	+5%	+5%	–2%	0%
Theft/handling	–8%	–13%	–9%	–3%
Change 1980–93:				
Violence against person	+6%	+5%	–3%	+1%
Theft/handling	–6%	–10%	–10%	–7%

(Percentages 1987 and 1993 from Table 5.12 in *Criminal Statistics* 1987 and 1993. Percentages for the age groups in 1980 derived from Tables 5.4 and 5.2 of *Criminal Statistics* 1980.)

The comparison in Table 5 with theft and handling of stolen goods reveals a different pattern of change to that for violence by ten- to sixteen-year-olds. Theft fell, from 69 per cent of all crimes committed by ten- to thirteen-year-olds in 1987 to 61 per cent in 1993 and from 61 per cent to 48 per cent in the fourteen- to sixteen-year-olds. Doubtless this reflects the large decreases in the amount of theft and handling of stolen goods recorded by the police as well as a change in criminal priorities.

Overall, this analysis of the juvenile criminal statistics strongly supports the thesis of this book. A final factor in analysing the violence-against-the-person statistics is the sharp fall in the total numbers of the most violently criminogenic group – fourteen- to twenty-year-olds.

THE FALL IN THE NUMBERS OF FOURTEEN- TO TWENTY-YEAR-OLD MALES SINCE 1987

THE RELATION BETWEEN YOUTH POPULATION AND CRIME

1987 was not only the year in which recorded violence against the person began its unprecedented rise; it was also the year in which the numbers of young men at large in England and Wales – the people who commit the majority of these crimes – began a sharp descent. Fewer young men should have meant less violence against the person as a whole, and less recorded juvenile violence. It did not. Although recorded juvenile crime as a whole decreased, juvenile violence increased substantially – even though there were one-fifth fewer juveniles to commit it.

There is compelling evidence that the amount of crime in a given community is directly affected by the number of young males in it (Maxim, 1986; Hirschi and Gottfredson, 1983) although the relationship is not crudely invariant (Farrington and West, 1993). Since most crime is committed by fifteen- to twenty-nine-year-olds this is only to be expected. Field's (1990) analysis of crime trends in Britain from 1950 to 1989 for the Home Office concluded that: 'growth in the numbers of young men (in Britain) was found to be positively related to growth in all types of crime . . . similar results have been obtained from research studies conducted in the USA'. A US government commission estimated that 40–50 per cent of the rise in recorded crime between 1960 and 1965 was directly caused by the increase in young men at that time (President's Commission on Law Enforcement and Administration of Justice, 1967). Gurr (1989) offers further support for the theory. The post-war baby-boom increased the numbers of fifteen- to twenty-nine-year-olds by 50 per cent in Britain and America, just when the rates of violent crime rose too. In Germany and Austria the baby-booms happened in the early 1950s once their post-war economic recovery had begun, rather than in the 1940s. Their crime rises were correspondingly later, as the theory would predict.

However, as Gurr points out: 'there is nothing automatic about the Youth/Crime connection' (Gurr, 1989). The violence of young men from different generations varies. If the relationship was invariant, for example, the 50 per cent baby-boom increase in the numbers of young men in Britain mentioned above would have resulted in a 50 per cent increase in violence against the person, not the thirtyfold that occurred. Economic, cultural and political factors influence the relation. In Communist bloc Eastern European nations large rises in the youthful population between 1964 and 1977 were not accompanied by an equivalent rise in violent crime. It seems highly probable this was due to the political system there (and a reluctance to record crime officially – however, the huge increases in violence against the person since the end of the Cold War are unlikely to be a mere artefact of recording). Nor is it only Communism that affects the relation. Switzerland's crime rate has remained constant since the Second World War, regardless of demographic changes, and in Japan the rate actually declined between 1950 and 1975 despite a burgeoning youth population (Gurr, 1989). Economic conditions are important as well (Field, 1990; Maxim, 1986). A large youth cohort increases competition for resources, with more young people chasing fewer jobs and employers able to offer lower wages, intensifying competition and stress.

Thus, a direct, invariant causal relation between size of the youth population and crime rates does not prevail under all conditions. None the less, the relation seems to be a strong one in the conditions found in most technologically-developed nations, including Britain.

THE EFFECT OF CHANGES IN POPULATION ON CAUTIONS/CONVICTIONS FOR VIOLENCE AGAINST THE PERSON

Between 1964 and 1976, with the end of the post-war baby-boom, the birth rate in England and Wales dropped steadily and, as a result, the numbers of young people fell from 1987 onwards (Table 6).

Table 6 Estimated resident male population at mid-1987 and mid-1993 by single year of age, England and Wales.

Age	Mid-1987	Mid-1993	Change
10	288400	326400	+38,000
11	299700	325900	+26,200
12	312700	330100	+17,400
13	323800	333500	+ 9,700
14	348400	322200	-26,200
15	370300	297200	-73,500
16	395200	293000	-102,200
17	389800	305200	-84,600
18	400200	317900	-82,300
19	403300	329700	-73,600
20	417800	354300	-63,500

(From Table 1, *Population Estimates*, 1987 and 1993.)

Table 6 reveals that in 1993, there were 22 per cent less fourteen- to sixteen-year-olds and 23 per cent less seventeen- to twenty-year-olds than in 1987. The number of ten- to thirteen-year-olds was rising and there were 7 per cent more in 1993. If the number of young people correlated exactly with the amount of crime recorded then there should have been 7 per cent more crime committed by ten- to thirteen-year-olds, 22 per cent less among fourteen- to sixteen-year-olds and 23 per cent less among seventeen- to twenty-year-olds compared with 1987. As we already know from Table 4, this is not what happened.

Table 7 contrasts the percentage changes in actual rates and numbers of crimes since 1987 with changes in population in the different age ranges. It reveals just how out-of-step with the rest of the juvenile crime statistics were those for violence against the person. Thus, what should have been a 7 per cent rise in the rate of offending per hundred thousand among ten- to thirteen-year-olds if the population rise had been precisely reflected was a 52 per cent rise, and among fourteen- to sixteen-year-olds what should have been a 22 per cent fall was a 29 per cent rise. The increase in rate of offending has therefore counteracted the fall in the number of offenders. This strongly supports the thesis that post-1987, juveniles behaved more violently.

By contrast, rates of offending for theft and handling of stolen goods fell by more than the population figures would have predicted; on the face of it suggesting that the post-1987 cohort have been less prone to thieving. Theft/handling among ten- to thirteen-year-olds should have risen by 7 per cent but fell by 40 per cent, and among fourteen- to sixteen-year-olds it fell by 16 per cent more than the 22 per cent it should have been. Rates for all offences among ten- to thirteen-year-olds fell by 32 per cent when they should have risen by 7 per cent. They were precisely the same as the 22 per cent population decrease among fourteen- to sixteen-year-olds.

Table 7 Rates per 100,000, numbers of offenders cautioned or found guilty (all courts) and change in population, boys aged 10–13 and 14–16, and men aged 17–20, violence against the person, theft and handling of stolen goods, and all offences compared, percentage changes 1987–93.

	Rate per 100,000			Number offenders		
	10–13	14–16	17–20	10–13	14–16	17–20
% change, 1987–93:						
Violence against person	+52%	+29%	–6%	+64%	+4%	–23%
% population change	+7%	–22%	–23%	+7%	–22%	–23%
Theft/handling goods	–40%	–38%	–19%	–35%	–50%	–27%
% population change	+7%	–22%	–23%	+7%	–22%	–23%
All offences	–32%	–22%	+15%	–27%	–35%	–10%
% population change	+7%	–22%	–23%	+7%	–22%	–23%

SUMMARY

Overall, our analysis of the juvenile violence-against-the-person statistics provides substantial support for the thesis that the cohort of juveniles since 1987 has been more violent than the preceding one. To recapitulate:

1 Between 1987 and 1993 the rate of juvenile violence increased by 40.5 per cent – despite the 26 per cent decrease for all juvenile offences – and the number of recorded violent juveniles increased by 34 per cent – despite the 31 per cent decrease for all offences.
2 In marked contrast, between 1980 and 1987, the rate of juvenile violent offending rose by only 2 per cent and the number of offenders fell by 15.5 per cent.
3 Between 1987 and 1993 theft/handling decreased by over 40 per cent – about as much as the increase in violence.
4 The proportion of juvenile crime that is violent has increased significantly since 1987. By contrast, it stayed at roughly the same proportion for juveniles between 1980 and 1987, and in older age groups (seventeen to twenty years old, and twenty-one and over) between 1987 and 1993.

HOW MUCH OF THE OVERALL INCREASE IN VIOLENCE CAN BE EXPLAINED BY THE INCREASE IN JUVENILE VIOLENCE?

Unfortunately, there is no certain way of establishing the contribution of juveniles to the overall increase in recorded violence against the person. This is because a record of the age of offenders is only kept if the case results in an official caution or a court conviction, of which over two-thirds of cases do not. Thus, the total number of crimes of violence-against-the-person recorded by the police in 1993 was 205,000 (both sexes), of which 63,000 led to a caution/conviction. Nothing is known about the age distribution of the remaining offenders involved in the 142,000 other offences recorded.

The simplest and most naive approach to answering our question would be to extrapolate directly from caution/conviction rates to numbers of crimes recorded – to assume that the recorded crimes for which we have no age-distribution data-breakdown spread in exactly the same proportions as cautions/convictions. Thus, if we use the same male–female ratios of the caution/conviction statistics to remove the females from the raw figures for recorded crime, and we apply the age distributions from cautions/ convictions, we can calculate the contribution of males in each age group to the recorded violence-against-the-person figures for 1987 and 1993 as follows:[1]

Table 8 Recorded male violence against the person by age, assuming the same age/gender patterns as found in cautions/convictions, 1980, 1987 and 1993.

	1987	1993	Change 1987–93	% of increase
10–16	20,304	29,623	= +9,319	19%
17–20	35,532	36,593	= +1,061	2%
21+	69,795	108,035	= +38,240	79%
Total	125,631	174,251	= +48,620	

	1980	1987	Change 1980–87	% of increase
10–16	14,003	20,304	= +6,301	16%
17–20	26,256	35,532	= +9,276	24%
21+	46,386	69,795	= +23,409	60%
Total	86,645	125,631	= +38,986	

(see note 1 for the full basis of these calculations)

On these calculations, there were 10,000 more crimes committed between 1987 and 1993 over and above the increase for 1980–87. Juveniles contributed a net 3 per cent more to the increase compared with 19 per cent from the over-twenty-one's. The net contribution of seventeen- to twenty-year-olds dropped by 22 per cent.

However, there are many reasons to doubt that these calculations have much, if any, scientific value. There is a considerable likelihood that the age distribution of those actually apprehended and subsequently cautioned/convicted is not the same as among those offenders who are involved in an incident that is merely recorded. Whereas the caution/conviction rates are based on offenders who get caught and against whom the police decide to act, the ones who were not caught or whom the police decided not to caution or prosecute may have an entirely different demographic profile.

Thus, there may be a tendency for police to take more action against adults compared with juveniles, giving them a greater preponderance in the caution/conviction figures than truly exists. There is little doubt that age is a major consideration in the decision to caution rather than prosecute. Home Office Circular 14/1985 (part 2, para. 1) which provides Home Office guidelines to chief constables made this explicit in stating that, while juveniles should be cautioned wherever possible rather than prosecuted, with adults: 'there is no general presumption that cautioning will be the normal course'.

If there is a greater overall likelihood for the police to take action against juveniles, it is likely that those who are prosecuted are only the hardest and thinnest end of a much larger wedge. Clear-up rates for violence against the person are around three-quarters (a clear-up does not mean the police necessarily prosecute; merely that they have identified the offender and dealt with him). This is also the proportion of thefts that are not cleared up. It is therefore much more likely if violence comes to the attention of the police that the assailant will be identified – yet further action is not taken on a great many occasions. The large disparity between the number of cautions/convictions for violence and the number of recorded crimes (63,000, versus 142,000 in 1993) suggests that in over two-thirds of cases the police take no further action (although part of the reason is the fact that some of the recorded crimes are by the same person; sometimes on the same occasion). There may be a much higher proportion of juveniles than adults in the recorded figures against whom the police have decided not to act. If this were so it would greatly increase the juvenile contribution to recorded crime compared with cautions/convictions.

Another effect on the age distribution of the violence statistics is the change that can occur between what is recorded and the crime for which the offender is actually convicted or cautioned. There may be a reduction from wounding to common assault, an offence that is summary rather than indictable, and therefore does not appear as part of the violence-against-the-person statistics. There may be large differences between age groups as to whether this adjustment is made. Thus, a juvenile whose first violent offence is wounding may be much more likely than an equivalent adult to have this reduced to assault, to try and minimize the sentence and seriousness of the crime in the hope of reducing the chance of reoffending. Every time this happens another juvenile drops out of the figures for cautions/convictions; likewise, every time an over-twenty-one is convicted/cautioned for wounding when he would have had the charge downgraded had he been younger, it enlarges the statistical impression that adults are more violent than juveniles.

Another imponderable is the use of informal cautioning. On the principle that once juveniles become part of the criminal justice system they are much more likely to continue to offend, the 1969 Children and Young Persons Act encouraged the police to keep children out of court wherever possible and led to a sharp increase in cautioning (Evans and Wilkinson, 1990). On top of these formal cautions, it has been argued by several relevant professional groups that the police have increasingly used their discretionary power to administer an informal caution, of which there might be no record. The National Association of Probation Officers submission to the HAC claimed that there has been an increase in juvenile informal cautioning and they were supported in this by the Police Federation and the Howard League (HAC, 1993). Increased use of informal cautions was one of the main reasons that Farrington (HAC, 1993) advanced in coming to the conclusion that the fall in all recorded juvenile crime since 1981 was 'only a statistical illusion'. Given (as discussed above) that cautions are much more likely to be used for juveniles than adults, it seems probable that the same would apply to informal cautions.

If so, it could affect the age distribution of recorded violence against the person.

Unfortunately, there is no reliable evidence on the extent of informal cautioning (the HAC recommended research into the subject). One study of police forces in England and Wales revealed that more than half do not have a formal policy on their use (Evans and Wilkinson, 1990). The same study suggested that informal street warnings, usually administered immediately after a crime, are only used for the most minor offences, such as dropping litter or riding bicycles on the pavement, which would suggest that their use would not affect violence statistics. There was no clear evidence on the extent of 'formal' informal warnings (the last step below a full caution) in the study.

There is a final reason for doubting that cautions/convictions are a sound basis for extrapolating the age distribution of recorded violence against the person. The proportions of different age groups contributing to cautions/convictions for violence against the person, on which these calculations all rely, do not necessarily indicate how violent or otherwise a group is. They reflect overall shifts in the age distribution of violence. Thus, more than anything else, the lowness of the 1 per cent rise in the juvenile contribution between 1987 and 1993 may reflect the substantial increase in the proportion of men over the age of twenty-one (from 55 per cent to 62 per cent), not whether juveniles have become more violent. If many more adults over the age of twenty-one act violently, because their raw numbers are so much greater anyway, it reduces the proportion of juveniles even if their numbers increase substantially as well.

All these considerations make the calculations in Table 8 largely redundant and lead to the conclusion that, in the absence of any other methods, it is currently impossible to estimate the age distribution of recorded crime. For this reason, we are unable to establish the extent of the contribution in the rise of juvenile violence to the increase in recorded violence against the person since 1987.

CONCLUSION

It has not been possible to answer the question with which this appendix is titled. However, it is clear that there has been a substantial increase in juvenile violence and that this must have contributed to some degree to the increase in all violence against the person recorded by the police.

APPENDIX 3

POSSIBLE EFFECTS OF THE WINNER–LOSER CULTURE OF THE MID TO LATE 1980s ON THE STATISTICS FOR VIOLENCE AGAINST THE PERSON SINCE 1987

During the early 1980s many people may have believed that the policies of the government would soon change, little realizing that they would be sustained for over fifteen years continuously. Until the Falklands War in the summer of 1982, the popularity of the government was extremely low. Afterwards, it was able to achieve a decisive majority in the 1983 general election. However, popularity again declined dramatically until the mid-1980s when the economic boom occurred which led to the re-election of the government in 1987. During this period large fortunes were made out of the property market and the stock exchange and the 'yuppie' became a part of popular culture. Tabloid newspapers both reflected and helped to create the spirit of the age – a nakedly materialistic one which specifically emphasized inequalities that already existed but which had not, until this point, been presented as a matter of 'winners' and 'losers'. This rhetoric became part of the everyday culture.

From early in the 1980s there were many TV drama series (mostly of American origin) in which wicked capitalists came off best. This was the decade of *Dallas* and JR Ewing and of Joan Collins's *Dynasty*. In recent years there have been a string of home-grown 'yuppie' dramas in which snake-in-the-grass British money makers were given a positive image, series like ITV's *Capital City* (about the dealing room of a merchant bank) and *Chancer* (a city whiz-kid's adventures running a motor car company). There have also been countless Hollywood feature-films which depicted get-rich-quick wide-boys winning out over 'wimps' (most famously the 1988 *Wall Street* which included one of its central characters, Gordon Gekko, famously pronouncing that 'greed is good').

By the mid-1980s it became common to use the word 'loser' to denote anyone with a low income, and the basic attitude behind such a word may have played a part in increasing violent behaviour. Many of these 'losers' may not have felt they were players in the first place; did not know the rules of the game (through lack of education and other disadvantages resulting from their upbringing) and would have stood little chance of succeeding had they competed. It can be argued that if you put someone in a situation where they are very likely to fail and then sneer at them for doing so, you must not be surprised if they react with hostility.

However, it is a matter of debate how widespread and well established the winner–loser culture really became in Britain and, of course, there are counter examples that can be offered in any speculative, ultimately anecdotal reviews of this kind. I first heard the expression 'loser' used to denote a person of low social status and income in America in 1985 at the FBI headquarters in Quantico, Virginia. The speaker was an FBI agent and he was summing up his view of the man who shot John Lennon: 'The guy was a real loser.' Five years later, I heard 'loser' used for the first time on mainstream British television without irony and intended to convey the same meaning, on the BBC1 soap opera *Eastenders* (17 January 1991). The 'yuppie' Ian Beale, a young catering entrepreneur, threw the word at the departing back of his cousin (Mark Fowler) who had just made a decision which put friendship before money. Ian could not conceal his derision at such sentimentality. However, this does not mean *Eastenders* has become a dramaturgical advocate of the entrepreneurial ethos – far from it. For the 'yuppie' Ian Beale is portrayed as a sad, bitter and twisted man whose addiction to hard work and money-making caused the breakup of his marriage and expresses deep emotional inadequacy. If anything, he is used as a parable for the cataclysmic consequences of the unbridled pursuit of 'yuppie' values (whose proponents might reasonably cite this as just one more example of the BBC's – or even, the whole nation that it serves –continued bias against entrepreneurs and commercial success).

In support of the idea that the British remain intractably hostile to and suspicious of entrepreneurial success, numerous similar examples could be cited from the other main home-grown soaps. The viewing figures for *Eastenders* are only bettered by those of *Coronation Street*, the highest-rating television programme in Britain. Its businessman, Mike Baldwin, had a particularly grim 1980s, frequently punished for displaying greed and ruthlessness – the grandiose and unattractive emotional roots of his need to succeed have been examined from almost every conceivable angle, with an unambiguous moral seen by 40 million viewers per week. Aficionados of *The Archers* on BBC Radio 4 will be aware that Brian Aldrich, a slave driving, philandering farmer with a half-a-million-pound turnover, was tormented like a character in a Greek tragedy during the 1980s (rather than one in 'an everyday tale of country folk', as the series is billed): numerous rejected adulterous advances; a miserable affair; a delinquent daughter and an accident resulting in epilepsy – to name but a few of the misfortunes that were rained upon his head by scriptwriters keen to show that no good comes to those who put material advancement before people.

This anecdotal glance in the mirror that popular culture holds up to us shows that a case can be made both for the view that the British are still highly resistant to the winner–loser culture and that we have come to accept it. Indisputably, the government sought to influence Britons in favour of it and they have had some success. To estimate the precise impact of something so nebulous on the violence statistics at the end of the decade seems impossible. None the less, it would be consistent with the overall evidence that inequality is a major correlate of violence, that as the gap between rich and poor during the 1980s steadily widened, there was a change in the way it felt to be poor and that this accounted for the lag in the rise in violence against the person. Thus, there were a great many more poor people in 1983 than there had been in 1979, but that may not have led to an increase in violence because of the cultural climate – what it felt like to be poor then. Subsequently, there may have been a subtle increase in the amount of rage and frustration felt by low-income males as a result of being dubbed failures for being of low income. This could have been a gradual, cumulative effect, increasingly acute as the 1980s wore on with no end in sight and an ever more visible cohort of newly wealthy men (most obviously in the tabloid newspapers) more-or-less flaunting the fact that they were 'winners' and that the low income male was a 'loser'.

NOTES

CHAPTER 1

1. Cummings, E.M. *et al.*, 1985; Porter, B. and O'Leary, K., 1980; Johnson, S.M. and Lobitz, G.K., 1974; Oltmans, T.F. *et al.*, 1977; Slater, P.E., 1962; Dodge, K.A., Bates, J.E. and Pettit, G.S., 1990; and four papers in Hinde, R.A. and Stevenson-Hinde, J., 1988, *Relationships Within Families*, Oxford: Clarendon Press: Meyer; Easterbrooks and Emde; Engfer; Christiansen and Margolin.
2. Block, J.H. *et al.*, 1986; Forehand, R. *et al.*, 1988; Hops, H. *et al.*, 1990; Emery, R.E., 1982; Hetherington, E.M. *et al.*, 1979; Brady, C.P. *et al.*, 1986; Hetherington, E.M., 1979; Jacobson, D.S., 1978.
3. Wolfe, D.A. *et al.*, 1985; Rosenbaum, A. and O'Leary, K.D., 1981; Kratcoski, P.C., 1985; Jaffee, P. *et al.*, 1986; Hughes, H. and Barad, S., 1983; Hilberman, E. and Mawson, K., 1978; Levine, M., 1975.
4. Widom, C.S., 1989a, lists 18 relevant studies on pages 166–173 of 'The intergenerational transmission of violence' in Weiner, N.A. and Wolfgang, M.E., 1989, *Pathways to Criminal Violence*, CA: Sage; to these I would add eight: Herrenkohl, R.C. and Herrenkohl, E.C., 1981; Patterson, G.R., 1986; Tizard, B. and Hodges, J., 1978; Tooley, K.M., 1977; Felthous, A.R., 1978; Trickett, P.K. and Kuczynski, L., 1986; Adams-Tucker, C., 1984; Lewis, D.O. *et al.*, 1985.
5. Wolfe, D.A. and Mosk, M.D., 1983; Rohrbeck, C.A. and Twentyman, C.T., 1986; Bousha, D.M. and Twentyman, C.T., 1984; Aragona, J.A. and Eyberg, S.M., 1981.
6. Jenkins, R.L., 1968; Jenkins, R.L., 1966; Widom, C.S., 1989; Reidy, T.J., 1977; Hoffman-Plotkin, D. and Twentyman, C.T., 1984; Burgess, R.L. and Conger, R.D., 1978; Crittenden, P.M., 1982; Mccord, J., 1983.
7. Geller, M. and Ford-Somma, L., 1984; Kratcoski, P.C., 1982; Jenkins, R.L., 1968; Lewis, D.O. *et al.*, 1979; Lewis, D.O. *et al.*, 1983; Alfaro, J.D., 1981; Tarter, R.E. *et al.*, 1984; Blount, H.R. and Chandler, T.A., 1979.
8. Widom, C.S., 1989; Climent, C.E. and Ervin, F.R., 1972; Bandura, A. and Walters, R.H., 1959; Sears, R.R., 1961.
9. Tanay, E., 1976; Pagan, D. and Smith, S.M., 1979; Duncan, J.W. and Duncan, G.M., 1971; Smith, S. and Topeka, K., 1965; Duncan, G.W. *et al.*, 1958; Tuteur, W. and Glotzer, J., 1959; Scott, P.D., 1973; Corder, B.F. *et al.*, 1976; Wille, W.S., 1974; Satten, J. *et al.*, 1960; Hill, D. and Pond, D.A., 1952; Sorrels, J.M., 1977; Boudouris, J., 1971; Frazier, S.H., 1974; Kahn, M.W., 1959; Sendi, I.B. and Blomgren, P.G., 1975; Humphrey, J.A., 1977; Langevin, R., 1983; Lewis, D.O. *et al.*, 1985.
10. Monane, M. *et al.*, 1984; Hunter, R.S. and Kilstrom, N., 1979; Smith, S.M. and Hanson, R., 1975; Herrenkohl, E.C. *et al.*, 1983; Straus, M.A., 1983; Herman, J. *et al.*, 1986.

CHAPTER 2

1. Patterson, 1982; two studies reported in Brody, G.H. and Forehand, R. (1988) 'Multiple determinants of parenting', in Hetherington, E.M. and Arasteh, J.D. *Impact of Divorce, Stepparenting and Single Parenting on Children*, NJ: Lawrence Erlbaum; Lewin, L. *et al.*, 1988; Griest, D. *et al.*, 1979; Christenson, A. *et al.*, 1983.

2. Brody, G.H. and Forehand, R., 1988; Furey, W.M. and Forehand, R., 1984; Seligman, M.E.P. and Peterson, C., 1986; Rickard, K.M. *et al.*, 1981; Patterson, G.R. and Fleischman, M.J., 1979; Forehand, R. *et al.*, 1980.

3. Five studies are reported on page 108 of Biglan, 1990, op cit; see also Biglan, A.,'Problem-solving interactions of depressed women and their husbands', Behaviour Therapy, *16*, 431–451.

4. Weissman and Paykel, 1974; Biglan *et al.*, 1990; Coyne, J.C. *et al.*, 1987; Bullock, R.C. *et al.*, 1972.

5. Weissman and Paykel, 1974; Panaccione, V.F. and Wahler, R.G., 1986; Brody, G.H. and Forehand, R., 1988; Estroff, T.W. *et al.*, 1984; Quinton, R. and Rutter, M., 1985; Cox, A.D. *et al.*, 1987; Altemeier, W.A. *et al.*, 1982.

6. Blehar, M.C. *et al.*, 1977; Cohen, S.E. and Beckwith, L., 1979; Fonagy *et al.*, 1993; Isabella, R.A. *et al.*, 1989; Lutkenhaus, P. *et al.*, 1985; Lewis, M. *et al.*, 1984; Main, M. *et al.*, 1985; Bates, J.E. *et al.*, 1985; Grossman, K. *et al.*, 1985; Myake, K. *et al.*, 1985; Hetherington, E.M., 1988; Rutter, M., 1988; Patterson, G.R., 1990.

7. George, C. and Main, M., 1979; Egeland, B. and Sroufe, L.A., 1981a; Egeland, B. and Sroufe, L.A., 1981b; Egeland, B. *et al.*, 1983; Manning, M. *et al.*, 1980; Schneider-Rosen, K. and Cicchetti, D., 1984; Schneider-Rosen, K. *et al.*, 1985; Gaensbauer, T.J. and Harmon, R.J., 1982.

8. Lieberman, A.F., 1977; Lewis, 1984; Stevenson-Hinde, J. *et al.*, 1986.

9. Radke-Yarrow, M. *et al.*, 1985; Gaensbauer, T.J. and Harmon, R.J., 1982; Cytryn, L. *et al.*, 1984; Zahn-Wexler, C. *et al.*, 1982; Zahn-Wexler, C. *et al.*, 1984b; Zahn-Wexler, C. *et al.*, 1984c.

10. Patterson, G.R., p. 37, 1980; Weintraub, S. *et al.*, 1986; Richman, N. *et al.*, p. 42, 1982; Brody and Forehand, pp. 125–7, 1988; Hops, H. *et al.*, pp. 344–6, 1987; Estroff, T.W. *et al.*, p. 649, 1984; Johnson, S.M. and Lobitz, G.K., 1974; Zahn-Wexler, C. *et al.*, 1984a; Billings, A.G. and Moos, R.H., 1985; Weissman, M.M. and Siegler, R., 1972; Wolkind, S., p. 208, 1985.

11. Patterson, 1980; Liverant, S., 1959; Goodstein, L.D. and Rowley, V.N.A., 1961; Wolkind, W. *et al.*, 1967; Karson, S. and Haupt, T.D., 1968; Anderson, L.M., 1969.

12. Kotelchuck, M., 1982; Mccord, J., 1983; Lahey, B.B. *et al.*, 1984; Mash, E.J. *et al.* 1987; Reid, *et al.*, 1981.

13. Beardslee, W.R. *et al.*, 1983; Weissman, M.M. *et al.*, 1986; Cox, A.D., 1988; Keller, M.B. *et al.*, 1986; Ghodsian, M. *et al.*, 1984; Gaensbauer, T.J. and Harmon, R.J., 1982; Wrate, R.M. *et al.*, 1985; Hammen, C. *et al.*, 1987; Orvaschel, H., 1983.

CHAPTER 5

1. The seventeen studies are listed in Table 2 on page 856 of Coid, J. (1983) 'The epidemiology of homicide and murder followed by suicide', *Psychological Medicine* 13:855–860; see also Palmer, S. and Humphrey, J.A. (1980) 'Offender–victim relationships in criminal homicide followed by offender's suicide, North Carolina, 1972–1977', *Suicide and Life Threatening Behaviour* 10:106–118; Hayes, E.M. (1983) 'And darkness closes in . . . a national study of jail suicides', *Criminal Justice and Behaviour* 10:461–484; Allen, N.H. (1983) 'Homicide followed by suicide: Los Angeles, 1970–1979', *Suicide and Life Threatening Behaviour* 13:155–165.
2. Straus, J.H and Straus, M., 1953; Lester, D., 1973; Pokorny, A.D., 1965; Brown, G. and Goodwin, F., 1986; Storr, A., 1968; Gold, M., 1958.
3. Kellam, S.G., 1990; Izard, C.E. and Schwartz, G.M., 1986; Fagot, B.I. *et al.*, 1986; Eme, R.F., 1984; Locksley, A. and Douvan, E., 1982; Widom, C.S., 1984; Sears, R., 1961; Achenbach, T.M., 1978; Cairns, R.B. and Cairns, B.D., 1986; Maccoby, E.E., 1986.
4. Rosenbaum, M. and Bennet, B., 1986; Bach-Y-Rita, G. and Veno, A., 1974a; Bach-Y-Rita, G. and Veno, A., 1974b; Climent, C.E. and Ervin, F.R., 1972; Martin, H.P. and Beezley, P., 1977; Burks, H.L. and Harrison, S.I., 1962; Anthony, H.S., 1968; Lesse, S., 1968; Chwast, J., 1967; Patterson, G.R., ch. 7, p. 37, 1990.
5. Green, A.H., 1978a; Green, A.H., 1978b; Martin, H.P. and Beezley, P., 1977; Gutierres, S.E. and Reich, J.W., 1981; Rolston, R.H., 1971; Galdston, R., 1965; Bender, B., 1980; Adams-Tucker, C., 1984; Timberlake, E.M., 1981.

APPENDIX 2

1. Basis of calculations for contribution of male juveniles to recorded violence against the person:

1980 figures: Percentage of females in caution/conviction rates = 10 per cent (from tables 5.2 and 5.5 of *Criminal Statistics* 1980). 10 per cent of total number recorded violence against the person (97,246) = 9725 females. Number recorded males = 97,246 - 9725 females = 87,521 males. Breakdown of ages 1980 = sixteen per cent 10–16, thirty per cent 17–20, fifty-three per cent 21+ (from tables 5.2 and 5.4 *Criminal Statistics* 1980).

1987 figures: Percentage of females in caution/conviction rates = ten per cent (from table 5.12 of *Criminal Statistics* 1987). Ten per cent of total number recorded violence against the person (141,000) = 14,100 females. Number recorded males = 141,000 – 14,100 females = 126,900 males. Breakdown of ages 1987 = sixteen per cent 10–16, twenty-eight per cent 14–16, fifty-five per cent 21+ (from table 5.12 of *Criminal Statistics* 1987).

1993 figures: Percentage of females in caution/conviction rates = fifteen per cent (from table 5.12 of *Criminal Statistics* 1993). Fifteen per cent of total number recorded violence against the person (205,000) = 30,750 females. Number recorded males = 205,000 – 30,750 females = 174,250 males. Breakdown of age groups = seventeen per cent 10–13, twenty-one per cent 17–20 and sixty-two per cent 21 + (from table 5.12 of *Criminal Statistics* 1993).

BIBLIOGRAPHY

Unless otherwise stated, place of publication London.

Achenbach, T. M. (1978) 'The child behaviour profile', *Journal of Consulting and Clinical Psychology* 46:478-88.

Adams-Tucker, C. (1984) 'The unmet psychiatric needs of sexually abused youths', *Journal of the American Academy of Child Psychiatry* 23:659-67.

Ainsworth, M. D. A. (1978) *Patterns of Attachment*. NJ: Lawrence Erlbaum.

Alfaro, J. D. (1981) 'Report on the relationship between child abuse and neglect and later socially deviant behaviour', in R. J. Hunner and Y. E. Walker, eds *Exploring the Relationship between Child Abuse and Delinquency*. Montclair, CA: Allanclair, Osmun.

Allan, E. A. and Steffensmeier, D. J. (1989) 'Youth, underemployment and property crime: differential effects of job availability and job quality on juvenile and young adult arrest rates', *American Sociological Review* 54:107-23.

Allen, N. H. (1983) 'Homicide followed by suicide: Los Angeles, 1970-1979', *Suicide and Life Threatening Behaviour* 13:155-65.

Altemeier, W. A. (1982) 'Antecedents of child abuse', *Journal of Paediatrics* 100:823-29.

Anderson, D. (1993) *The Loss of Virtue*. Social Affairs Unit.

Anderson, L. M. (1969) 'Personality characteristics of parents of neurotic, aggressive and normal preadolescent boys', *Journal of Consulting and Clinical Psychology* 33:575-81.

Anderson, T. F. (1984) 'Persistence of social and health problems in the welfare state: A Danish cohort experience from 1948 to 1979', *Social Science and Medicine* 18(7).

Anthony, H. S. (1968) 'The association of violence and depression in a sample of young offenders', *British Journal of Criminology* 8:346-65.

Aragona, J. A. and Eyberg, S. M. (1981) 'Neglected children: mothers' report of child behaviour problems and observed verbal behaviour', *Child Development* 52:596-602.

Archer, D. (1978) 'Cities and homicide: a new look at an old paradox', *Comparative Studies in Sociology* 1(84).

—— and Gartner, R. (1976) 'Violent acts and violent times: a comparative approach to postwar homicide rates', *American Sociological Review* 41:937-63.

Bach-Y-Rita, G. and Veno, A. (1974a) 'Habitual violence: a profile of 62 men', *American Journal of Psychiatry* 131:1015-20.

Badinter, E. (1980) *The Myth of Motherhood – an Historical View of the Maternal Instinct*. Souvenir.

Balasubramaniam, V. (1972) 'Stereotaxic surgery for behaviour disorders', in E. Hitchcock, *Psychosurgery*. II: Thomas.

Bandler, R. (1982) 'Neural control of aggressive behaviour', *Trends in Neuroscience* 5:390-94.

Bandura, A. and Walters, R. H. (1959) *Adolescent Aggression*. New York: Roland.

—— (1966) *Adolescent Aggression*, pp. 39-41. New York: Roland.

Bates, J. E; (1985) 'Attachment security, mother–child interaction and temperament as predictors of behaviour-problem ratings at age three years', in I. Bretherton and E. Waters, eds *Growing Points of Attachment*, monographs of the Society for Research in Child Development 209 (50): 1-2.

Beardslee, W. R. (1983) 'Children of parents with major affective disorder', *American Journal Of Psychiatry* 140:825-32.

Bebbington, P. E. (1988) 'The social epidemiology of clinical depression', in A. S. Henderson and G. Burrows, eds *Handbook of Social Psychiatry*. Oxford: Elsevier.

Bender, B. (1980) 'Self-chosen victims: scapegoating behaviour sequential to battering', in J. V. Cook and R. T. Bowles, eds *Child Abuse: Omission and Commission*. Toronto: Butterworth.

Bernal, M. E. (1974) 'Comparison of boys' behaviour in homes and classrooms', in E. J. Marsh, L. A. Hamerlynck, and L. C. Handy, eds *Behaviour Modification and Families*. New York: Brunner Mazel.

Biglan, A. (1985) 'Problem-solving interactions of depressed women and their husbands', *Behaviour Therapy* 16:431-51.

—— (1990) 'A contextual approach to the problem of aversive practices in families', in G. R. Patterson, ed *Depression and Aggression in Family Interaction*. NJ: Lawrence Erlbaum.

Billings, A. G. and Moos, R. H. (1985) 'Children of parents with a unipolar depression', *Journal of Abnormal and Clinical Psychology* 14:149-66.

Binns, D. and Mars, G. (1984) 'Family, community and unemployment', *Sociological Review* 32:662-95.

Blackburn, R. (1986) 'Patterns of personality deviation among violent offenders', *British Journal of Criminology* 26:254-69.

—— (1988) 'Psychopathy and personality disorder', in E Miller and P. J. Cooper, eds *Adult Abnormal Personality: the Major Disorders*. Edinburgh: Churchill Livingstone.

—— and Lee-Evans, J. M. (1985) 'Reactions of primary and secondary psychopaths to anger-evoking situations', *British Journal of Clinical Psychology* 24:93-100.

Blaus, J. and Blaus P. (1982) 'The cost of inequality: Metropolitan structure and violent crime', *American Sociological Review* 47:121.

Blehar, M. C. (1977) 'Early face-to-face interaction and its relation to later infant–mother attachment', *Child Development* 48:182-94.

Block, J. H. (1986) 'The personality of children prior to divorce', *Child Development* 57:827-40.

Blount, H. R. and Chandler, T. A. (1979) 'Relationship between childhood abuse and assaultive behaviour in adolescent male psychiatric patients', *Psychological Report* 44:1126.

Bohman, M. (1978) 'Some genetic aspects of alcoholism and criminality: apopulation of adoptees', *Archives of General Psychiatry* 35:269-76.

Boudouris, J. (1971) 'Homicide and the Family' *Journal of Marriage and The Family* November 1971.

Bousha, D. M. and Twentyman, C. T. (1984) 'Mother-child interactional style in abuse, neglect and control groups: naturalistic observations in the home', *Journal of Abnormal Psychology* 93: 106-14.

Bowlby, J. (1944) 'Forty four juvenile thieves: their characters and their home lives', *International Journal of Psychoanalysis* 25:19-52, 107-27.

Box, S. (1983) *Power, Crime and Mystification*. Routledge & Kegan Paul.

—— (1988) *Recession, Crime and Punishment*. Macmillan.

Brady, C. P. (1986) 'Behaviour problems of clinic children: Relation to parental marital status, age and sex of child', *American Journal of Orthopsychiatry* 56:399-412.

Braithwaite, J. (1981) 'The myth of social class and criminality reconsidered', *American Sociological Review* 46:36-57.

—— and Braithwaite, V. (1980) 'The effect of income inequality and social democracy on homicide', *British Journal of Criminology* 20(1).

British Medical Journal (1994) Special Edition on Health Inequalities, 308.

Brody, G. (1968) 'Socioeconomic differences in stated maternal child rearing practices and in observed maternal behaviour', *Journal of Marriage and the Family* 30:656-60.

—— and Forehand, R. (1988) 'Multiple determinants of parenting', in E. M. Hetherington and J. D. Arasteh, eds *Impact of Divorce, Stepparenting and Single Parenting on Children*. NJ: Lawrence Erlbaum.

Bronfenbrenner, U. (1958) 'Socialization and social class through time and space', in E. Maccoby, ed *Readings in Social Psychology*. New York: Holt Rinehart.

Brown, G. and Harris, T. (1978) *Social Origins of Depression*. Tavistock Publications.

Brown, G. L. and Goodwin, F. K. (1986) 'Human aggression and suicide', *Suicide and Life Threatening Behaviour* 16:141-57.

Brown, G. W. (1972) 'Influence of family life on the course of schizophrenic disorders: a replication', *British Journal of Psychiatry* 121:241-58.

Brown, G. (1989) *Where there is Greed*. Edinburgh: Mainstream Publishing.

Brown, J. C. (1989) 'Why don't they go back to work? Mothers on benefit', *Social Security Advisory Committee* 2. HMSO.

Bullock, R. C. (1972) 'The weeping wife: marital relations of depressed women', *Journal of Marriage and the Family* 39:488-95.

Burgess, R. L. and Conger, R. D. (1978) 'Family interactions in abusive, neglectful and normal families', *Child Development* 49:1163-73.

Burghes, L. (1994) *Lone Parenthood and Family Disruption: The Outcomes for Children*. Family Policy Studies Centre.

Burks, H. L. and Harrison, S. I. (1962) 'Aggressive behaviour as a means of avoiding depression', *American Journal of Orthopsychiatry* 32:416-22.

Cairns, R. B. and Cairns, B. D. (1986) 'The developmental- interactional view of social behaviour: four issues of adolescent aggression', in D. Olweus, ed *Development of Antisocial and Prosocial Behaviour* Academic Press.

Camara, K. A. and Resnick, G. (1989) 'Interparental conflict and cooperation: Factors moderating post-divorce adjustment', in E. M. Hetherington and J. D. Arasteh, eds *Impact of Divorce, Single Parenting and Stepparenting on children*. NJ: Lawrence Erlbaum.

Campbell, B. (1993) *Goliath*. Methuen.

Cantor, D. and Land, K. (1985) 'Unemployment and crime rates in the post-World War II United States', *American Sociological Review* 50:317-32.

Carey, G. (1989) 'Genetics and violence: human studies'. Commissioned paper for the Panel on the Understanding and Control of Violent Behaviour; Committee on Research in Law Enforcement and the Administration of Justice; Commission on Behavioural and Social Sciences and Education; National Academy of Sciences/National Research Council.

Carlson, B. E. (1983) 'Children's observations of interparental conflict', in A. R. Roberts, ed *Battered Women and Their Families*. New York: Springer Verlag.

Carr-Hill, R. and Stern, N. (1979) *Crime, the Police and Criminal Statistics*. Academic Press.

Cater, J. and Easton, P. (1980) 'Separation and other stress in child abuse', *Lancet* i:972-3.

Chodorow, N. (1994) *Femininities, Masculinities, Sexualities*. Free Association Press.

Christenson, A. (1983) 'Parental characteristics and interactional dysfunction in families with child behaviour problems', *Journal of Abnormal Psychology* 11:153-66.

Christoffel, K. and Kiang, L. (1983) 'Homicide death rates in 23 countries: U.S. rates atypically high', *Child Abuse and Neglect* 7(3).

Chwast, J. (1967) 'Depressive reactions as manifested among adolescent delinquents', *American Journal of Psychiatry* 21:574-84.

Cicchetti, D. and Rizley, R. (1981) in *New Directions for Child Development 11*. Jossey-Bass.

Climent, C. E. and Ervin, F. R. (1972) 'Historical data in the evaluation of violent subjects', *Archives of General Psychiatry* 27:621-4.

Clinard, M. (1975) *Cities with Little Crime*. New York: Sage.

—— and Abbott, D. (1973) *Crime in Developing Countries: A Comparative Perspective.* New York: John Wiley.

Cloninger, C. R. and Gottesman, I. (1987) 'Genetic and environmental factors in antisocial behaviour disorders', in S. A. Mednick, ed *The Causes of Crime; New Biological Approaches.* New York: Cambridge Univ. Press.

Cockett, M. and Tripp, J. (1994) *The Exeter Family Study: Family Breakdown and its Impact on Children.* Exeter: University of Exeter Press.

Cohen, S. E. and Beckwith, L. (1979) 'Preterm infant interaction with the caregiver in the first year of life and competence at age two', *Child Development* 50:767-76.

Coid, J. (1983) 'The epidemiology of homicide and murder followed by suicide', *Psychological Medicine* 13:855-60.

Coles, R. (1968) 'Violence in ghetto children', in S. Chess and A. Thomas eds *Annual Progress in Child Psychiatry and Child Development.* New York: Brunner/Mazel.

Colletta, N. D. (1981) 'Social support and the risk of maternal rejection by adolescent mothers', *Journal of Psychology* 109:191-7.

Comstock, G. W. and Helsing K. J. (1976) 'Symptoms of depression in two communities', *Psychological Medicine* 6:551-63.

Corder, B. F. (1976) 'Adolescent parricide: a comparison with adolescent murderer', *American Journal of Psychiatry*, 133: 957-61;

Cox, A.D. (1988) 'Maternal depression and impact on children's development', *Archives of Disease in Childhood* 63:90-95.

—— Puckering, C., Pound, A. and Mills, M. (1987) 'The impact of depression in young children', *Journal of Child Psychology and Psychiatry* 28:917-28.

Coyne, J. C. (1987) 'Living with a depressed person', *Journal of Consulting and Clinical Psychology* 55:347-52.

Crellin, E., Kellmer-Pringle, M. and West, P. (1971) *Born Illegitimate: Educational and Social Implications.* NFER.

Criminal Statistics 1970. HMSO.

—— 1980. HMSO.

—— 1987. HMSO.

—— 1989. HMSO.

—— 1993. HMSO.

Crittenden, P. M. (1982) 'Abusing, neglecting, problematic and adequate dyads: differentiating by patterns of interaction', *Merril-Palmer Quarterly* 27:201-18.

Crockenberg, S. B. (1981) 'Infant irritability, mother responsiveness and social support influences on the security of infant-mother attachment', *Child Development* 52:857-65.

Cummings, E. M. (1985) 'Influence of conflict between adults on the emotions and aggression of young children', *Developmental Psychology* 21:495-507.

Currie, E. (1985) *Confronting Crime.* New York: Pantheon.

Curtis, G. C. (1963) 'Violence breeds violence – perhaps?', *American Journal of Psychiatry* 120:386-7.

Cutrona, C. E. and Troutman, B. R. (1986) 'Social support, infant temperament and patenting self efficacy: a mediational model of postpartum depression', *Child Development* 57:1507-18.

Cytryn, L. (1984) 'Affective disturbances in the offspring of affectively ill patients', *American Journal of Psychiatry* 141:219-22.

Daniels, J., Hampton, R. and Newberger, E. (1983) 'Child abuse and accidents in black families: A controlled comparative study', *American Journal of Orthopsychiatry* 53(4).

Davidoff, L. and Dowds, L. (1990) 'Recent trends in crimes of violence against the person in England and Wales', *Home Office Research Bulletin* 27:11-17.

Davies, C. (1983) 'Crime, bureaucracy and equality', *Policy Review* winter.

Dawkins, R. (1976) *The Selfish Gene*. Oxford: Oxford University Press.

De Baryshe, B. D., Patterson, G. R. and Capaldi, D. M. (1993) 'A performance model for academic achievement in early adolescent boys', *Developmental Psychology* 29:795-804.

De Mause, L. (1974) *The History of Childhood*. Condor.

DeFronzo, J. (1983) 'Economic assistance to impoverished Americans: relationship to incidence of crime', *Criminology* 21(1).

Dennis, N. and Erdos, G. (1992) *Families without Fatherhood*. Institute of Economic Affairs Health and Welfare Unit.

Dodge, K. A. (1980) 'Social cognition and children's aggressive behaviour', *Child Development* 51:162-70.

——, Bates, J. E. and Pettit, G. S. (1990) 'Mechanisms in the cycle of violence', *Science* 250:1678-83.

Dohrenwend, B. P. and Dohrenwend, B. S. (1974) *Stressful Life Events: Their Nature and Effect*. New York: John Wiley.

Dore, R. P. (1958) *City Life in Japan* Berkeley, CA: University of California Press.

Dornbusch, S. M. (1985) 'Single parents, extended households and the control of adolescents', *Child Development* 56:326-41.

Downes, D. (1993) 'Employment opportunities for offenders'. London School Of Economics, Department of Social Administration.

Drugs Supplement (1992) 43(2).

Duncan, G. W. (1958) 'Etiological factors in first degree murder'. *Journal of the American Mental Association* 168:1755-58.

Duncan, J. W. and Duncan, G. M. (1971) 'Murder in the Family: a study of some homicidal adolescents'. *American Journal of Psychiatry* 127:1498-1502.

Durkheim, E. (1952) *Suicide*, trans. J. A. Spaulding. Routledge.

Durkheim, E. (1933) *The Division of Labour in Society*. New York: Free Press.

Egeland, B. and Sroufe, L. A. (1981a) 'Attachment and early maltreatment', *Child Development* 52:44-52.

—— (1981b) 'Developmental sequelae of maltreatment in infancy', in R. Rizley, ed *Developmental Perspectives on Child Maltreatment*. Jossey-Bass.

—— (1983) 'The developmental consequences of different patterns of maltreatment', *Child Abuse and Neglect* 7:459-69.

Elder, G. H. (1985) 'Linking family hardship to children's lives', *Child Development* 56:361-75.

Elliott, B. J. and Richards, M. P. M. (1991) 'Children and divorce: Educational performance and behaviour before and after parental separation', *International Journal of Law and the Family* 5:258-76.

Eme, R. F. (1984) 'Sex-role stereotypes and the epidemiology of child psychopathology', in C. S. Widom, ed *Sex Roles and Psychopathology*. New York: Plenum Press.

Emery, G. N. (1986) 'The nurturant acts of very young children', in D. Olweus; ed *Development of Antisocial and Prosocial Behaviour*. Academic Press.

Emery, R. E. (1982) 'Interparental conflict and the children of discord and divorce', *Psychological Bulletin* 92:310-30.

Erickson, M. F., Egeland, B. and Sroufe, L.A. (1985) 'The relationship between quality of attachment and behaviour problems in preschool in a high risk sample', *Monograph Social Research Child Development* 50:147-66.

Eron, L. D. (1963) 'Social Class, parental punishment for aggression and child aggression', *Child Development* 34:849-67.

Estroff, T. W. (1984) *Journal of the American Academy of Child Psychology* 23:649-53.

Evans, R. and Wilkinson, C. (1990) 'Variations in police cautioning policy and practice in England and Wales', *Howard Journal of Criminal Justice* 29:155-76.

Fagan, J. (1987) 'Neighbourhood education, mobilization and organization for juvenile crime prevention', *Annals of the American Academy of Political and Social Science* 494:54-70.

Fagin, L. and Little, M. (1984) *Forsaken Families*. Penguin.

Fagot, B. I. (1986) 'Gender labelling and the adoption of sex-typed behaviours', *Developmental Psychology* 22:440-3.

Farrington, D.P. (1975) 'The family backgrounds of aggressive youths', in L. A. Hersov, ed *Aggression and Antisocial Behaviour in Childhood and Adolescence*. Pergamon.

—— (1982), pp. 175-6 'Longitudinal analyses of criminal violence', in M. E. Wolfgang, ed *Criminal Violence*. CA: Sage.

—— (1987) 'Early precursors of frequent offending', in J. Q. Wilson and G. C. Loury, eds *From Children to Citizens Vol. III: Families, Schools and Delinquency Prevention*. Springer-Verlag.

—— (1989a) 'Childhood aggression and adult violence: early precursors and later life outcomes', in K. H. Rubin and D. Pepler, eds *The Development and Treatment of Childhood Aggression*. NJ: Lawrence Erlbaum.

—— (1989b) 'Early predictors of adolescent aggression and adult violence', *Violence and Victims* 4:79-99.

—— (1991) 'Antisocial personality from childhood to adulthood', *The Psychologist* 4:389-94.

—— (1986) 'Unemployment, school-leaving and crime', *British Journal of Criminology* 26:335-56.

—— (1988) 'Are there any successful men from criminogenic backgrounds?', *Psychiatry* 51:116-30.

—— and West, D. (1993) 'Criminal, penal, and life histories of chronic offenders: risk and protective factors and early identification', *Criminal Behaviour and Mental Health* 3:482-523.

Felthous, A. R. (1978) 'Childhood cruelty to cats, dogs and other animals', *Bulletin of the AAPL* 9:48-53.

Field, F. (1989) *Losing Out*. Oxford: Blackwell.

Field, S. (1990) 'Trends in crime and their interpretation: a study of recorded crime in post-war England and Wales', *Home Office Research Study* 119.

Field, T., Healy, B., Goldstein, S., Perry, S. and Bendell, D. (1988) 'Infants of depressed mothers show "depressed" behaviour even with nondepressed adults', *Child Development* 59:1569-79.

Fonagy, P., Steele, H. and Steele, M. (1991) 'Maternal representation of attachment during pregnancy predict the organization of infant-other attachment at one year of age', *Child Development* 62:891-905.

Forehand, R. (1975) 'Mother-child interactions: comparison of a noncompliant clinic group and a nonclinic group', *Behaviour Research and Therapy* 13:79-84.

Forehand, R. (1980) 'An examination of the social validity of a parent training programme', *Behaviour Therapy* 11:488-502.

Forehand, R. (1988) 'Divorce and marital conflict', in E. M. Hetherington and J. D. Arasteh, eds *Impact of Divorce, Single Parenting and Stepparenting on Children*, NJ: Lawrence Erlbaum.

Frazier, S. H. (1974) 'Murder – Single and Multiple', *Association for Research in Nervous and Mental Disease* 52:304-12.

Freud, S. (1900) *The Interpretation of Dreams*. Penguin.

Friedrich, W. H. and Wheeler, K. K. (1982) 'The abusing parent revisited: a decade of psychological research', *Journal of Nervous and Mental Diseases* 170:577-88.

Fuchs, V. R. (1986) 'Sex differences in economic well-being', *Science* 232: 459-64.

Furey, W. M. and Forehand, R. (1984) 'An examination of predictors of mothers' perceptions of satisfaction with their children', *Journal of Social and Clinical Psychology* 2:230-43.

Gaensbauer, T. J. and Harmon, R. J. (1981) 'Social-affective development in infants of manic depressive parents', *American Journal of Psychiatry* 141:223-9.

—— (1982) 'Attachment behaviour in abused/neglected and premature infants', in R. N. Emde and R. J. Harmon, eds *The Development of Attachment and Affiliative Systems*. Plenum.

Gaines, R. (1978) 'Etiological factors in child maltreatment', *Journal of Abnormal Psychology* 87:531-40.

Galdston, R. (1965) 'Observations on children who have been physically abused and their parents', *American Journal of Psychiatry* 122:440-3.

Gallwey, P. (1985) 'The psychodynamics of borderline personality', in D. P. Farrington and J. Gunn, eds *Aggression and Dangerousness*. John Wiley.

Gayford, J. J. (1975) 'Wife battering: a preliminary survey of 100 cases', *British Medical Journal* 25 January.

Geller, M. and Ford-Somma, L. (1984) *Violent Homes, Violent Children*. The State Of New Jersey Department of Correction, Division of Juvenile Services.

Gelles, R. J. and Cornell, C. P. (1985) p. 56, *Intimate Violence in Families*. CA: Sage.

—— and Hargreaves, E. F. (1981) 'Maternal employment and violence towards children', *Journal of Family Issues* 2:509-30.

George, C. and Main, M. (1979) 'Social interactions of young abused children: approach, avoidance and aggression', *Child Development* 50:306-18.

Ghodsian, M. (1984) 'A longitudinal study of maternal depression and child behaviour problems', *Journal of Child Psychology and Psychiatry* 25:91-109.

Glaser, M. (1987) 'Some psychodynamic ingredients of violence'. Paper presented to the Portman Clinic, London, Golden Jubilee conference.

Glueck, S. and Glueck, E. (1950) *Unravelling juvenile delinquency*. New York: The Commonwealth Fund.

Gold, M. (1958) 'Suicide, homicide and the socialization of aggression'. *American Journal of Sociology* 63:651-61.

Goodstein, L. D. and Rowley, V. N. A. (1961) 'A further study of MMPI differences between parents of disturbed and nondisturbed children', *Journal of Consulting Psychology* 25:460-4.

Gornick, V. and Moran, B. K. (1971) *Woman in a Sexist Society*. Basic.

Gottfredson, M. R. and Hirschi, T. (1983) *A General Theory of Crime*. Stanford: Stanford University Press.

Gove, W. R. (1979) 'Sex differences in the epidemiology of mental disorders: evidence and explanations', in E. S. Gomberg and V. Franks, eds *Gender and Disordered Behaviour: Sex Differences in Psychopathology*. New York: Brunner/Mazel.

Gray, J.D. (1979) 'Prediction and prevention of child abuse and neglect', *Journal of Social Issues* 35:127-39.

Green, A. H. (1978a) 'Psychopathology of abused children', *Journal of the American Academy of Child Psychiatry* 17:92–103.

—— (1978b) 'Self-destructive behaviour in battered children', *American Journal of Psychiatry* 135:579–82.

—— (1979) 'Child abusing fathers', *Journal of the American Academy of Child Psychiatry* 18(2).

Griest, D. (1979) 'An examination of predictors of maternal perception of maladjustment in clinic-referred children', *Journal of Abnormal Psychology* 88:277–81.

Grossman, K. (1985) 'Maternal sensitivity and newborns' orientation responses as related to quality of attachment in Northern Germany', in I. Bretherton and E. Waters, eds *Growing Points of Attachment*, Monographs of the Society for Research in Child Development 209(50): 1–2.

Guerry, A. M. (1833) *Essai sur la Statistique Morale de la France*. Paris.

Gurr, T. B. (1989) 'Historical trends in violent crime: Europe and the United States', in Gurr, T. B. *Violence in America Vol. 1: The History of Crime*. Sage.

—— (1977) *The Politics of Crime and Conflict: A Comparative History of Four Cities*. Sage.

Gutierres, S. E. and Reich, J. W. (1981) 'A developmental perspective on runaway behaviour: its relationship to child abuse', *Child Welfare* 60:89–94.

Hagan, J., Simpson, J. and Gillis, A. R. (1987) 'Class in the household: a power-control theory of gender and delinquency', *American Journal of Sociology* 92:788–816.

Hagell, A. and Newburn, T. (1994) *Persistent Young Offenders*. Policy Studies Institute.

Hakim, C. (1990) 'The social consequences of high unemployment', *Journal of Social Policy* 11:433–67.

Hammen, C. (1987) 'Maternal affective disorders, illness and stress: risk for children's psychopathology', *American Journal of Psychiatry* 144:736–41.

Hanushek, E. (1979) 'Ethnic income variations: magnitudes and explanations', in T. Sowell, ed *American Ethnic Groups*. Washington DC: Urban Institute.

Harris, T. 'Social Support and Depression', in Henderson, A.S. and Burrows, G.D. *Handbook of Social Psychiatry*. Oxford: Elsevier.

Hartjen, C. (1982) 'Delinquency, development and social integration in India', *Social Problems* 29(2):471.

Haskey, J. (1983) 'Social class patterns in marriage', *Population Trends* 34.

—— (1984) 'Social class and socioeconomic differentials in divorce in England and Wales', *Population Trends* 35.

Haverson, C. F. and Waldrop, M. F. (1970) 'Maternal behaviour towards own and other preschool children: the problem of ownness', *Child Development* 41:839-45.

Hayes, E. M. (1983) 'And darkness closes in . . . a national study of jail suicides', *Criminal Justice and Behaviour* 10:461-84.

Heady, P. and Smyth, M. (1989) *Living Standards During Unemployment*. HMSO.

Heilbrun, A. B. (1979) 'Psychopathy and violent crime', *Journal of Consulting and Clinical Psychology* 47:509-16.

Henderson, A. H. and Brown, G. (1988) p. 76 'Social support: the hypothesis and the evidence', in A. H. Henderson and G. D. Burrows, eds *Handbook of Social Psychiatry*. Oxford: Elsevier.

Henry, A. F. and Short, J. F. (1954) *Suicide and Homicide*. Glencoe, IL: Free Press.

Herman, J. (1986) 'Long term effects of incestuous abuse in childhood', *American Journal of Psychiatry* 143:1293-6.

Hernandez, D. J. (1989) 'Demographic trends and the living arrangements of children' in E. M. Hetherington and J. D. Arasteh, eds *Impact of Divorce, Single Parenting and Stepparenting on Children*. NJ: Lawrence Erlbaum.

Herrenkohl, E. C. (1983) 'Perspectives on the intergenerational transmission of abuse', in D. Finkelhor, ed *The Dark Side of Families*. CA: Sage.

—— (1984) 'Parent-child interactions in abusive and nonabusive families', *Journal of the American Academy of Child Psychiatry* 23:641-8.

Herrenkohl, R. C. and Herrenkohl, E. C. (1981) 'Some antecedents and developmental consequences of child maltreatment', *New Directions for Child Development: Number 11*. Jossey-Bass.

Herrnstein, R. and Murray, C. (1994) *The Bell Curve*. New York: Free Press.

—— to Oliver James at the Centre for Policy Studies Conference on Crime, May 1990. Cited in a newspaper article by O. James, 'Crime and the American mind', *The Independent* features page, 21 May 1990.

Hetherington, E. M. (1972) 'Effects of father absence on personality development in adolescent daughters', *Developmental Psychology* 7:313-26.

—— (1979) 'Divorce: a child's perspective', *American Psychologist* 34:851-8.

—— (1988) 'Parents, children and siblings: Six years after divorce', in R. A. Hinde and J. Stevenson-Hinde, eds *Relationships within Families*. Oxford: Clarendon Press.

—— (1979) 'Play and social interaction in children following divorce', *Journal of Social Issues* 35:26-49.

Hewitt, J. D. and Hoover, D. W. (1982) 'Local Modernization and crime: The effects of modernization on crime in middletown, 1845-1910', *Law and Human Behaviour* 6.

Hilberman, E. and Mawson, K. (1978) 'Sixty battered wives', *Victimology* 2:460–70.

Hill, D. and Pond, D. A. (1952) 'Reflections on one hundred capital cases submitted for electroencephalography', *Journal of Mental Science* 98:23–43.

Hinde, R. A. and Stevenson-Hinde, J. (1988) *Relationships within Families.* Oxford: Clarendon Press.

Hineline, P. N. (1977) 'Negative reinforcement and avoidance', in W. Honig, ed *Handbook of Operant Behaviour.* NJ: Prentice Hall.

Hirschfield, R. A. and Cross, C. K. (1982) 'Epidemiology of affective disorders', *Archives of General Psychiatry* 39:35–46.

Hirschi, T. and Gottfredson, M. R. (1983) 'Age and the explanation of crime', *American Journal of Sociology* 89.

Hock, E., Coady, S. and Cordero, L. (1973) 'Patterns of attachment to mothers' one year olds'. Paper presented to the biennial meeting of the Society for Research in Child Development. Philadelphia, USA.

Hoffman-Plotkin, D. and Twentyman, C. T. (1984) 'A multimodal assessment of behavioural and cognitive deficits in abused and neglected preschoolers', *Child Development* 55:794–802.

Home Office Statistical Bulletin (1990) 19.

—— (1991) 18/91.

Hops, H. (1987) pp. 344–6 'Home observations of family interactions of depressed women', *Journal of Consulting and Clinical Psychology* 55:341–6.

—— (1990) 'Maternal depression, marital discord and children's behaviour: a developmental perspective', in G. R. Patterson, ed *Aggression and Depression in Family Interaction.* NJ: Lawrence Erlbaum.

Hough, M. and Mayhew, P. (1983) 'The British crime survey: first report', *Home Office Research Study* 76. HMSO.

—— (1985) 'Taking account of crime', *Home Office Research Study* 85. HMSO.

Households below average income, a statistical analysis, 1981–7. HMSO.

Huesman, L. R., Eron, L. D. and Yarmel, P. W. (1987) 'Intellectual function and aggression', *Journal of Personality and Social Psychology* 52:232–40.

Hughes, H. and Barad, S. (1983) 'Psychological functioning of children in a battered woman's shelter', *American Journal of Orthopsychiatry* 55:525–31.

Humphrey, J. A. (1977) 'Social loss: A comparison of suicide victims, homicide offenders and non violent individuals', *Disease of the Nervous System* 38:157–60.

Hunter, R. S. and Kilstrom, N. (1979) 'Breaking the cycle in abusive families', *American Journal of Orthopsychiatry* 136:1320–2.

Hutchings, B. and Mednick, S. A. (1975) 'Registered criminality in the adoptive and biological parents of registered male criminal adoptees', in R. R. Fieve, ed *Genetic Research in Psychiatry*. Baltimore MD: John Hopkins University Press.

Inciardi, J. and Faupel, C. (1980) *History and Crime*. CA: Sage.

Isabella, R. A. (1989) 'Origins of infant-mother attachment: an examination of interactional synchrony during the infant's first year', *Developmental Psychology* 25:12- 21.

Izard, C. E. and Schwartz, G. M. (1986) 'Patterns of emotion in distress', in M. Rutter, ed *Depression in Young People*. London: Guildford Press.

Jacobs, P. A. (1965) 'Aggressive behaviour, mental subnormality and the XYY male', *Behaviour Genetics* 208:1351-2.

Jacobson, D. S. (1978) 'The impact of marital separation/divorce on children: Interparental hostility and child adjustment', *Journal of Divorce* 2:3-19.

Jaffee, P. (1986) 'Similarities in behavioural and social maladjustment among child victims and witnesses to family violence', *American Journal of Orthopsychiatry* 56:142-6.

Jason, J. and Andereck, N. (1983) 'Fatal abuse in Georgia: The epidemiology of severe physical child abuse', *Child Abuse and Neglect* 7(1).

Jenkins, R. L. (1966) 'Psychiatric syndromes in children and their relation to family background', *American Journal of Orthopsychiatry* 36:450-7.

—— (1968) 'The varieties of children's behavioural problems and family dynamics', *American Journal of Psychiatry* 124:1440-5.

Johnson, P. and Webb, S. (1990) *Poverty in Official Statistics*. Institute of Fiscal Studies.

Johnson, S. M. (1973) p. 50 'How deviant is the normal child?', in R. D. Rubin *Advances in Behavioural Therapy*. New York: Academic Press.

—— and Lobitz, G. K. (1974) 'The personal and marital adjustment of parents as related to observed child deviance and parenting behaviours', *Journal of Abnormal Psychology* 2:193-207.

Johnstone, L. (1993) 'Family management in "schizophrenia": its assumptions and contradictions', *Journal Of Mental Health* 2:255-69.

Jones, A. D. (1965) *Ictal and Subictal Neurosis: Diagnosis and Treatment*, IL: Thomas.

Joseph Rowntree Foundation (1995) *Inquiry Into Income and Wealth*. York: Joseph Rowntree Foundation.

Jukes, A. (1993) *Why Men Hate Women*. Free Association Press.

Kagan, J. (1977) 'The child in the family', *Daedalus* 106:33-56.

Kahn, M. W. (1959) 'A comparison of personality, intelligence, and social history of two criminal groups', *Journal of Social Psychology* 49:33-40.

Kalmuss, D. (1984) 'The intergenerational transmission of marital aggression', *Journal of the Marriage and the Family* 46:11-49.

Kandel, D. B. and Davies, M. (1982) 'Epidemiology of depressive mood in adolescents', *Archives of General Psychiatry* 39:1205-12.

Kaplan, G. A. (1987) 'Psychosocial predictors of depression', *American Journal of Epidemiology* 125:206-20.

Karson, S. and Haupt, T. D. (1968) 'Second-order personality factors in parents of child guidance clinic patients', *Multivariate Behaviour Research*, Special Issue, 97-106.

Kaufman, J. and Zigler, E. (1987) 'Do abused children become abusive parents?', *American Journal of Orthopsychiatry* 57:186-92.

Kellam, S. G. (1990) 'Developmental epidemiological framework for family research on depression and aggression', in G. R. Patterson *Depression and Aggression in Family Interaction*. Lawrence Erlbaum.

—— (1982) 'The long term evolution of the family structure of teenage and older mother', *Journal of Marriage and the Family*. August.

Keller, M. B. (1986) Impact of severity and chronicity of parental affective illness on adaptive functioning and psychopathology in children', *Archives of General Psychiatry* 43:930-7.

Kempson, E., Bryson, A. and Rowlinson, K. (1994) *Hard Times: How Poor Families Make Ends Meet*. Policy Studies Institute.

Kendell, R. E. (1970) 'Relationship between aggression and depression', *Archives of General Psychiatry* 22:308-18.

Kiernan, K. E. (1986) 'Teenage marriage and marital breakdown: A longitudinal study', *Population Studies* 40:35-44.

—— and Estaugh, V. (1993) *Cohabitation: Extramarital Childbearing and Social Policy*. Family Policy Studies Centre.

—— and Wicks, M. (1990) *Family Change and Future Policy*. Family Policy Studies Unit.

Kinard, E. M. (1978) 'Emotional development in physically abused children: a study of self concept and aggression'. Doctoral Dissertation, Brandeis University.

Kolvin, I., Miller, F. J. W., Scott, D. McI., Gatzanis, S. R. M. and Fleeting, M. (1990) *Continuities of Deprivation? The Newcastle 1000 Family Study*. Aldershot: Avebury.

Korbin, J. (1981) *Child Abuse and Neglect: Cross-cultural Perspectives*. Berkeley CA: University of California Press.

Kotelchuck, M. (1982) 'Child abuse and neglect', in R. H. Starr *Child Abuse Prediction*. Cambridge, MA: Ballinger.

Kratcoski, P. C. (1982) 'Child abuse and violence against the family', *Child Welfare* 61:435-44.

—— (1985) 'Youth violence directed towards significant others', *Journal of Adolescence* 8:145-57.

Krohn, M. (1976) 'Inequality, unemployment and crime: a cross-national analysis', *Sociological Quarterly* 17.

Kuczynski, I. (1987) 'A developmental interpretation of young children's noncompliance', *Developmental Psychology* 23:799-806.

Kuipers, L. and Bebbington, P. (1988) 'Expressed emotion research in schizophrenia: theoretical and clinical implications', *Psychological Medicine* 18:893–909.

Lahey, B. B. (1984) 'Parenting behaviour and emotional status of physically abusive mothers', *Journal of Consulting and Clinical Psychology* 52:1062–71.

Langevin, R. (1983) 'Childhood and family backgrounds of killers seen for psychiatric assessment: a controlled study', *Bulletin of the American Academy of Psychiatry Law* 2(4).

Layard, R. and Nickell, S. (1989) The Thatcher miracle?', Discussion paper 315. Centre For Labour Economics.

Lefkowitz, M. M. (1977) *Growing Up to be Violent: A Longitudinal Study of the Development of Aggression*. Pergamon.

Lesse, S. (1968) 'The multivariate masks of depression', *American Journal of Psychiatry* 124:35–40.

Lester, D. (1973) 'National homicide and suicide rates as a function of political stability', *Psychological Reports* 33:298.

Levine, M. (1975) 'Interparental violence and its effect on the children: a study of 50 children in General Practice', *Medicine, Science and the Law* 15:172–6.

Levinson, D. (1983) 'Physical punishment of children and wifebeating in cross-cultural perspective', in Gelles, R.J. and Cornell, C.P., *International perspectives on family violence*. Lexington DC: Heath.

Lewin, L. (1988) 'Predictors of maternal satisfaction regarding clinic-referred children: methodological considerations', *Journal of Clinical Child Psychology* 17:159–63.

Lewis, D. O. and Santok, S. S. (1977) 'Medical histories of delinquent and nondelinquent children: an epidemiological study', *American Journal of Psychiatry* 134:1020–5.

—— (1979) 'Violent juvenile delinquents', *Journal of the American Academy of Child Psychiatry* 18:307–19.

—— (1983) 'Homicidally aggressive young children: Neuropsychiatric and experiential correlates', *American Journal of Psychiatry* 140:148–53.

—— (1985) 'Biopsychological characteristics of children who later murder', *American Journal of Psychiatry* 142:1161–7.

Lewis, M. (1984) 'Predicting psychopathology in six year olds from early social relations', *Child Development* 55:123–36.

Lieberman, A. F. (1977) 'Preschoolers' competence with a peer: influence of attachment and social experience', *Child Development* 48:1277–87.

Light, R. J. (1973) 'Abused and neglected children in America', *Harvard Educational Review* 43:556–98.

Linnoila M. (1983) 'Low cerebrospinal fluid 5 -Hydroxyincoleacetic acid concentration differentiates impulsive from nonimpulsive violent behaviour' *Life Sciences* 33:2609–14.

Liverant, S. (1959) 'MMPI differences between parents of disturbed and nondisturbed children', *Journal of Consulting Psychology* 23:256-60.

Locksley, A. and Douvan, E. (1979) 'Problem behaviour in adolescents', in E. S. Gomberg and V. Franks, eds *Gender and Disordered Behaviour Sex Differences in Psychopathology*. New York: Brunner/Mazel.

Loeber, R. and Stouthamer-Loeber, M. (1987) pp. 333-4, list eleven studies showing that delinquents are more aggressive than non-delinquents in childhood, in 'Prediction', H. C. Quay, ed *Handbook of Juvenile Delinquency*. John Wiley.

Loftin, C. and Hill, R. (1974) 'Regional subculture and homicide', *American Sociological Review* 39(5).

Lorenz, K. (1966) *On Aggression*. Methuen.

Lutkenhaus, P. (1985) 'Infant-mother attachment at twelve months and style of interaction with a stranger at the age of three years', *Child Development* 56:1538-42.

Lyons, H. A. (1972) 'Depressive illness and aggression in Belfast', *British Medical Journal* 1:342-4.

Maccoby, E. E. (1986) 'Social groupings in childhood: Their relationship to prosocial and antisocial behaviour in girls and boys', in D. Olweus, ed *Development of Antisocial and Prosocial Behaviour*. Academic Press.

—— (1989) 'Social-emotional development and response to stressors', in N. Garmezy and M. Rutter, eds *Stress, Coping and Development in Children*. Baltimore MD: John Hopkins University Press.

Macdonald, J. S. and Macdonald, L. (1978) 'The black family in the Americas: a review of the literature', *Sage Race Relations Abstracts* 3.

Madge, N. (1983) 'Unemployment and its effects on children', *Journal of Child Psychology and Psychiatry* 24:311-19.

Magnusson, D. (1983) 'Aggression and criminality in a longitudinal perspective', in K. T. Van Duren and S. A. Mednick, eds *Prospective Studies of Crime and Delinquency*. New York: Academic Press.

Main, M. (1977) 'Avoidance in the service of proximity', in K. Immelman, ed *Behavioural Development*. New York: Cambridge University Press.

—— (1985) 'Security in infancy, childhood and adulthood: a move to the level of representation', in I. Bretherton and E. Waters, eds *Growing Points of Attachment*, monographs of the Society for Research in Child Development, serial no. 209, vol. 50, 1-2.

Manning, M. and Herrman, J. (1981) 'The relationships of problem children in nursery schools', in R. Gilmour and S. Duck, eds *Personal Relationships in Disorder*. Academic Press.

—— (1980) 'Styles of hostility and social interaction at nursery, at school and at home', in L. Hersov and M. Berger, eds *Aggression and Conduct Disorder in Childhood and Adolescence*. New York: Pergamon.

—— (1985) 'Styles of hostility and social interactions at nursery, at school and at home. An extended study', in D. P. Farrington and J. Gunn, eds *Aggression and Dangerousness*. John Wiley.

Mark, V. H. (1978) 'Sociobiological theories of abnormal aggression', in S. B. Kutash, *Violence: Perspectives on Murder and Aggression*. San Francisco, CA: Jossey-Bass.

Marshall, J. R. (1984) 'The genetics of schizophrenia revisited', *Bulletin of the British Psychological Society* 37:177–81.

Martin, H. P. and Beezley, P. (1977) 'Behavioural observations of abused children', *Developmental Medicine and Child Neurology* 19:373–87.

Mash, E. J. 'A comparison of the mother–child interactions of physically abused and non-abused children during play and task situations', *Journal of Clinical Child Psychology* 12:337–46.

Maury, A. (1860) 'Du mouvement moral des societes, d'apres les derniers resutoaos de la statistique', *Review Deux Mondes* 29:468.

Mawson, A. R. (1980) 'Aggression, attachment behaviour and crimes of violence', in T. Hirschi and M. Gottesman, eds *Understanding Crime*. CA: Sage.

Maxim, P. S. (1986) 'Cohort size and juvenile delinquency in England and Wales', *Journal of Criminal Justice* 14:491–9.

Mayhew, P.; Elliott, D. and Dowds, L. (1989) 'The 1988 British Crime Survey', *Home Office Research Study* 111. HMSO.

——, Maung, N. A. and Mirrlees-Black, C. (1993) *The 1992 British Crime Survey*. HMSO.

Mcadoo, H. P. (1978) 'Factors related to stability in upwardly mobile black families', *Journal of Marriage and the Family* November.

Mccord, J. (1979) 'Some child-rearing antecedents of criminal behaviour in adult men', *Journal of Personality and Social Psychology* 37:1477–86.

—— (1983) 'A forty year perspective on effects of child abuse and neglect', *Child Abuse and Neglect* 7:265–70.

Mcgahey, R. M. (1986) 'Economic conditions, neighbourhood organisation and urban crime', in A. J. Reiss Jr and M. Tonry, eds *Communities and Crime*. Chicago IL: The Chicago University Press.

McKee, L. and Bell, C. (1985) 'Marital and family relations in times of male unemployment', in B. Roberts and D. Gallie, eds *New Approaches to Economic Life*. Manchester: Manchester University Press.

Mednick, S. A. (1982) 'Biology and violence', in M. E. Wolfgang and N. A. Weiner, eds *Criminal Violence*. CA: Sage.

—— (1984) 'Genetic influences in criminal convictions: evidence from an adoption cohort', *Science* 224:891–4.

Menninger, K. (1942) *Love Against Hate*. New York: Harcourt Brace.

Menzies, R. J. and Webster, C. D. (1989) 'Mental disorder and violent crime', in N. A. Weiner and M. E. Wolfgang, eds *Pathways to Criminal Violence*. CA: Sage.

Messner, S. F. (1982a) 'Income inequality and murder rates: Some cross-national findings', *Comparative Social Research* 3.

—— (1982b) 'Societal development, social equality and homicide', *Social Forces* 61.

Miedzian, M. (1992) *Boys Will Be Boys*. Virago.

Miller, A. (1991) *Banished Knowledge*. Virago.

Mirowsky, J. and Ross, C. E. (1989) *Social Causes of Distress*. New York: Aldine De Gruyter.

Mischzek, K. (1993) 'Wot U lookin' at?', BBC1 TV *Horizon*.

Mitchell, J. (1974) *Psychoanalysis and Feminism*. Penguin.

Moffitt, T. E. (1993) 'Adolescence-limited and life-course persistent antisocial behaviour: a developmental taxonomy', *Psychological Review* 100:674–701.

—— and Henry, B. (1989) 'Neuropsychological assessment of executive functions in self-reported delinquents', *Development and Psychopathology* 1:105–19.

Monane, M. (1984) 'Physical abuse in psychiatrically hospitalized children and adolescents', *Journal of the American Academy of Child Psychiatry* 23:653–8.

Morselli, E. (1879) 'Il suicidio, saggio di statistica moale comporata'.

Moyer, K. E. (1976) p. 41 *The Psychobiology of Aggression*. New York: Harper & Row.

Murray, C. (1984) *Losing Ground: American Social Policy 1950–1980*. New York: Basic.

—— (May 1990) speaking at a conference organized by the Centre for Policy Studies, London.

—— (1989) 'Underclass – a disaster in the making'. *Sunday Times Magazine*, 26 November.

Murray, L. (1993) 'The role of infant irritability in postnatal depression in a Cambridge community population', in J. K. Nugent, *The Cultural Context of Infancy* Vol 3. NJ: Ablex.

Myake, K. (1985) 'Infant temperament, mothers' mode of interaction and attachment in Japan', in I. Bretherton and E. Waters, eds *Growing Points of Attachment*, monographs of the Society for Reseach in Child Development 209(50): 1–2.

NSPCC, June 1990, London.

Newell, H. W. (1934) 'The psychodynamics of maternal rejection', *American Journal of Orthopsychiatry* 4:3887–4001.

Newson, J. and Newson, E. (1976) *Seven Years Old in the Home Environment*. Penguin.

—— (1989) 'The extent of parental physical punishment in the UK'. Approach.

Office of Population and Census, London.

Oltmans, T. F. (1977) 'Marital adjustment and the efficacy of behaviour therapy with children', *Journal of Consulting and Clinical Psychology* 45:724-9.

Olweus, D. (1979) 'Stability of aggressive reaction patterns in males: a review', *Psychological Bulletin* 86:852-75.

—— (1986) 'Aggression and hormones: relationship with testosterone and adrenaline', in D. Olweus, ed *Development of Antisocial and Prosocial Behaviour*. Academic Press.

Oppenheim, C. (1990) *Poverty: the Facts*. Child Poverty Action Group.

Orvaschel, H. (1983) 'Parental depression and child psychopathology', in S. B. Guze, ed *Childhood Psychopathology and Development*. New York: Raven.

Pagan, D. and Smith, S.M. (1979) 'Homicide: A medico legal study of thirty cases', *Bulletin of the American Academy of Psychiatry Law* 7:272-85.

Palmer, S. and Humphrey, J. A. (1980) 'Offender-victim relationships in criminal homicide followed by offender's suicide, North Carolina, 1972-1977', *Suicide and Life Threatening Behaviour* 10:106-18.

Panaccione, V. F. and Wahler, R. G. (1986) 'Child behaviour, maternal depression, and social coercion as factors in the quality of child care', *Journal of Abnormal Child Psychology* 14:263-78.

Parker, H., Bakx, K. and Newcombe, R. (1988) *Living with Heroin*. Milton Keynes: Open University Press.

Parker, R. N. and Smith, N. D. (1979) 'Deterrence, poverty and type of homicide', *American Journal of Sociology* 85(3).

Pastor, D. (1981) 'The quality of mother-infant attachment and its relationship to toddlers' initial sociability with peers', *Developmental Psychology* 17:326-35.

Patterson, G. R. (1980) p. 37 *'Mothers: The unacknowledged victims'*, Monographs of the Society for Research in Child Development 186(45):5.

—— (1982) *Coercive Family Processes*, Eugene. OR: Castalia Publishing.

—— (1986) 'The contribution of siblings to training for fighting: a microsocial analysis', in D. Olweus, ed *Development of Antisocial and Prosocial Behaviour*. Academic Press.

—— (1990) 'Maternal rejection: determinant or product for deviant child behaviour?', in W. Hartup and Z. Rubin, eds *Relationships and Development*. Lawrence Erlbaum.

—— (1994) 'Some alternatives to seven myths about treating families of antisocial children', in C. Henricson, ed *Crime and the Family*. Occasional Paper 20. Family Policy Studies Centre.

—— and Forgatch, M. S. (1990) 'Initiation and maintenance of process disrupting single-mother families', in G. R. Patterson, ed *Depression and Aggression in Family Interaction*. NJ: Lawrence Erlbaum.

—— and Fleischman, M. J. (1979) 'Maintenance of treatment effects', *Behaviour Therapy* 10:168-85.

—— (1990) *Antisocial Boys*. Eugene, OR: Castalia Publishing.

——, Reid, J. B. and Dishion, T. J. (1992) *A Social Learning Approach: Vol. 4 Antisocial Boys*. Eugene, OR: Castalia Publishing.

Paykel, E. S. and Dienelt, M. N. (1971) 'Suicide attempts following acute depression', *Journal of Nervous and Mental Disease* 153:234–43.

Pearson, G. (1987) *The New Heroin Users*. Oxford: Blackwell.

Petersen, R. (1980) 'Social class, social learning and wife abuse', *Social Services Review* 54:390–406.

Philip, A. E. (1970) 'Traits, attitudes and symptoms in a group of attempted suicides', *British Journal of Psychiatry* 116:475–82.

Plomin, R. and Daniels, D. (1987) 'Why are children in the same family so different from one another?', *Behavioural and Brain Science* 10:1–60.

—— and McCleary (1994) *Nature, Nurture and Psychology*. Washington DC: American Psychological Association.

——, Owen, M. J. and McGuffin, P. (1994) 'The genetic basis of complex human behaviours', *Science* 264:1733–9.

Pokorny, A. D. (1965) 'Human violence: a comparison of homicide, aggravated assault, suicide and attempted suicide', *Journal of Criminal Law and Police Science* 56:488–97.

Porter, B. and O'Leary, K. (1980) 'Marital discord and child behaviour problems', *Journal of Abnormal Child Psychology* 8:287–95.

Poyner, B. (1980) 'A study of street crime'. (Tavistock Institute, London. Unpublished.)

Prescott, S. and Letko, C. (1977) 'Battered women: A social psychological perspective', in *Battered Women: a Psycho Social Study of Domestic Violence*. New York: Van Nostrund Rheinhold.

President's Commission on Law Enforcement and Administration of Justice, 1967, 'Task force report: crime and its impact', 25. Washington DC: US Government Printing Office.

Quiggle, N. L., Garber, J., Panak, W. F. and Dodge, K. A. (1992) 'Social information process in aggressive and depressed children', *Child Development* 63:1305–20.

Quinton, R. and Rutter, M. (1985) 'Family pathology and child psychiatric disorder: a four year prospective study', in A. R. Nicol, ed *Longitudinal Studies in Child Psychiatry and Psychology*. Chichester: John Wiley.

Radke-Yarrow, M. (1983) 'Children's prosocial dispositions and behaviour', in P. H. Mussen, ed *Manual of Child Psychology*. New York: John Wiley; Rheingold, H.L.

—— (1985) 'Patterns of attachment in two and three year olds in normal families and families with parental depression', *Child Development* 56:884–93.

Ratcliffe, S. G. and Paul, N. (1986) *Prospective Studies on Children with Sex Chromosome Aneuploidy*. New York: Alan R Liss.

Reich, R. B. (1983) *The Next American Frontier*. New York: Random House.

158   JUVENILE VIOLENCE IN A WINNER-LOSER CULTURE

Reid, (1981) 'A social interactional approach to the treatment of abusive families', in Stuart, R. B., *Violent Behaviour*. New York: Brunner/Mazel.

Reidy, T. J. (1977) 'The aggressive characteristics of abused and neglected children', *Journal of Clinical Psychology* 33:1140–45.

Richman, N. (1982) p. 42 *Pre-school to School*. Academic Press.

Rheingold, H. L. and Emery, G. N. (1986) 'The nurturant acts of very young children', in D. Olweus, ed *Development of Antisocial and Prosocial Behaviour*. Academic Press.

Rickard, K. M. (1981) 'Factors in the referral of children for behavioural treatment: a comparison of mothers of clinic-referred deviant, clinic-referred non-deviant and non-clinic children', *Behaviour Research and Therapy* 19:201–5.

Robins, L. N. (1978) 'Sturdy predictors of adult antisocial behaviour: replications from longitudinal studies', *Psychological Medicine* 8:611–22.

—— (1975) 'Arrests and delinquency in two generations: a study of black urban families and their children', *Journal of Child Psychology and Psychiatry* 16:125–40.

Rogers, T. R. and Forehand, R. (1983) 'The role of depression in interactions between mothers and their clinic referred children', *Cognitive Therapy and Research* 7:315–24.

Rohner, R. P. (1975) 'Parental acceptance-rejection and personal development: a universalist approach to behavioural science', in R. W. Brislin, ed *Cross-cultural Perspectives on Learning*. CA: Sage.

Rohrbeck, C. A. and Twentyman, C. T. (1986) 'Multimodal assessment of impulsiveness in abusing, neglecting and nonmaltreating mothers and their preschool children', *Journal of Consulting and Clinical Psychology* 54:231–6.

Rolston, R. H. (1971) 'The effect of physical abuse on the expression of overt and fantasy aggressive behaviour in children'. Louisiana State University, Doctoral Dissertation.

Rosenbaum, A. and O'Leary, K. D. (1981) 'Children: the unintended victims of marital violence', *American Journal of Orthopsychiatry* 51:692–9.

Rosenbaum, M. and Bennett, B. (1986) 'Homicide and suicide', *American Journal of Psychiatry* 143:367–70.

Rounsaville, B. J. (1978) 'Theories in marital violence: evidence from a study of battered women', *Victimology: An International Journal* 3:11–31.

Rutter, M. (1979) *Changing Youth in a Changing Society*. Nuffield Provincial Hospitals Trust.

—— (1986) 'The developmental psychopathology of depression', in M. Rutter, C. E. Izard and P. B. Read, eds *Depression in Young People*. The Guildford Press.

—— (1988) 'Functions and consequences of relationships', in R. A. Hinde and J. Stevenson-Hinde, eds *Relationships within Families*. Oxford: Clarendon.

—— and Quinton, D. (1977) 'Psychiatric disorder', in H. Mcgurk, ed *Ecological Factors in Human Development* Amsterdam: North Holland.

Satten, J. (1960) 'Murder without apparent motive: a study in personality disorganisation', *American Journal of Psychiatry* 17:48-53.

Sawyer, M. (1978) *Income Distribution in OECD Countries*. Paris: OECD.

Schneider-Rosen, K. and Cicchetti, D. (1984) 'The relationship between affect and cognition in maltreated infants: quality of attachment and the development of visual self-recognition', *Child Development* 55:648-58.

—— (1985) 'Current perspectives in attachment theory: illustration from the study of maltreated infants', in I. Bretherton and E. Waters, eds *Growing Points of Attachment Theory and Research*, Monographs of the Society for Research in Child Development 209, vol(50): 1-2.

Scott, P. D. (1973) 'Fatal battered baby cases', *Medicine, Science and the Law* 13:197-206.

Sears, R. R. (1961) 'Relations of early socializing experience to aggression', *Journal of Abnormal and Social Psychology* 63:466-92.

Seligman, M. E. P. and Peterson, C. (1986) 'A learned helplessness perspective on childhood depression', in M. Rutter, C. E. Izard and P. B. Read, eds *Depression in Young People*. Guildford Press.

Sendi, I. B. and Blomgren, P. G. (1975) ' A comparative study of predictive criteria in the predisposition of homicidal adolescents', *American Journal of Psychiatry* 132:423-7.

Serbes, J. M. (1986) 'Defining high risk', in J. Garbarino *Troubled Youth, Troubled Families*. New York: Aldine.

Shafii, M. (1985) 'Psychological autopsy of competed suicide in children and adolescents', *American Journal of Psychiatry* 142:1061-4.

Shannon, L. W. (1978) 'A longitudinal study of crime and delinquancy', in C. Wellford, ed. *Quantitative Studies in Criminology*. CA: Sage.

Sian, G. (1985) *Accounting for Aggression*. Allen & Unwin.

Simon, R. J. and Baxter, S. (1989) 'Gender and violent crime', in N. A. Weiner and M. E. Wolfgang, eds *Violent Crime, Violent Criminals*. CA: Sage.

—— and Sharma, N. (1979) 'Women and crime: Does the American experience generalize', in F. Adler and R. J. Simon, eds *Criminology of Deviant Women*. Boston, HA: Houghton Mifflin.

Skogan, W. (1989) 'Social change and the future of crime', in T. B. Gurr, ed *Violence in America: Vol. 1 The History of Crime*. Sage.

Slater, P. E. (1962) 'Parental behaviour and the personality of the child', *Journal of Genetic Psychology* 101:53-68.

Smith, S. and Topeka, K. (1965) 'The Adolescent Murderer', *Archives of General Psychiatry* 13:310-19.

Smith, S. M. and Hanson, R. (1975) 'Interpersonal relationships and child-rearing practices in 214 parents of battered children', *British Journal of Psychiatry* 127:513-25.

Snyder, J. J. (1977) 'Reinforcement analysis of interaction in problem and nonproblem families', *Journal of Abnormal Psychology* 86:528-35.

Sorrels, J. M. (1977) 'Kids who kill', *Crime and Delinquency* 23:312-20.

Sowell, T. (1979) 'Three black histories', in T. Sowell, ed *American Ethnic Groups*. Washington DC: Urban Institute.

Spinetta, J. J. and Rigler, D. (1972) 'The child-abusing parent: a psychological review', *Psychological Bulletin* 77:296-304.

Sroufe, L. A. (1983) 'Infant-caregiver attachment and patterns of adaptation in preschool: the roots of maladaptation and competence', *Minnesota Symposium on Child Psychology* 16:41-81.

Stark, E. and Flitcroft, A. (1985) 'Woman battering, child abuse and social heredity: what is the relationship?', *Marital Violence: Sociological Review Monograph* 31:147-71.

Steinberg, L. (1981) 'Economic antecedents of child abuse and neglect', *Child Abuse* 52:975-85.

Stevenson-Hinde, J. (1986) 'Behaviour at home and friendly or hostile behaviour in preschool', in D. Olweus, ed *Development of Antisocial and Prosocial Behaviour*. Academic Press.

Stevenson, M. R. and Black, K. N. (1995) *How Divorce Affects Offspring*. Madison, WI: Brown & Benchmark.

Storr, A. (1968) *Human Aggression*. Penguin.

Straus, J. H. and Straus, M. (1953) 'Suicide, homicide and social structure in Ceylon', *American Journal of Sociology* 11:461-9.

Straus, M.A. (1983) 'Ordinary violence, child abuse and wife beating: what do they have in common?', in D. Finkelhor, *The Dark Side of Families*. CA: Sage.

—— and Gelles, R. J. (1988) pp. 14-36, in J. T. Kirkpatrick and M. A. Straus, eds *Family Abuse and its Consequences*. CA: Sage.

—— and Hotaling, G. T. (1980) *The Social Causes of Husband-Wife Violence*. Minneapolis, MN: University of Minnesota.

—— (1980) *Behind Closed Doors - Violence in the American Family*. New York: Anchor.

——, Cater, J. and Easton, P. (1980) 'Separation and other stress in child abuse', *Lancet* 1:972-3.

Sugarman, D. B. and Hotaling, G. T. (1986) 'Violent men in intimate relationships', *Journal of Applied Social Psychology*.

Sullivan, M. L. (1984) *Youth Crime and Employment Patterns in Three Brooklyn Neighbourhoods*. New York: Vera Institute of Justice.

—— (1989) *Getting Paid: Youth Crime and Work in the Inner City*. Ithaca, NY: Cornell University Press.

Sunday Times Magazine, 26 November 1989, 'Underclass - a disaster in the making', p. 39.

Symonds, P. M. (1938) 'A study of parental acceptance and rejection', *American Journal of Orthopsychiatry* 8:679-88.

Tanay, E. (1976) *The Murderers*. Indianapolis/New York: The Bobbs-Merril Company Inc.

Tarling, R. (1993) *Analysing Offending*. HMSO.

Tarter, R. E. (1984) 'Neuropsychological, personality and familial characteristics of physically abused delinquents', *Journal of the American Academy of Child Psychiatry* 23:668-74.

Thornberry, T. B. and Farnworth, M. (1982) 'Social correlates of criminal involvement: further evidence on the relationship between social status and criminal behaviour', *American Sociological Review* 47:505-18.

Timberlake, E. M. (1981) 'Child abuse and externalized aggression', in R. J. Hunner and Y. E. Walker, eds *Exploring the Relationship Between Child Abuse and Delinquency*. Montclair , CA: Allanheld, Osmun.

Tittle, C. R. (1973) 'The myth of social class and criminality: an empirical assessment of the empirical evidence', *American Sociological Review* 43:643-56.

Tizard, B. and Hodges, J. (1978) 'The effect of early institutional rearing on the development of eight year old children', *Journal of Child Psychology and Psychiatry* 19:99-118.

Tooley, K. M. (1977) 'The young child as victim of sibling attack', *Social Casework* 58:25-8.

Tonge, W., James, D. and Hillam, S. (1975) *Families Without Hope*, British *Journal of Psychiatry* Special publication no. 11.

Trickett, P. K. and Kuczynski, L. (1986) 'Children's misbehaviours and parental discipline strategies in abusive and nonabusive families', *Developmental Psychology* 22:115-23.

Troy, M. and Sroufe, L. A. (1987) 'Victimization among preschoolers: Role of attachment relationship history', *Journal of the American Academy of Child Adolescent Psychiatry* 26:166-72.

Tuck, M. (1989) *Drinking and Disorder: a Study of Non- Metropolitan Violence*. HORS: HMSO.

Turner, C. W. (1981) 'A social psychological analysis of violent behaviour', in R. B. Stuart, ed *Violent Behaviour*. New York: Brunner/Mazel.

Tuteur, W. and Glotzer, J. (1959) 'Murdering mothers', *American Journal of Psychiatry* 116:447-52.

Virkunnen, M. (1989) 'Psychobiological concomitants of history of suicide attempts among violent offenders and impulsive firesetters', *Archives of General Psychiatry* 46:604-6.

Wagstaff, A. and Maynard, A. (1988) 'Economic aspects of the illicit drug market and drug enforcement policies in the United Kingdom', *Home Office Research Study* 95: HMSO.

Wahler, R. G. (1980) 'The insular mother: her problems in parent–child treatment', *Journal of Applied Behaviour Analysis* 13:207-19.

—— and Dumas, J. E. (1986) p. 20 'Maintenance factors in coercive mother-child interactions: the compliance and predictability hypothesis', *Journal of Applied Behaviour Analysis* 19:13-22.

Wallerstein, J. S. (1988) 'Children of divorce: a 10 year study', in E. M. Hetherington and J. D. Arasteh, eds *Impact of Divorce, Single Parenting and Stepparenting on Children.* , NJ: Lawrence Erlbaum.

Warheit, G. (1984) 'An analysis of social class and racial differences in depressive symptom-aetiology: a community study', *Journal of Health and Social Behaviour* 4:921-99.

Waters, E., Vaughan, B. E. and Egeland, B. R. (1980) 'Individual Differences in infant-mother attachment relationships at age one', *Child Development* 51:208-16.

Watson, D. and Tellegren, A. (1985) 'Towards a consensual structure of mood', *Psychological Bullletin* 98:219-35.

Weintraub, S. (1986) Competence and vulnerability in children with an affectively disordered parent', in M. Rutter, ed *Depression in Young People*. London: Guildford Press.

Weissman, M. M. and Siegler, R. (1972) 'The depressed woman and her rebellious adolescent', *Social Casework* November.

—— and Klerman, G. L. (1977) pp. 99-101, 'Sex differences and the epidemiology of depression', *Archives of General Psychiatry* 34:98-111.

—— and Myers, J. K. (1978) 'Rates and risks of depressive symptoms in a United States urban community', *Acta Psychiatrica Scandinavia* 57:219-31.

—— and Paykel, E. S. (1974), *The Depressed Woman*. University of Chicago Press.

—— (1986) 'Depressed parents and their children', *American Journal of Diseases of Childhood* 140:801-4.

—— (1987) 'Children of depressed parents', *Archives of General Psychiatry* 44:847-53.

Weitzman, L. J. (1986) *The Divorce Revolution*. Free Press.

West, D. J. (1965) *Murder Followed by Suicide*. Heinemann.

—— (1969) *Present Conduct and Future Delinquency*. Heinemann.

Whiffen, V. E. and Gotlib, I. H. (1989) 'Infants of postpartum depressed mothers: temperament and cognitive status', *Journal of Abnormal Psychology* 98(3): 1-6.

Widom, C.S. (1984) 'Sex roles, Criminality and psychopathology', in C. S. Widom *Sex Roles and Psychopathology*. New York: Plenum.

—— (1989a) 'The intergenerational transmission of violence', in N. A. Weiner and M. E. Wolfgang, eds *Pathways to Criminal Violence*. CA: Sage.

—— (1989b) 'The cycle of violence', *Science* 244:160-6.

Wille, W. S. (1974) *Citizens who Commit Murder*. St. Louis, MO: Warren H. Green Inc.

Wilson, J. Q. and Herrnstein, R. J. (1985) *Crime and Human Nature*. New York: Torchstone.

Wilson, M. I. (1980) 'Household composition and the risk of child abuse and neglect', *Journal of Biosocial Science* 12:333–40.

Wilson, M. N. (1984) 'Mothers' and grandmothers' perceptions of parental behaviour in three-generational black families', *Child Development* 55:1333–9.

—— and Tolson, T. F. J. (1989) 'Single parenting in the context of three-generational black families', in E. M. Hetherington and J. D. Arasteh, eds *Impact of Divorce, Single Parenting and Stepparenting on Children*. NJ: Lawrence Erlbaum.

Wolberg, L. R. (1944) 'The character structure of the rejected child', *Nervous Child Journal* 3:74–88.

Wolfe, D. A. and Mosk, M. D. (1983) 'Behavioural comparisons of children from abusive and distressed families', *Journal of Consulting and Clinical Psychology* 51:702–8.

—— (1985) 'Children of battered women: the relation of child behaviour to family violence and maternal stress', *Journal of Consulting and Clinical Psychology* 53:657–65.

Wolfgang, M. E. (1981) 'Surveying violence across nations: a review of the literature, with research and policy recommendations', *International Review of Criminal Policy* 37:62–95.

—— and Ferracuti, F. (1967) *The Subculture of Violence*. Tavistock.

—— (1982) *Delinquency in a Birth Cohort*. Chicago, IL: Chicago University Press.

Wolkind, S. (1985) p. 208 'The first years: Pre-school children and their families in the inner city', in J. E. Stevenson, ed *Recent Research in Developmental Psychopathology*. Pergamon.

Wolkind, W. (1967) 'Multivariate analyses of parents' MMPI's based on the psychiatric diagnoses of their children', *Journal of Consulting Psychology* 31:521–4.

Wrate, R. M. (1985) 'Postnatal depression and child development', *British Journal of Psychiatry* 146:622–7.

Yarrow, M. D. (1970) 'Recollections of childhood', *Monographs of the Society for Research in Child Development* 138(35), no. 5.

Zahn-Wexler, C. (1982) 'Cognitive and social development in infants and toddlers with a bipolar parent'. Presented at the annual meeting of the American Academy of Child Psychiatry.

—— (1984a) 'Altruism, aggression and social interaction in young children with a manic-depressive parent', *Child Development* 55:112–22.

—— (1984b) 'Affective arousal and social interactions in young children of manic-depressive parents', *Child Development* 55:112–22.

—— (1984c) 'Problem-behaviours and peer interactions of young children with a manic-depressive parent', *American Journal of Psychiatry* 141:236–40.

Zillman, D. (1979) *Hostility and Aggression*. NJ: Lawrence Erlbaum.

INDEX

168